Social Theory

POLITICS: A WORK IN CONSTRUCTIVE SOCIAL THEORY

by Roberto Mangabeira Unger

SOCIAL THEORY: ITS SITUATION AND ITS TASK

FALSE NECESSITY: ANTI-NECESSITARIAN SOCIAL THEORY IN THE SERVICE OF RADICAL DEMOCRACY

PLASTICITY INTO POWER: COMPARATIVE-HISTORICAL STUDIES ON THE INSTITUTIONAL CONDITIONS OF ECONOMIC AND MILITARY SUCCESS

SOCIAL THEORY: ITS SITUATION AND ITS TASK

A CRITICAL INTRODUCTION TO
POLITICS
A WORK IN CONSTRUCTIVE SOCIAL THEORY

ROBERTO MANGABEIRA UNGER

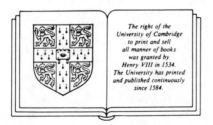

*The right of the
University of Cambridge
to print and sell
all manner of books
was granted by
Henry VIII in 1534.
The University has printed
and published continuously
since 1584.*

CAMBRIDGE UNIVERSITY PRESS

CAMBRIDGE

NEW YORK   NEW ROCHELLE   MELBOURNE   SYDNEY

Published by the Press Syndicate of the University of Cambridge
The Pitt Building, Trumpington Street, Cambridge CB2 1RP
32 East 57th Street, New York, NY 10022, USA
10 Stamford Road, Oakleigh, Melbourne 3166, Australia

First published 1987

Printed in the United States of America

Library of Congress Cataloging-in-Publication Data
Unger, Roberto Mangabeira.
Social theory: its situation and its task.
"A critical introduction to Politics, a work in
constructive social theory."
1. Sociology. 2. Political science. 3. Philosophy.
I. Unger, Roberto Mangabeira. Politics, a work in
constructive social theory. II. Title.
HM24.U536 1987 301'.01 86–7882

British Library Cataloging in Publication Data
Unger, Roberto Mangabeira.
Social theory : its situation and its
task : critical introduction to Politics,
a work in constructive social theory.
1. Political sociology. I. Title 320'.01 JA76
ISBN 0 521 32974 4 hard covers
ISBN 0 521 33862 x paperback

Contents

1

Introduction

Society as Artifact

MODERN social thought was born proclaiming that society is made and imagined, that it is a human artifact rather than the expression of an underlying natural order. This insight inspired the great secular doctrines of emancipation: liberalism, socialism, and communism. In one way or another, all these doctrines held out the promise of building a society in which we may be individually and collectively empowered to disengage our practical and passionate relations from rigid roles and hierarchies. If society is indeed ours to reinvent, we can carry forward the liberal and leftist aim of cleansing from our forms of practical collaboration or passionate attachment the taint of dependence and domination. We can advance the modernist goal of freeing subjective experience more fully from a pre-written and imposed script. We may even be able to draw the left-liberal and modernist goals together in a larger ambition to construct social worlds whose stability does not depend on the surrender of our society-making powers or on their confiscation by privileged elites. The practical point of the view of society as made and imagined is to discover what is realistic and what illusory in these objectives and to find guidance for their execution.

No one has ever taken the idea of society as artifact to the hilt. On the contrary, the social theories that provided radical politics with its chief intellectual tools balanced the notion that society is made and imagined against the ambition to develop a science of history, rich in lawlike explanations. This science claimed to identify a small number of possible types of social organization, coexisting or succeeding one another under the influence of relentless developmental tendencies or of deep-seated economic, organizational, or psychological constraints. Marxism is the star example.

Such theories have become ever less credible. A mass of historical knowledge and practical experience has battered them. Inconvenient facts have discredited their characteristic beliefs in a short list of types of social organization and in laws that determine the identity of these types or govern their history.

But the most visible result of this battering has not been to extend the idea of society as artifact. On the contrary, it has been to abandon more and more of the field to a style of social science that seeks narrowly framed explanations for narrowly described phenomena. This social science – positivist or empiricist as it is sometimes called – rejects the search for comprehensive social or historical laws in favor of a more limited explanatory task. In so doing, it comes to see society as a vast, amorphous heap of conflicting individual or group interests and exercises in interest accommodation, of practical problems and episodes of problem solving. Such a social science lacks the means with which to address the institutional and imaginative assumptions on which routine problem solving and interest accommodation take place. Whatever the adepts of this social science may say, their practice has a built-in propensity to take the existing framework of social life for granted and thereby to lend it a semblance of necessity and authority. In this respect, positivist social science is even more dangerous than the ambitious social theories of the nineteenth and early twentieth centuries. These theories at least defined the present institutional and imaginative order of society as a transitory though necessary stage of social evolution or as only one of several possible types of social organization.

Meanwhile the radical project – the shared enterprise of liberal and leftist doctrines and of the political movements that embraced them – has also suffered a daunting series of setbacks. The communist revolutions, despite their economic and redistributive achievements, failed to establish social institutions that could credibly claim to carry the radical project beyond the point to which it has already been brought by the rich Western democracies and market economies. At the same time, party politics in these democracies has settled down to a series of routine struggles over marginal economic redistribution, within an institutional and imaginative ordering of social life that remains largely unchallenged. Third world countries continue to be the playing ground of predatory oligarchies that often can scarcely be distinguished from self-appointed revolutionary vanguards. It becomes hard to continue hoping that poorer and more fluid societies might stage promising experiments in the advancement of the radical project.

Such defeats have produced a sense of social life combining an awareness that nothing has to be the way it is with a conviction that nothing important can be changed by deliberate collective action. All revolutionary programs are made to seem utopian reveries, bound to end in despotism and disillusionment. This experience of faithless prostration, the stigma and shame of our time, provides an ironic commentary on the conception of society as artifact: while respecting the literal truth of this conception, it eviscerates the idea of its force.

The message of this book is that these disheartening intellectual and political events tell only half the story, the half that evokes intellectual entropy and social stagnation. *Social Theory: Its Situation and Its Task* deals chiefly with the other, hidden half. It shows how the criticism and self-criticism of received traditions of social theory have prepared the way for a practice of social and historical understanding that extends even further than the ambitious European social theories of the past the idea of society as artifact and enables us to broaden and refine our sense of the possible. The resulting insights inform efforts to carry both liberal and socialist commitments beyond the point to which contemporary societies have taken them. Thus, what seems to be a circumstance of theoretical exhaustion and political retrenchment can be redefined as a gathering of forces for a new and more powerful assault upon superstition and despotism.

The critical argument of this book leads directly into constructive explanatory and programmatic ideas. The character and concerns of the critical diagnosis may best be outlined by suggesting the orientation of the constructive view it prepares.

This constructive view includes both an explanatory approach to society and a program for social reconstruction. The explanatory proposals of *Politics* cuts the link between the possibility of social explanation and the denial or downplaying of our freedom to remake the social worlds we construct and inhabit. Like classic doctrines such as Marxism but unlike traditional, positivist social science, these explanations assign central importance to the distinction between routine deals or quarrels and the recalcitrant institutional and imaginative frameworks in which they ordinarily occur. Such frameworks comprise all the institutional arrangements and imaginative preconceptions that shape routine conflicts over the mastery and use of key resources. These resources enable the occupants of some social stations to set terms to what the occupants of other stations do. They include economic capital, governmental power, technical expertise, and even prestigious ideals. (The terms context, structure, and framework are employed synonymously throughout this book.)

In the contemporary Western democracies the social framework includes legal rules that use property rights as the instrument of economic decentralization, constitutional arrangements that provide for representation while discouraging militancy, and a style of business organization that starkly contrasts task-defining and task-executing activities. In the industrial democracies the formative structure of social life also incorporates a series of models of human association that are expected to be realized in different areas of social existence: a model of private community applying to the life of family and friendship, a model of democratic organization guiding the activities of governments and political parties, and a model of private contract combined with impersonal technical hierarchy addressing the prosaic realm of work and exchange.

The explanatory theory developed in *Politics* differs from positivist social science in its insistence that the distinction between formative structures and formed routines is central to our understanding of society and history. The institutional and imaginative frameworks of social life supply the basis on which people define and reconcile interests, identify and solve problems. These frameworks cannot be adequately explained as mere crystallized outcomes of interest-accommodating or problem-solving activities. Until we make the underlying institutional and imaginative structure of a society explicit we are almost certain to mistake the regularities and routines that persist, so long as the structure is left undisturbed, for general laws of social organization. At the very least, we are likely to treat them as the laws of a particular type of society and to imagine that we can suspend them only by a revolutionary switch to another type. Superstition then encourages surrender.

If the explanatory theory of *Politics* is incompatible with positivist social science, it is also irreconcilable with some of the characteristic tenets of the classic social theories. Like the view for which *Politics* argues, these theories assigned a central explanatory role to the contrast between frameworks and routines. Thus, for example, the Marxist studies modes of production (his frameworks) and the distinctive laws of each mode (his routines). The approach anticipated in this book nevertheless repudiates two major assumptions with which the contrast between frameworks and routines, formative structures and formed routines, has traditionally been associated.

One of these assumptions is the belief in the existence of a limited number of types or stages of social organization, all of whose parts combine to form an indivisible package. The style of social analysis to which this work contributes dispenses with ideas about such types and stages. Each framework is unique rather than an example of a general type that can be repeated in different societies at different times. The components of such an institutional and imaginative order are only loosely and unevenly connected. They can be replaced piece by piece rather than only as an inseparable whole.

The other repudiated assumption with which the contrast between frameworks and routines has ordinarily been connected is the thesis that general explanations of the genesis, workings, and reinvention of these frameworks must take the form of appeals to deep-seated economic, organizational, and psychological constraints or to irresistible developmental forces supposedly underlying the chaos of historical life. The theory advocated and anticipated here shows how we can develop an account of context making whose generality does not depend upon laws that generate a closed list or a preordained sequence of forms of social life.

A third idea extends the two sets of necessitarian assumptions that have traditionally accompanied the distinction between frameworks and routines. This third assumption is less directly connected to the other two than they are to each other, and it represents more an unexamined prejudice than a considered belief. This prejudice is the belief that structures will be structures. They always have the same relation to the practical and discursive routines that they influence and to the constraints and tendencies that in turn shape them. The arguments of *Politics* claim, however, that we can diminish the power of these all-important structures to impose a script upon people's practical or passionate relations and weaken the contrast between structure-preserving routines and structure-transforming conflicts.

We have an important stake in changing our relation to the formative institutions and preconceptions of our societies. Less entrenched and more revisable sets of arrangements and beliefs help us empower ourselves individually and collectively. They encourage the development of productive capabilities by enabling us to experiment more freely with the practical forms of production and exchange. They free group life of some of its characteristic dangers of dependence and depersonalization by diminishing the hold of rigid hierarchies and roles over our dealings with one another. They allow us to engage in group life without becoming the victims of compulsions we do not master and hardly understand.

Nothing in the development of the effort to disengage the framework—routine distinction from its inherited associations requires a solution to the metaphysical problem of free will and determinism. The aim is not to show that we are free in any ultimate sense and somehow unrestrained by causal influences upon our conduct. It is to break loose from a style of social understanding that allows us to explain ourselves and our societies only to the extent we imagine ourselves helpless puppets of the social worlds we build and inhabit or of the lawlike forces that have supposedly brought these worlds into being. History really is surprising; it does not just seem that way. And social invention, deliberate or unintended, is not just an acting out of preestablished and narrowly defined possibilities.

A view of the institutional and imaginative contexts of social life, of how these contexts stick together, come apart, and get remade, lies at the center of the explanatory theory of *Politics*. From such a view we can hope to get critical distance on our societies. We can disrupt the implicit, often involuntary alliance between the apologetics of established order and the explanation of past or present societies. We can find an explanatory practice that, by providing us with a credible account of discontinuous change and social novelty, inspires rather than subverts the advancement of the radical project: the effort, shared by liberals and socialists, to lift the burden of rigid hierarchy and division that weighs on our practical and passionate relations with one another.

The approach to social and historical explanation for which this book argues has practical implications. Our beliefs about ideals and interests are shaped by the institutional and imaginative frameworks of social life. But they are not shaped completely. The formative contexts of social life never entirely control our practical dealings and passionate attachments. We regularly invest our recognized interests and ideals with ill-defined longings that we cannot satisfy within the limits imposed by current institutional and imaginative assumptions. But we just as regularly fail to grasp the conflict between longings and assumptions because of our failure to imagine alternative possibilities of social organization. This failure in turn prompts us to underestimate the wealth of materials available for context-transforming use: the surviving residues of past institutional arrangements and imaginative worlds, the stubborn anomalies of a social order, and the endless, petty practical and imaginative quarrels that may escalate at any time into structure-subverting fights. A believable social theory teaches the imagination how to take these deviations seriously and how to use them as starting points for the inauguration of new forms of social organization and personal experience.

The explanatory view of *Politics* goes hand in hand with a program for social reconstruction. Like the explanatory theory that informs it, the program is anticipated in this introductory book. The program takes sides with the cause that modernist and liberal or leftist radicals contentiously and half-consciously share. But in siding with this cause and in trying to justify, to develop, and to unify it, the argument also changes it. The change affects both the conception of what the cause is for and the view of its practical implications for the reordering of society.

The programmatic arguments of *Politics* reinterpret and generalize the liberal and leftist endeavor by freeing it from unjustifiably restrictive assumptions about the practical institutional forms that representative democracies, market economies, and the social control of economic accumulation can and should assume. At the heart of this vision of alternative institutional forms lies an appreciation of the link between the extent to which an institutional and imaginative framework of social life makes itself available to revision in the midst of ordinary social activity and the success with which this framework undermines rigid social roles and hierarchies. *Politics* argues for a particular way of reorganizing governments and economies that promises to realize more effectively both aspects of the radical commitment: the subversion of social division and hierarchy and the assertion of will over custom and compulsion. The traditional disputes between leftists and liberals are seen to be based on a misunderstanding, once we recognize that the present forms of decentralized economies and pluralistic democracies (markets based on absolute property rights, democracies predicated on the skeptical quiescence of the citizenry) are neither the necessary nor the best expressions of inherited ideals of liberty and equality. They frustrate the very goals for whose sake we uphold them.

The same ideas that change our view of the institutional message of radical politics also revise and clarify our conception of their purpose. We come to recognize the ideal of social equality, for example, as a partial, subsidiary aspect of our effort to free ourselves from a social script that both subordinates us unnecessarily to an overpowering scheme of class, communal, gender, and national divisions and denies us as individuals, as groups, and as whole societies a greater mastery over the institutional and imaginative contexts of our lives. This enlarged view of the radical cause in turn allows us to connect leftism and modernism, the radical politics of institutional reform and the radical politics of personal relations, a political vision obsessed with issues of dependence and domination and a moral vision concerned with the inability of the individual to gain practical, emotional, or even cognitive access to other people without forfeiting his independence.

The programmatic and explanatory arguments of *Politics* stand much more closely connected than our inherited preconceptions about facts and values suggest is possible. One of the many connections should be singled out here because it illuminates the direction of this introductory work. The explanatory ideas of *Politics* focus on what may at first seem a mere embarrassment to the pretensions of general social theory. We sometimes act as if our shared institutional and imaginative contexts did not in fact bind us. We hold on to deviant examples of human association, often the left-overs of past or rejected bids to establish a settled ordering of social life. We pass occasionally and often unexpectedly from context-respecting disputes to context-defying struggles. This endless, baffling experience of hidden or open defiance eludes the explanatory styles favored by both the classical social theories and the positivist social sciences. But the apparent obstacle to our explanatory capacities in fact points the way to a better strategy of explanation. The failure of our social contexts, or of the tendencies and constraints that help shape them, to prevent or to govern their own revision is the very fact that supplies the cornerstone for the approach of *Politics* to social and historical explanation.

What the explanatory argument takes as an opportunity for insight, the programmatic argument sees as a source of practical and ideal benefits. A central thesis of *Politics* is that all the major aspects of human empowerment or self-assertion depend on our success at diminishing the distance between context-preserving routine and context-transforming conflict. They rely on our ability to invent institutions and practices more fully respectful of the same context-revising freedom that provides the explanatory view of *Politics* with both its problem and its opportunity.

Why a critical assessment of the situation of social thought? Why not pass directly to the constructive explanatory and programmatic ideas?

The conception of intellectual history underlying this critical diagnosis is not the image of intellectual systems eventually collapsing under the weight of contrary evidence until a theoretical revolution replaces them with alternative theories. It is rather the picture of a twofold process of dissolution and construction: as the intellectual traditions dissolve, they also provide the materials and the methods for their own substitution. In this view of the situation of social thought, we need to explicate and to extend the fragments of an alternative social theory already implicit in the self-subverting activities of contemporary social thought. Thus, for example, the disintegration of Marxism is often misinterpreted by conservatives or antitheorists as the punishment due to overweening theoretical ambition. In fact, however, the internal controversies of the Marxist tradition have produced many of the insights needed to develop the idea that society is made and imagined and that it can therefore be remade and reimagined. The reluctance to push to extremes the criticism of an inherited tradition of social and historical analysis is habitually justified by the fear that its outcome will be nihilism. But this fear is misplaced not only because it makes us cling to confused and mistaken ideas but also because it deprives us of the constructive insights that help prevent the feared nihilistic result.

A great deal more than a hypothesis about intellectual history is at stake in this approach to the constructive implications of what may appear to be a purely disintegrative process. The practical issue is whether we must begin the reconstruction of social theory as nearly from scratch as possible. In the view that emphasizes the creation and overthrow of entire theoretical systems, we must not only formulate a brand new set of categories and methods but also laboriously develop a new empirical basis for our theories. Past observations will have been more or less contaminated by the flawed theoretical assumptions that partly shaped them. But in the conception of intellectual history employed here, the materials for an alternative vision – methods, insights, and interpreted observations – already lie at hand, though in undeveloped, fragmentary, and distorted form.

Another reason to preface the constructive explanatory and programmatic argument of *Politics* with a discussion of the contemporary situation of social and historical studies is to identify alternative though similarly motivated responses to the same intellectual and political circumstance. Though the critical discussion developed in this introductory book foreshadows the affirmative explanatory and programmatic ideas of the larger work, the relation between criticism and construction remains loose. The explanatory and programmatic argument of *Politics* is certainly not the sole promising response to the intellectual predicament described here. At least one rival line of development deserves attention. This alternative, which this book labels ultra-theory, also pushes to extremes the conception of society as artifact. But it does so by abandoning rather than by transforming the effort to formulate general explanations and comprehensive proposals for social reconstruction. It puts in place of such explanations and proposals not positivist social science but an array of critical and constructive practices, which range from the trashing of particular necessitarian explanations to the utopian evocation of forms of social life more responsive to the radical project. The argument of this book remains neutral between this skeptical, antinecessitarian approach and the equally antinecessitarian but aggressively theoretical tack pursued in *Politics*.

Social Theory: Its Situation and Its Task does not merely show intellectual and political opportunities arising from apparent theoretical disorientation and social blockage. It also seeks to convey a sense of the variety of constructive possibilities existing even within a field of thought defined by commitments to the view of society as artifact and to the radical project in politics.

A final aim of this introductory book is to enlist the reader's help in the theoretical campaign that this work initiates. *Politics* sets out to execute a program for which no ready-made mode of discourse exists. It changes the sense of terms and problems drawn from other bodies of thought, inspired by other intentions. It raids many disciplines and imposes on its inquiry an order no discipline acknowledges as its own. It develops, as it moves forward, a language for a vision. When the larger argument falls into confusion and obscurity, when I stagger and stumble, help me. Refer to the purpose described in this book and revise what I say in the light of what I want.

Social Theory: Its Situation and Its Task does not follow a single continuous argument. Instead, it proposes several points of departure from which to arrive, by convergent routes, at the same theoretical outcome. By far the most extensively considered of these points of departure is the internal situation of social thought, understood to include the whole field of social and historical studies. The discussion advances through a criticism of two intellectual traditions. One tradition, represented by positivist social science, disregards or downplays the contrast between the institutional and imaginative contexts, frameworks, or structures of social life and the routine activities, conflicts, and deals that these frameworks help shape. The other tradition accepts the distinction but subordinates it to unjustifiably restrictive assumptions about how frameworks change, what frameworks can exist, and what relations may hold between a framework and the freedom of the agents who move within it.

Marxism is the most cogent and elaborate example of this second class of theories. Yet both in Marx's own writings and in the later tradition of Marxist self-criticism we find the most uncompromising statements of the idea that society is made. We also discover many of the most powerful instruments with which to free this idea from the necessitarian assumptions about frameworks and their history that have played so large a role in Marxist thinking. Thus, the confrontation with Marxism remains a continuing concern – explicit in this preliminary book, largely implicit in the constructive work that follows.

The discussion of the internal situation of social theory suggests two parallel but distinct responses. One of these agendas, pursued in the main body of *Politics*, is intellectually ambitious. The other response is skeptical of the usefulness of general explanations and detailed proposals for reconstruction. But both carry to new extremes the conception of society as artifact. Both take sides with the people who, when faced with claims that current forms of social organization reflect inflexible economic, organizational, or psychological constraints, answer: No, they do not; they are just politics. Both show how the seemingly voluntaristic and nihilist claim that it is all politics permits a deeper insight into social life and even a better grasp of constraints upon transformative action.*

Preconceptions about scientific method have influenced practices of social description and explanation. The major traditions of social thought have modeled social explanation on their view of a scientific

---

*Throughout this book and its constructive sequel I use the term "politics" in both a narrower and a broader sense. The narrower sense is the conflict over the mastery and uses of governmental power. The broader sense is the conflict over the terms of our practical and passionate relations to one another and over all the resources and assumptions that may influence these terms. Preeminent among these assumptions are the institutional arrangements and imaginative preconceptions that compose a social framework, context, or structure. Governmental politics is only a special case of politics in this larger sense. In a theory that carries to extremes the view of society as artifact, this larger notion of politics merges into the conception of society making. The slogan "It's all politics" adds a further twist to this more inclusive idea. The additional twist is the notion that this society-making activity follows no preestablished plot and that its outcomes are not chiefly to be understood as the results of lawlike economic, organizational, and psychological constraints or overpowering developmental tendencies.

method most fully manifest in the natural sciences. The cruder versions of large-scale social theory and positivist social science have tried to come as close as possible to natural science. The subtler versions have seen in the historical, particularistic, and relatively contingent quality of social phenomena a reason to moderate the imitation of science. But they have then also moderated their explanatory and critical ambitions. Finally, those who have rebelled against the intimidating example of natural science have often done so by assimilating social theory to the humanities. The result has been to abandon the causal explanation of social facts and historical events to people who hold up the example of a single-minded view of science.

An antinecessitarian social theory must reject the choice between a scientistic social theory and a causally agnostic understanding. Thus, a discussion of the broader philosophical and scientific setting of social and historical studies caps my analysis of the internal situation of social theory. This discussion begins as an attempt to enlist certain discoveries of modern philosophy, psychology, and natural science in the endeavor to break the scientistic obsession. But it ends as an effort to use these same discoveries to make the constructive implications of the earlier criticism of social and historical studies clearer and more powerful.

The analysis of the internal situation of social thought and of its philosophical and scientific setting is preceded in this book by a discussion of three other themes. These themes deal with aspects of contemporary practical experience and ideology. Nevertheless, they too provide points of departure for the development of a social theory capable of carrying to extremes the view of social order as frozen politics. They highlight the practical importance of the effort to work out a body of ideas faithful to the insight that society is made and imagined. They suggest the diversity of paths for arriving at the same intellectual position.

The first such starting point is the diffusion to ever broader numbers of people of an idea of work once restricted to tiny numbers of leaders, artists, and thinkers and not always and everywhere shared even by them. In this view of work, true satisfaction can be found only in an activity that enables people to fight back, individually or collectively, against the established settings of their lives – to resist these settings and even to remake them. The dominant institutional and imaginative structure of a society represents a major part of this constraining biographical circumstance, and it must therefore also be a central target of transformative resistance. Those who have been converted to the idea of a transformative vocation cannot easily return to the notion of work as an honorable calling within a fixed scheme of social roles and hierarchies, nor can they remain content with a purely instrumental view of labor as a source of material benefits with which to support themselves and their families.

The attraction of the ideal of a transformative vocation depends on the satisfaction of elementary material needs. Moreover, the distinctive traditions of particular nations and classes influence both the interpretation of this ideal and its persuasive force. Nevertheless, something in this conception of work represents the combination of a deeper insight with a more defensible aim of human striving, deeper and more defensible than the empirical and normative assumptions on which other available views of work depend. The social theory anticipated in this book is, among other things, an effort to develop the ideas that make sense of the transformative vocation and to justify its claim to allegiance.

A second starting point for my argument is the effort to develop ideas that elucidate and support what this book calls the radical project or the project of the modernist visionary. I do not claim that leftist liberal, or modernist radicals understand their cause in the precise terms by which it is described in these pages. On the contrary, the conception of the radical project already presupposes a criticism, a revision, and a reconciliation of separate and even antagonistic traditions: liberal and leftist proposals for social reconstruction and modernist attitudes toward rigid roles and conventions. The criticism of these loosely related traditions can lead us to rethink our ideas about society. This rethinking can converge with the intellectual agenda developed from the other points of departure discussed in this book. For in every instance the deficiencies of inherited leftist or liberal ideas turn out to be closely related to failures of our empirical understanding of society.

Institutional fetishism vitiates the most familiar liberal and leftist ideas. The classical liberal mistakenly identifies a particular group of makeshift compromises in the organization of representative democracies and market economies with the very nature of a free democratic and market order. The orthodox Marxist subsumes these same unique institutional arrangements under a general type of social organization that supposedly represents a well-defined stage of world history. He then excuses himself from the need to describe in detail the next, socialist stage of social evolution.

The modernist critic of roles and conventions often makes a different empirical mistake, at a higher level of abstraction. Human freedom, he is prone to believe, consists in the repeated defiance of all established institutions and conventions. We may not be able to purge social life of its structured and repetitious quality; but only so long as we continue trying can we hope to affirm our transcendence over the confining and belittling worlds in which we find ourselves.

This version of the modernist creed hopes for both too much and too little. It hopes for too much because it fails to see that we can never perform the act of defiance often enough or relentlessly enough to save ourselves from having to settle down in a particular social order. But it also hopes for too little. For all its negativism it fails to see that the relation of our context-revising freedom to the contexts we inhabit is itself up for grabs. The institutional and imaginative frameworks of social life differ in their quality as well as in their content, that is to say, in the extent to which they remain available for revision in the midst of ordinary social life. The adherent to the negativistic heresy within modernism believes that structures will be structures. But this belief imposes an unjustifiable restriction on the principle of historical variability that this same modernist ardently espouses.

The effort to correct and to unify the radical project by disengaging it from these errors holds an interest even for those who entertain little sympathy for any part of the radical commitment. The general insights and the concrete proposals that result from this exercise contribute to the solution of a dilemma that has increasingly overshadowed our debates about social and personal ideals. We lose faith in the existence of a transcendent, secure place above particular collective traditions from which to evaluate these traditions. Yet we also rebel against the idea that we must merely choose a framework, or accept the framework we are in, and take for granted its preconceptions about the possible and desirable forms of human association. A social theory capable of informing a revised and unified version of the radical cause shows that this rebellion is justified and that it can be carried out without either promoting nihilism or perpetuating belief in an uncontroversial and definitive foundation for normative thought.

Here, as elsewhere, *Social Theory: Its Situation and Its Task* merely suggests a route that *Politics* actually clears and follows. The modest beginning serves as a reminder that we do not need a developed social theory to begin criticizing and correcting liberal, leftist, and modernist ideas. Instead, our attempts to combine, step by step, revised ideals and changed understandings can themselves help build such a theory.

A third point of departure for the intellectual enterprise launched in this book is the effort to rethink the implications of the setbacks and obstacles the radical project has encountered in recent history. (For the present purpose I have in mind the liberal and leftist rather than the modernist side of radicalism.) The disappointments of the communist revolutions and of third world experiments present the most dramatic admonitory fables. Wherever it has gained power the organized left has proved more successful at achieving economic growth, at redistributing wealth, and even at exciting nationalist fervor than at realizing the participatory self-government of which its leaders so often speak. We can glean more subtle and no less revealing lessons from the experience of leftist and liberal movements in the rich Western democracies.

In these countries the leftist and progressive liberal forces stand divided into two camps. One camp maintains the purity of its radical views at the cost of increasing difficulty in winning or maintaining electoral majorities. This left interprets radicalism from the vantage point of Marxist ideas that commit it to a rigid set of class alliances and to a narrow conception of transformative possibilities. It continues to present itself as the spokesman of an organized industrial working class, entrenched in mass-production industries that represent an ever weaker and smaller sector of the advanced economies. It remains committed to a contrast between a capitalist present whose place in world history it professes to understand and a socialist future to whose contours it can give little content other than redistribution and nationalization.

A second camp seeks to break into the mainstream and to become, or remain acceptable to, majorities. But it usually does so at the cost of abandoning its framework-transforming commitments. It settles down to a program of social democracy. This social-democratic program accepts the current institutional forms of representative democracies and regulated markets. It favors economic redistribution and grassroots participation in local government and in the workplace. And it argues that a more technical management of social problems has superseded great ideological conflicts over social life.

Social democrats regularly come face-to-face with the constraints that the existing institutional framework imposes on their redistributive and participatory aims. If they continue to take these institutional arrangements for granted they find their goals frustrated. If, on the other hand, they advocate and begin to realize alternative ways of institutionalizing representative democracies, market economies, and the social control of economic accumulation, their conception of their goals, and of their relation to familiar adversaries and allies, undergoes a drastic change.

For all its disappointments social democracy has become by default the most attractive political agenda in the world, the one with the broadest and most faithful following. Even parties whose orthodox leftist or classical-liberal rhetoric commits them to oppose the social-democratic program have, once in power, regularly contributed to its extension. The great political question of our day has become: Is social democracy the best that we can reasonably hope for?

The belief that social democracy is the best program we can expect to achieve rests on assumptions about what forms of governmental and economic organization are possible and how they change – the same assumptions criticized in other parts of this introductory book. If we are serious about assessing the claims of social democracy, we must subject these assumptions to criticism. When we do so, we discover that they do not hold up.

The explanatory and programmatic social theory into which this book leads formulates ideas that can help us push the radical project beyond the point to which social democracy has carried it. The explanatory ideas account for the failures of the radical project in ways that do not make current institutional arrangements appear to be the necessary outcomes of intractable organizational, economic, or psychological constraints. They help us find transformative opportunity in the midst of apparently insuperable constraint. They provide a credible view of social change and social invention, freeing us from the temptation to describe as realistic only those proposals that stick close to current practice. The programmatic ideas informed by these explanatory conjectures present a detailed alternative to social democracy and describe both the justifications that support this alternative and the style of transformative practice that can bring it into being. *Social Theory: Its Situation and Its Task* emphasizes the elements of the problem rather than the terms of the proposed solution. But the description of the problem anticipates the terms of the solution.

A clear connection links the three starting points that precede my discussion of the internal situation of social thought: the idea of the transformative vocation, the reinterpretation of the radical cause, and the discontent with social democracy. For the first represents the repercussion of the radical project on our expectations about work while the second shows the influence of this project on the imagination of possible social futures.

It is not surprising that a more credible social theory assists the modernist, liberal, and leftist radicals. We must be realists in order to become visionaries, and we need an understanding of social life (whether or not a theoretical understanding) to criticize and enlarge our view of social reality and social possibility. But the reverse claim that the radical perspective has a unique cognitive value, that it contributes to the development of a non-necessitarian social theory, seems far more controversial. Why, indeed, should the progress of our insight into social life be tied up with the concerns and fortunes of a particular program for the reconstruction of society? The main text of *Politics* argues that an explanatory social theory has a far closer connection to our normative commitments than modern philosophical preconceptions about facts and values allow. A fully developed social theory interprets our efforts at individual and collective self-assertion. This interpretation can prompt us to revise our preexisting beliefs about where to find self-assertion and how to achieve it. Given certain additional assumptions, which are themselves as factual as they are normative, it can even persuade us to change our ideals and commitments.

The case for the convergence of explanatory and prescriptive ideas is intricate and contentious. This argument plays no major role in this introductory work. But there is a looser and less doubtful link between the explanatory and the programmatic ideas prefigured in this book. As reinterpreted here, the radical project seeks to change the relation between formative structures and formed routines. It sees the disruption of the social mechanisms of dependence and domination as inseparable from the achievement of this objective. The basic puzzle of social explanation, the chief obstacle to generalization about society and history, the reason why social understanding remains so hard to square with scientific method, is that we are not governed fully by the established imaginative and institutional contexts of our societies and that such contexts are not interestingly determined by general laws or inflexible constraints. The radical is the person who can least afford to disregard this vocation for indiscipline. He wants to use it, to extend it, and even – by an apparent paradox – to embody it in a set of practices and institutions. He must therefore also comprehend it. Thus, to look at society and history from his standpoint (even though the onlooker may be a conservative) is to force yourself to confront the central explanatory scandal of social and historical studies in the hope of turning this embarrassment into a source of insight.

The discussion does not begin immediately with the points of departure enumerated in the preceding pages. Instead, it turns first to the description of a view of human activity – a picture of our relation to our contexts – that inspires all the programmatic and explanatory arguments of *Politics*. The social frameworks or structures with which these arguments deal are only a special case of the contexts addressed by this preliminary conception.

I do not mean this initial view of our relation to the mental or social contexts we construct and inhabit to be taken on faith. It is rather to be justified retrospectively by the relative success of the explanatory and programmatic ideas it informs. Its defense is what can be accomplished under its aegis. Nevertheless, the tentative statement of this picture of our relation to our contexts at the outset of the long, taxing, and implausible project that this book begins may help dispel ambiguities by clarifying intentions. It locates this theoretical venture in a speculative setting broader than any of the discrete points of departure for the argument.

This conception of our relation to our contexts gives a new twist to one of the oldest and most puzzling themes of our civilization: the idea that man is the infinite caught within the finite. His external circumstances belittle him. His ardors and devotions are misspent on unworthy objects. An adherent to this view of our basic circumstance is hopeful when he thinks that this disproportion between the quality of our longings and the nature of our circumstances can be diminished. He is doubly hopeful when he thinks that the methods for diminishing this disproportion are the same as the means for cleansing our relations to one another of their characteristic dangers of subjugation and of disrespect for the originality in each of us.

The social theory foreshadowed here gives a detailed social and historical content to this speculative conception and provides reasons for this double hope. Reconsidered from the perspective of this theory, the radical project has a moral significance that goes beyond the liberal or leftist aim of freeing society from structures of dependence and domination and beyond the modernist goal of rescuing subjectivity and intersubjectivity from rigid roles and unexamined conventions. This greater ambition is to make our societies more responsive to that within us which ultimately rejects these limited experiments in humanity and says that they are not enough.

2

The Conditional and the Unconditional

OUR thoughts and desires and our relations to one another never fit, completely or definitively, within the structures we impose upon belief and action. Sometimes we conduct ourselves as exiles from a world whose arrangements exclude no true insight and no worthwhile satisfaction. But more often we treat the plain, lusterless world in which we actually find ourselves, this world in which the limits of circumstance always remain preposterously disproportionate to the unlimited reach of striving, as if *its* structures of belief and action were here for keeps, as if *it* were the lost paradise where we could think all the thoughts and satisfy all the desires worth having. When we think and act in this way, we commit the sin the prophets called idolatry. As a basis for self-understanding, it is worse than a sin. It is a mistake.

Occasionally, however, we push the given contexts of thought, desire, and practical or passionate relations aside. We treat them as unreal and even as if our apparently unfounded devotion to them had been just a ploy. We think the thoughts and satisfy the desires and establish the relationships excluded, in the world we inhabit, by all the practical or conceptual structures to which we had seemed so thoroughly subjugated. We think and act, at such moments, as if we were not ultimately limited by anything. Our practical, theoretical, and spiritual progress is largely the record of these repeated limit breakings. The experience of freedom and achievement implied in such acts of defiance is iconoclastic: it works by doing things that cannot be dreamt of in the established mental or social world rather than by creating the world that could realize all dreams.

You can take the social theory anticipated in this book as the systematic development of this conception of human activity into a view of society and personality. The conception includes three elements.

The first element is the idea of the contextual or conditional quality of all human activity. To say that extended conceptual activity is conditional is to say that its practice depends on taking for granted, at least provisionally, many beliefs that define its nature and limits. These assumptions include criteria of validity, verification, or sense; a view of explanation, persuasion, or communication, and even an underlying ontology – a picture of what the world is really like. It may even include a set of premises about whether and in what sense thought and language have a structure.

Our representations cannot be both significant and open to complete revision within the framework of assumptions about sense, validity, or verification on which the significance of the representation depends. The impossibility of correcting our representations without having to change our frameworks is hardly self-evident. After all, people have often believed that they lived in a world where assumptions are never at risk. These people have not been confused. They have, however, been mistaken. It just turns out that our world is really not like this. The contextual quality of thought is a brute fact. But it is not an isolated fact. It fits in with some of the other most important facts about ourselves.

All sustained practical activity takes for granted certain terms of the access that people have to one another: material, cognitive, emotional. These assumed terms appear most decisively as established powers and rights. Such rights and powers draw the outline within which people can make claims upon one another's help. Whatever its origins in conflict and coercion, a stable system of powers and rights must also work as the practical expression of a certain way of imagining society: of conceiving what the relations among people can and should be like in different areas of existence. Unless the rights and powers are read against such a background, they will not be respected and, in the end, they will not even be understood.

Society works and assumes a definite form because the fighting over all these terms of order is partly interrupted and contained. The ordinary modes of exchange and attachment, dependence and dominion, take the terms as given and derive from them both their basic shape and their accepted meaning. These facts constitute the contextual or conditional quality of social life.

There is no ordering of life in society of which we can say at the same time, first, that it can shape people's access to one another and second, that it can be compatible with all the forms of human association people might come to imagine and want. Again, this is no self-evident impossibility: you might imagine a natural form of society where the terms, though specific, were compatible with all the feasible and desirable forms of association. In such a view, the apparent departures from this natural form would turn out to be practically or morally disastrous and self-defeating. Throughout history many of the most influential social doctrines have taught some version of the belief in an authoritative model of society. Most of the modern thinkers who pretended to scorn this belief continued and continue faithful to embrace it in diluted and vestigial form.

The second element in this conception of human activity is the idea that we can always break through all contexts of practical or conceptual activity. At any moment people may think or associate with one another in ways that overstep the boundaries of the conditional worlds in which they had moved till then.

You can see or think in ways that conflict with the established context of thought even before you have deliberately and explicitly revised the context. A discovery of yours may be impossible to verify, validate, or even make sense of within the available forms of explanation and discourse; or it may conflict with the fundamental pictures of reality embodied in these forms. It may nevertheless be true. It may turn out to be a truth in the very fields that had no room for it. In the contest between the incongruous insight and the established context, the context may go under, and the proponents of the insight may discover retrospectively the terms that justify the forbidden idea.

What is true of different areas of thought, taken one by one, also holds for the work of the mind as a whole. Put together all the forms of discourse in science, philosophy, and art. Define their formative contexts however you like, so long as you define them with enough precision to save them from emptiness. The powers of the mind will never be exhaustively defined by this catalog. There will continue to be insights that do not fit any member of the list – and not just separate insights accommodated by casual adjustments here and there but whole lines of belief, explanation, or expression. No final balance can be achieved, either in the mind's life as a whole or in any segment of it, between possible insight and available discourse; the power of insight outreaches all the statable contexts of thought.

The same principle applies to the contexts of human association. People will always be able to order their relations to one another – from the most practical forms of collective labor to the most disinterested sorts of communal attachment – in ways that conflict with established terms of mutual access. Most of this deviation will be sufficiently fragmentary and truncated to seem a mere penumbra of distraction and uncertainty around the fundamentals of social order. But intensify the deviations far enough – either generalize or radicalize the local experiments – and the conflict becomes unmistakable.

What is true for any given society is true as well for all societies put together, no matter what our historical vantage point may be. There is no past, existent, or statable catalog of social orders that can accommodate all the practical or passionate relationships that people might reasonably and realistically and rightly want to establish. So the power to make society always goes beyond all the societies that exist or that have existed, just as the power to discover the truth about the world cannot keep within the forms of discourse that are its vehicles.

The second part of this view – the idea that all contexts can be broken – may seem incompatible with the first element – the idea that all activity is contextual. If, having broken the context they are in, people could simply remain outside any context, the thesis that all activity is contextual would be overturned. But the paradox is apparent. Context breaking remains both exceptional and transitory. Either it fails and leaves the preestablished context in place, or it generates another context that can sustain it together with the beliefs or relationships allied to it. An insight may enter into conflict with established criteria of validity, verification, and sense, or with a settled conception of fundamental reality. But if it tells a truth, then there will be criteria that can be retrospectively constructed with the aim of preserving it. A form of practical or passionate association may be incompatible with the established terms of mutual access. But unless it does irremediable violence to some demand of personal or collective existence, there must be a remade and reimagined social world in which it might figure. In the context of association as in the context of representation, every act of limit breaking either fails or becomes an incident in a quick movement toward a reconstructed order.

We never overcome context dependence. But we may loosen it. For contexts of representation or relationship differ in the severity of the limits they impose on our activity. The acknowledgment of this difference is the third element in this picture of our relation to our contexts.

A conceptual or social context may remain relatively immunized against activities that bring it into question and that open it up to revision and conflict. To the extent of this immunity, a sharp contrast appears between two kinds of activities: the normal activities that move within the context and the extraordinary transformative acts that change the context itself. This contrast is both a truth and lie. Though it describes a reality, it also conceals the relativity of the distinction between context-preserving and context-breaking activities. Pushed far enough, the small-scale adjustments and revisions that accompany all our routines may turn into chances for subversion. Once you disregard this potential, the conditionality of the contexts becomes easy to forget. You can mistake the established modes of thought and human association for the natural forms of reason or relationship: that limitless plain where mind and desire and society making could wander freely without hitting against any obstacle to their further exertions.

But you can also imagine the setting of representation or relationship progressively opened up to opportunities of vision and revision. The context is constantly held up to light and treated for what it is: a context rather than a natural order. To each of its aspects there corresponds some activity that robs it of its immunity. The more a structure of thought or society incorporates the occasions and instruments of its own revision, the less you must choose between maintaining it and abandoning it for the sake of the things it excludes. You can just remake or reimagine it. Suppose, for example, a society whose formative system of powers and rights is continuously on the line, a system neither invisible nor protected against ordinary conflict; a society in which the collective experience of setting the terms of social life passes increasingly into the tenor of everyday experience; a society that therefore frees itself from the oscillation between modest, aimless bickering and extraordinary revolutionary outbursts; a society where, in some larger measure, people neither treat the conditional as unconditional nor fall to their knees as idolaters of the social world they inhabit. Imagine a scientific or artistic representation that extends the boundaries within which the mind can move without coming into conflict with the premises of the representation. Imagine, further, that this extension comes about by making the forms of representation themselves increasingly apparent, controversial, and revisable.

The cumulative change I describe in the conditions of reason or relationship neither hides nor abolishes context dependence. It recognizes it with a vengeance and, in so doing, changes its nature. To live and move in the conditional world is, then, constantly to be reminded of its conditionality. To gain a higher freedom from the context is to make the context more malleable rather than to bring it to a resting point of universal scope. Thus, the third element in the picture of human activity elucidates the coexistence of the other two elements – that everything is contextual and that all contexts can be broken.

The conception of human activity made up of these three elements confronts the mind with a central difficulty. It also helps shape an understanding of the ideal for the person and the society.

All our major problems in the understanding of society arise from the same source. They have to do with the difficulty of accounting for the actions of a being who, individually and collectively, in thought and relationship, might break through the contexts within which he ordinarily moves. The perennial temptation in the understanding of society and personality is to equate the very nature of explanation with an explanatory style that treats people's actions and thoughts as governed by a describable structure. When we make this mistake, we deny the power to discover truth and establish association beyond the limits of the available contexts. Or we treat these episodes of structure breaking as if they were themselves governed by metastructures. The metastructure may be a set of ultimate constraints upon possible social worlds accompanied by more specific accounts of why certain possible worlds become actual at given times. Or it may be the scheme of a lawlike evolution that controls the passage from one social order to the next. To disengage the idea of explanation from the exclusive hold of these styles of explanation is the beginning of insight in social thought. Indeed, for the theorist of society it is the most exacting and delicate of tasks.

The same picture of human activity transforms our vision of the ideal for society and personality if it does not generate an ideal by its own force. Because we do not move in a context of all contexts, there is the danger that our views of the social ideal will turn out to be a projection of the particular society into which we happen to have been thrown. The objectivity possible in the formulation of a social ideal must have something to do with its ability to incorporate the next best thing to absolute knowledge and fulfilled desire: not to be a prisoner of the context. The pursuit of this demand is intimately entangled with our desire not to be prisoners of one another. It is even bound up with the history of our practical capabilities.

The conception of human action I have outlined must be justified, in part, by its fruits. *Politics* turns it into a general view of society and personality. The spirit of this view is to understand reality from the perspective of transformation. The little, endless quarrels within contexts will be shown to contain the secret of the great struggles over contexts. The scheme of transformative variation that enables us to explain events must not be one that mythologizes society and history by treating the breaking of contexts either as if it were itself a context-governed activity or, to the extent it is not so governed, as if it were unintelligible, a gap in the powers of explanation and judgment. The truth of human freedom, of our strange freedom from any given finite structure, must count, count affirmatively, for the way we understand ourselves and our history.

The social theory that develops this view of our relation to our contexts is a theory that unrelentingly rejects what might be called the naturalistic premise about society. Because the discussion of this premise and of the consequences of its rejection plays a central role in the arguments of this introductory book, I now define it tentatively. The definition will be enriched, gathering both precision and richness of connotation, as the analysis moves forward.

The naturalistic premise represents a denial of the conditionality of social worlds. It takes a particular form of social life as the context of all contexts – the true and undistorted form of social existence. By repudiating the first element in the account of our relation to our contexts sketched earlier, the naturalistic thesis also rejects the other elements. The natural context of social life may pass through decay or renascence, but it cannot be remade. Nor is there, in this view, any sense in which the defining context of social life can become less contextual – less arbitrary and confining. It is already the real thing.

The naturalistic thesis may now be defined in slightly greater detail and more independently of this view of human activity. It holds up the picture of an ordering of human life that is not the mere product of force and fraud. This ordering, sustained by a system of powers and rights, includes a practical scheme of coordination, contrast, and ranking. It makes each individual's membership in the division of labor an occasion to reaffirm the general scheme of order. It constantly draws new life from the pursuit of ordinary interests within the terms it establishes. It claims to see into the innermost core of society and personality. This authentic pattern of social life can undergo corruption and regeneration. But it can never be rearranged. To uphold the natural social order is the basic social piety.

The canonical form of society is natural in the sense that the distinction between what it prescribes and what force and fraud conspire to establish is given: given in the truth about personality and society rather than merely chosen or brought about by fighting; changeless and only partly intelligible, like the great natural world around us. The reconstructive will and imagination can make only a modest dent on this natural order, when indeed they can exercise any influence on it at all.

Again, the canonical form of social life is natural in that it emerges when ravenous and fragmentary interests, and the partiality of viewpoint they favor, have been either effectively tamed or wisely combined. Natural society is society understood and established beyond the perspective of the will, always the perspective of one-sidedness and self-assertion.

Finally, the canonical form of social life is natural because it is seen as connecting fundamental truth about society to equally basic truth about personality. The import of this correspondence must be left deliberately loose: it bears different philosophical interpretations. All clear-cut versions of the naturalistic premise, however, attribute to the personality some proper order of emotions, or of virtues and vices. This order sustains, and is in turn renewed by, the arrangements of the larger society. A person's repeated willingness to meet the claims that the natural social order assigns to him exercises a shaping, incantatory, even redemptive influence upon the dark, labile force of his emotions.

The naturalistic premise has been the central element in most of the forms of social thought throughout history. Modern social theory rebelled against the naturalistic idea. It did so, however, incompletely. Many of its contradictions and inadequacies arise from the incompleteness of this rebellion. We must find a way to complete it.

3
The Idea of the Transformative Vocation
A First Point of Departure

THREE basic ideas about work are now available in the world. These ideas are not just about jobs; seen from a wide enough perspective, they involve people's views of what they can expect to do with their lives, and they put in question the tie between the family and society. The rivalry of these conceptions, as they have been variously developed by different classes and among different peoples, gives rise to an obscure but decisive spiritual struggle. People wage this struggle all over the world, through contrasting visions of society and secret movements of the heart.

Each of these visions of work finds its chief home in the experience and outlook of a part of society. But the groups responsible for developing the idea vary from one moment in history, and even from one society, to another.

Work may be seen as an honorable calling within society. So conceived, labor enables the individual (at first the man but then others as well) to support the family that provides him with his most important sustaining relations. The job as honorable calling helps shape a person's view of his own dignity. He can do something that fulfills one of the natural needs of society. He fulfills it by performing, or preparing for, work that requires proficiency or experience. His job, and the trained and learned capacities with which he performs it, singles him out from the shifting, the dependent, and the useless.

The idea of work as an honorable calling usually accompanies certain preconceptions about society and the family. There exists a catalog of natural needs: social demands that have to be met for a society to go on as it always has. To this catalog of impersonal jobs, there corresponds an equally natural list of occupations, each with its distinctive skills and rewards. The person who occupies one of these positions can expect to live with his family in a certain way. He also has, at work, a distinctive relation to the people who do other jobs. Thus, an idea of natural ranks accompanies the notion of natural social needs and natural jobs.

The social world that these honorable callings keep going knows its share of conflict. But its quarrels – according to this view of social life – deal more with peripheral matters. People may feel that they have been done an injustice. They may try to grab more for themselves and their co-workers than what they are properly entitled to. In either event there will be trouble. But the basic order of needs, jobs, and ranks is not, in its fundamentals, the outcome of such struggles. It is just part of the way things are. You can go a long way toward qualifying this view of social life without giving up its central tenets. For the naturalistic attitude to society seems far more persuasive in the nuance of active belief than in the caricature of exposition.

The image of work as an honorable calling and the larger vision of society that extends and justifies it have often been accompanied by a view of the family. The honorable worker is, above all, the adult man. His performance of the honorable job outside the family lends moral authority as well as economic support to his position within the family. The family itself amounts to a softened, smaller-scale version of the social world. The wife and the children occupy a recognized place within the family. By performing their roles scrupulously, they earn the respect of their wider social milieu. When all goes well, the greater world of society and the smaller realm of the family display a fundamental harmony both in their economic requirements and in their moral principles.

Today, this idea of work flourishes most vigorously among the skilled and semiskilled working classes of the rich Western and the communist societies. It survives better among those who do something with their hands or who apply techniques with tangible results than among the lower ranks of paper pushers and commodity circulators. But until recently in the history of the West, and of many of the civilizations whose life the Western peoples have interrupted, all ranks of society shared this conception of work. Even the most privileged groups embraced it. The gentleman landowner might disclaim anything that looked like a job. But his view of himself included the idea of occupying a natural station that both entitled and obligated him to perform valuable social tasks. He showed he was up to it by exhibiting in his person and his deeds the qualities proper to his caste.

Another, more chastened idea of work is also loose in the world. According to this conception, work lacks any intrinsic authority, any power of its own to confer dignity or direction on a human life. You have to do it to achieve or support the things that count: your family and your community or, if worse comes to worst, your own self. If labor can still be said to be honorable in this instrumental view, the honor lies solely in the activities its earnings support.

The instrumental view of work represents drastically diminished expectations of what a person can make of his life. It is in fact, and is understood to be, an aberration: the stigma of a terrible defeat or the price of a transition to a higher mode of life. In the rich Western countries of the present day, three types of workers seem most often to share this vision of work.

Some are people who have been defeated in their attempt to grow up into the honorable working class or who have been cast out of this class after having gotten into it. They float from one unstable and dead-end job to another, and pine in the suffering underclass.

Others who hold this instrumental view of work also occupy the worst and least secure jobs. They often come from a foreign country or a backward region, to which they hope to return. For them, work is a purgatory governed by rules they can barely understand. They analogize its arrangements as best they can to the ideas of obligation and reward they have brought with them to a new land. Their over-riding goal remains to go back home to a better life that includes the experience of labor as an honorable calling. This hope may eventually be frustrated. It may also be replaced by the desire to stay where they are and there to become the honorable workers they had at first thought of becoming back home. Meanwhile, they live in their com-munities and find in these communal bonds the consolations and the self-respect their jobs deny them.

Still others who hold the instrumental conception of work are young people or married women willing to take on temporary jobs. For them, too, the immediate conception of work can be unashamed-ly instrumental because it remains ancillary to their main concern: a future career or the life of the family.

In other parts of the globe – in some of the communist and third world countries – access to the experience of work as an honorable calling remains barred to vast numbers of people. These people may be driven to a purely instrumental vision of labor. But, at every opportunity, they may also put up a rearguard struggle and demand something better.

For to conceive of your workaday activity in this manner is to view the social world as utterly oppressive or alien. If the personality is not discredited and crushed by this world, it is at least (with the exception of the part-time workers) denied any sense of belonging to it. Confidence in a natural order of needs, jobs, and ranks is shaken, though not dissipated. The defeated and the excluded understand more easily what the self-deception of the honorable workers tends to conceal: that the entire order of jobs and ranks—not just its details and adjustments – results from fighting and from the containment of fighting. They have seen the fist without the glove and have looked in through the window, with the undeceived eyes of the outcast, at the indifference of the fortunate. But they would gladly exchange this insight—which is, in part, a discovery of the falsehood of the naturalistic premise – for a reprieve from their defeat or their exclusion.

A third idea of work has appeared in the world, and it is turning things inside out. It connects self-fulfillment and transformation: the change of any aspect of the practical or imaginative setting of the individual's life. To be fully a person, in this conception, you must engage in a struggle against the defects or the limits of existing society or available knowledge. The goals of self-fulfillment and service to society combine with the notion that such service requires you to press against things and conceptions as they are. The quarrel may be pursued in imaginative work rather than out in the open. Even when it involves real-life conflict, it may be moderated and concealed under the appearance of faithful service. But it cannot be abandoned altogether without exacting a price in disappointment and failure. Resistance becomes the price of salvation. Only when you move away from the concern with the terms of collective life toward the more impersonal endeavors of art, philosophy, and science or give yourself over to the immediate care of individuals does the weight of this command diminish.

This idea of work – and of what you can most valuably do with your life – has taken root most strongly among the educated and the privileged, and especially among the young who are educated for privilege. You can find it most unequivocally among intellectuals, agitators, artists, and scientists. But it extends as well into the great professions. Each profession does more than link a privileged exercise of power to a claim of expertise. It also serves as the scene of a conflict between the idea of the honorable calling and the more ambitious standard of the transformative vocation.

The people who have been converted to this view of what they should do with themselves run into trouble in their experience of their own lives and in their relations to all the groups who have stuck with another vision of what work and life are for. Even after you have tried to understand, with a clear mind and a quiet heart, what the trouble means, you cannot easily tell. Is there a flaw in the idea of the transformative vocation that condemns it to futility and self-deception? Is it, in this respect, like a certain romantic view of love with which it has been historically associated? Or are these difficulties and surprises the unavoidable road to higher insight?

A person may come under the influence of the idea of the transformative vocation in his youth. Much may bring him over to it. Even for those who deny that it conveys any ultimate truth about mind and activity, its presence, its omnipresence, in the productions of high culture is hard to miss. The works of literature and social thought, of speculative theory and moral sloganeering, revel in it.

The broader popular culture speaks it back in a thousand diluted but still recognizable forms. Both the political heroes and the modernist antiheroes of the age seem to embody one aspect or another of its central concerns.

The more seriously someone takes these ideas, the greater his difficulties are likely to be. As soon as he begins to face the resistances and the entanglements of the social world, the effort to realize the idea of the transformative vocation starts to seem an unrealistic and self-destructive program. It seems to demand both a favorable opportunity and corresponding gifts. If either are absent, what begins in high purpose may end as mere anxiety.

As the obstacles to an actual transformative involvement pile up, the would-be transformer faces ever more clearly a destructive dilemma. He may trim his sails and look for more modest and "realistic" expectations. But it is not easy to pass from the idea of the transformative vocation to the notion of the honorable calling. The former implies an insight into the relation between self and society that strikes at the foundations of the latter. This insight is just too convincing to forget, once the individual has recognized it and acted it out, however incompletely or unsuccessfully.

The assumptions that underlie the idea of the transformative vocation combine an idea about society with an idea about the self. Society lacks natural needs, jobs, and ranks; whatever the social order is, it is as a result of the fights that have taken place and of the fights that have been avoided. Your work may serve a human need whose claim to attention you regard as unquestionable. But what people make of you, your station, and your work is not something that you can take for granted as the natural order of things. This given context may confirm, distort, or defeat your intention.

The idea about self that joins this notion of society is the primacy of transforming denial in all human activities. You satisfy desires by changing something in the world. You understand a portion of reality by passing it, in fact or fantasy, through transformative variations: by imagining it other than what it is or seems to be. All the more complicated enterprises of the personality involve equally complicated revisions of the practical or imaginative setting through which the individual moves. Through such efforts, and through them alone, you discover and make yourself.

These ideas about self and society betray a disbelief in what I earlier called the naturalistic premise as well as revealing a particular view of the purpose of a working life. The notion of an honorable calling cannot easily be made plausible again without resurrecting the vision of self and society implicit in the naturalistic premise.

The person who can neither make good on his commitment to a transformative vocation nor gain faith in the idea of the honorable calling soon finds himself driven down to the instrumental conception of work. He seeks in the family or the spectacles of an ornamental culture compensatory solace for his incompensable loss. He cannot view his own instrumental work as the necessary transition to a higher form of experience.

When the idea of the transformative vocation runs into trouble it can take another direction. It may escalate rather than diminish its ambitions. Beyond the give-and-take of ordinary social life lie the great redemptive exercises of revolutionary thought, practice, and art. The artist sitting in his cork-lined room holds out the only true promise of happiness and salvation (but for himself or for everybody else as well?). Someone grinds away at his desk in the British Museum systematizing views about which most of his informed contemporaries hardly know what to think. A few generations later, people will be slaughtering one another in Manchuria in the name of his doctrines. Someone else arrives suddenly at a train station in the midst of violent civic commotion, seizes the state with the support of a disciplined following and an indignant mass, and inaugurates a new order of social life.

As escape routes for an embattled idea of transformative vocation, these images serve as corrupting delusions. They exclude all but a tiny band of extraordinary people. They cover up the actual texture of compromise, circumstance, resistance, and disappointment, the fantastic incongruity between intention and result, even in these unusual experiences. The heart, in its despair, wants to forget such indignities.

The two directions in which the idea of the transformative calling can move amount to two complementary ways of losing sanity. For the cognitive element in madness is precisely the alternation between two experiences of perception and reasoning. Perceptions and ideas are frozen in place; they cannot be recombined or replaced. At the same time, everything can be effortlessly broken down and combined with everything else. The simultaneous coexistence of these experiences makes all perceptions and thoughts appear arbitrary.

But suppose a person manages to keep the idea of transformative work from falling off in either of these directions. He soon finds himself at odds not only with people who share a different perspective on the aims of transformation but also with people who have a completely different view of work. He then has to recognize that activity inspired by such intentions contains, directly or indirectly, a claim to power that others resist and that he himself may be unable to justify or to confess. He may even try to get them to act in ways justified by his idea of work but opposed by them, in the name of their own ideals of labor and community, as a surrender to selfishness.

For example, a militant in a rich Western country fights to vindicate rights of abortion for unmarried women. He does so in part because he has an idea of personal dignity connected to his own idea of vocation. He wants to imagine, or to make, this idea universal. The working class family fights back not only out of religious belief but out of the desire to preserve, through the repression of occasional sexual unions, its own hierarchic authority, the accompaniment to its own ideas of work as honorable calling. After all, what more inclusive and more perfect form of social solidarity does the self-appointed champion have to put in place of the one he is trying to destroy?

If the would-be transformer is someone who acts in the world, he may fantasize that he belongs to a mass of people who increasingly share his vision of history and work. The existence of factions, the dense confusions of personal animosity and programmatic difference, the struggle for leadership, the elements of self-aggrandizement in his own conception of his calling – each of these amounts to a knock on the door that he would rather not answer. Once he has tasted power, however, he may find such fantasies convenient. He may present himself as the voice of those to whom he gives orders.

The idea of the transformative vocation has begun to influence large numbers of people all over the world. It wages a largely mute spiritual struggle against the other two notions of work. Where did this demanding and even dreamlike view come from? What is its essential human meaning? You would be misguided to see it merely as the result of local episodes in the history of thought. In some parts of the Western world, the idea bears the imprint of a secularized version of Protestant ideas of calling. But it has advanced everywhere, independently as well as by contagion. The conception of an honorable calling has been undermined by the insights into self and society described earlier. Through them, the idea of the transformative vocation connects to everything that shows people the made-up, remakable, and reimaginable quality of social life, to everything that frees the conception and the ordeal of personality from rigid social constraints. People seize on traditional religious, political, and moral doctrines and reinterpret them from the perspective of the new dispensation.

Once you view the idea of the transformative vocation from this more general standpoint you can identify in it a still larger human meaning. This meaning clarifies the hidden ambiguities, aspirations, and dangers of the idea, so carefully concealed in the ordinary thoughts and deeds of its adherents. The less the individual sees himself as occupying a natural position within a society that itself has a natural order, the more acutely he feels a certain aspect of his situation in his world. He feels it, ordinarily, less in its abstract and general statement than in particular and concrete ramifications. The person experiences himself as the center of his own world. He knows himself in a way that he can know no other mind. He feels, in his less guarded moments, a will to self-assertion and to the satisfaction of a desire that knows no fixed boundaries other than the limits imposed by temporary satiation, apathy, or despair. When he imagines the world without himself, after his own death, he still hovers there as a disembodied onlooker. But the individual is also made to confront the world as a subject among many others. He must develop introspection by participating in a practical and discursive give-and-take that constantly denies his claim to be the center of things. He must satisfy his material and spiritual needs by performing activities that force him to deal with people who do not see him as the center and in whose lapses into self-centeredness he sees the barely suppressed traces of his own self-absorption.

But when all the taunting correctives have piled up, the individual's claim to be the center still refuses to go away. How can we even call it a mistake? It is built into the most elementary pretheoretical moments of perception and desire. It belongs to the intimate and ultimate though ill-defined experience of selfhood. Our reflective ideas may refine this experience but they can never repudiate it without ceasing to be persuasive or even intelligible.

That we lay claim to the center while recognizing at the same time that we are not the center is more than a natural fact about us, like our susceptibility to certain optical illusions. It is just as basic to our experience as the structure of conceptual thought whose preconceptions about sameness and difference prohibit us from saying that we both are and are not the center. By what standard can we choose between the conceptual structure and the counterconceptual experience? Though we disbelieve the latter in certain contexts of understanding and action or when certain interests seem paramount, we put aside the former in other settings and for other purposes. A person incapable of making this switch would be judged more insane than many of the madmen we actually meet. For his madness would not be simply the exaggeration of a conflict, a self-division, in ordinary experience. It would be a denial of one of the enabling conditions of our routine perceptions and responsibilities.

The contrast between these two aspects of personality cannot become acute so long as the views of society and self that underlie the idea of work as an honorable calling survive. For these views prevent the experience of subjectivity, and therefore of the self as center, from reaching desperate and anxious lengths. They teach people to understand their internal world of passion and the outward order of society as two complementary realms that display the same principles of order and that, when well ordered, lend each other indispensable support. These naturalistic ideas cannot abolish the contrast in our experience between self-centeredness and the overcoming of self-centeredness. The ideas can, however, deny this experience a voice and make its occasional manifestations look like mere outbreaks of delusory self-regard. When, however, people no longer adhere to the naturalistic view underlying the idea of work as an honorable calling, the conflict between the two poles of experience breaks out into the open.

Personal love and transformative work enable people to escape selfishness and isolation without denying the weight of subjectivity. In love, they find a connection to another person that simultaneously confirms them in their sense of self-possession. Transformative action offers them a way to establish an alternative connection: an engagement with the larger collective context of their lives that gives the acting or imagining self a chance for self-assertion while refusing to sanctify the resistant context. Whichever route of connection you follow, you have surprises in store.

The pursuit of the transformative solution faces two obstacles, which are also riddles. The first embarrassment is the coexistence of constant resistance to all the transforming efforts of the imagination and the will with our failure ever fully to understand the sources of this resistance. This failure plagues us in every area of experience. Some of the reasons for this inability are distinctive to each field of activity; others are common to all fields.

Nonhuman nature remains imperfectly knowable and manageable because of its vast disproportion to our own selves. We know nature only in part, through forms of practice and imagination that, though they imitate transformative variations of the natural world, do so from the limiting perspective of our interests and faculties. One level of insight falls down into another, more basic or universal, without any hope of reaching a place of rest.

Society remains imperfectly intelligible and pliable because it is made up of distinct selves, each with its power to resist submission and disclosure. Moreover, no practical or imaginative ordering of human life represents the definitive, complete form of personality or society, nor do all the orderings that have ever existed, when put together. In every realm of society or nonhuman nature, our ideas suffer from an incurable instability: we may always discover at the next moment something that is not just novel but incompatible with our assumptions. Not only may we have ignored this truth before, but we may have ignored the whole way of thinking, or seeing, or talking that its full exploration requires.

The recalcitrance of our circumstances to complete mastery by the imagination and the will has an important corollary in political action: the inability fully to comprehend or control the consequences of action. William Morris described the ironic pathos of every transformative conflict over the terms of social life: "Men fight and lose the battle, and the thing they fought for comes about in spite of their defeat, and when it comes turns out to be not what they wanted, and other men must fight for what they wanted under another name."

The other problem with transforming action comes from within. The transformative deed fails completely to bridge the gap between the self as center and the self as one among others. It remains a bid for self-aggrandizement as well as a form of self-renunciation. The vicissitudes of the transformative vocation in society bring out this two-sidedness. The would-be transformer wants to shine and even to rule while portraying himself as the humble and responsive servant of an impersonal good. The self-appointed revolutionary vanguard, lording it over a frightened or passive populace in the name of a doctrine of virtual representation, is simply the extreme case of what appears, less starkly, in countless other disguises.

Most great social theories of the last two centuries accepted and attempted to explicate and develop the ideas underlying this revolutionary conception of work. But they did so in a way that concealed the embarrassments just described. They thereby limited the reach of the idea of the transformative vocation. They viewed the obstacles to transformation as the products of lawlike constraints that a fully informed mind would render fully intelligible. The would-be transformers could present themselves as agents of a historical necessity. The claim to be the unchosen agents of the oppressed and the voiceless remained their characteristic response to the suspicion of self-aggrandizement.

One way to understand the constructive social theory anticipated by this book is to read it as an attempt to carry to the hilt the view of society and personality within which the idea of the transformative vocation makes sense. We must reason about constraints without seeing them as the superficial expression of intelligible, lawlike necessities. We must describe how the antinaturalistic conception of self and society can inform the life projects of an individual. We must even try to show how it can guide these projects in ways that contain and ennoble the self-aggrandizing impulse.

4

Credible Ideals and Transformative Insight

A Second Point of Departure

I F you set out to participate in discussions of the social ideal, you find, in the rich countries of the West, three main conceptions of the capabilities of normative thought. Though these debates are carried on in a confined atmosphere, it is worth trying to understand their basic structure. This structure reveals the hidden implications of the failure of a visionary imagination of human possibility. It shows how the failure connects with a refusal to face the contingency of social worlds, a refusal that has marred even the most liberating social theories.

One setting for normative debates, within and outside the West, has been Marxism. In one view, Marxist doctrine simply rejected the sense of discussions about what ought to be: it told you what, in the end, had to be. The only possible choice left to the individual conscience was the decision whether voluntarily to collaborate with the arrow of history or to force it to detour before it hit its preestablished target. But you might well ask why you ought to collaborate with this history machine rather than resist it as best you could. Then the other theme in Marxism and other evolutionary social theories comes to the fore: historical development expresses an immanent moral rationality. This rationality amounts to a discontinuous but relentless progression toward higher levels of productive capacity but also, in the end, toward the disengagement of community and self-expression from dependency and domination. The appeal to such a rationality drastically underestimates the surprises of history – the indeterminacy of the actual constraints and the multiplicity of the possible sequences – while failing to develop any conception of personality and community. Consequently, it also downgrades the role of the imagination of associative possibility in awakening people to the belief that there are uncreated social worlds worth fighting for.

A second view of the foundations of normative thought appeals to the idea of a tragedy of incompatible ideals. This tragic liberalism claims that the ultimate issues of moral and political controversy are matters of commitment to one form of life against others. Each society or tradition embodies a scheme of ordered human life that gives primacy to certain values. In the end, the most a conscientious individual can do, on this account, is to take a stand for the overriding authority of some of these values against others. Such ultimate choices supposedly require a sacrifice of human possibilities with a legitimate claim on the social imagination: all the possibilities contained in the social worlds that you had finally opted against. This unavoidable sacrifice is the tragic element in this tragic liberalism. The liberal element is the belief that the best you can do is to avoid unnecessary exclusions and to safeguard the free institutions that would allow ideas and practices to change. These civilizing institutions are then more or less tacitly identified with those of the Western democracies of the day.

This view certainly has the advantage of recognizing the tentative, partial, and dangerous qualities of commitments and the importance of preserving an institutional context that makes the criticism and invention of social forms possible. But the conception of a tragedy of ultimate values drastically understates the transformability of society through politics. Take two supposed conflicting values like freedom and community. Each is understood against a tacit background of social practice in particular areas of life. The values simply have no determinate reference apart from these implied contexts. So the belief in a tragic conflict of values implies that the settings which give these values their detailed meaning cannot be remade.

If, for example, communal ideals were worked out in areas of social life from which they had, till then, been excluded, the tacit meaning of the idea of community would be enlarged or revised. Community cannot mean the same thing in a cooperative work team that it does in a family. As a result, the terms on which it comes into conflict with another equally contextualized value (like freedom) must also change.

Either the tragedy-of-values doctrine fails to recognize the way in which social ideals get their content from practical schemes of association, or it takes these schemes as given, as beyond the reach of the will and the imagination. You do not need to believe in the millennium to discount these preconceptions. They imply an arbitrary limit upon collective experiments in the forms of common life. They survive through the concealment of this implication.

A third position is the search for objective principles of evaluation. These principles may be derived from an appropriately defined situation of choice. Or they may be inferred from the direct scrutiny of our own or other people's moral intuitions and from the search for their underlying principles. Actually, these two methods are not that different from each other: to define the constraints that apply to the ideal choice situation – the motives, the knowledge, and the decision procedures of the people who are in it – you first have to choose among values or ideals. These decisions must then be justified by a similar mutual adjustment of intuition and principle, until you reach a condition of relative assurance and coherence in your moral and political ideas. Then, the whole body of principles promulgated in this ideal choice situation has to be compared with your intuitions. Though the principles may lead you to revise some of the intuitions, pushing you toward greater objectivity and self-understanding, you cannot expect to revise too many of them. For, in this view, the intuitions represent the ultimate givens of moral insight. This quest for objective principle always flounders on two related difficulties.

For one thing, there is a fatal hesitation between alternative views of the basis of intuitions and principles. Does their authority come from widespread agreement or from a transcendent source? The theorists cannot bring themselves to name such a higher authority, the kind that may require not just the marginal adjustment but the radical subversion of established opinions. (What could have been more antagonistic to moral common sense than Christianity or Buddhism at the time of their origin or, for that matter, at any time?) But the effort to base the intuitions and principles on consensus within a particular society or tradition is also unsatisfactory. In this era of mass politics and world history, people who think about such things can no longer easily believe – as much as they may want to – that their own society or tradition serves as the natural embodiment of civilization and the privileged channel of moral insight. They are therefore barred from continuing in the vein of most of the classic social doctrines of other times and places: the belief that, at its heart, the social order contains a scheme of right and necessary association and that the spiritual task of rulers, priests, and philosophers is to defend such schemes against corruption.

When the philosophers of our day look to consensus, they try to find values and decision procedures as little tainted as possible by the distinctive opinions of any one class or period. Here the other major problem with the search for objective principles becomes clear. To the extent that the values or decision procedures are defined in very loose and abstract terms, they remain vacuous. Any number of concrete ways of dealing with a discrete problem of choice may be inferred from them. When such guiding values are presented in greater detail their entanglement in the moral ideas of a limited social situation becomes unmistakable. And when a decision procedure – a philosophical method or a constitutional system – is made determinate, you discover that, both in construction and outcome, it implies a strong preference for some particular vision of society. Though it may never have been intended to be entirely neutral, it is even less neutral than it seemed.

If you refuse to speak solely with the adepts of one of the three normative positions described, but hear all these people out, follow them around, and patiently study their ideas, you begin to understand that their confusions and mistakes grow out of the same root. All these doctrines have been affected by the awareness of the contingency of forms of social life. This awareness has made it impossible for them to carry on work in the spirit of the dominant social doctrines of past civilization: the naturalistic idea that there exists a natural scheme of association, inherent in the available experience of social life, though perhaps corrupted, undeveloped, or unintelligible. Yet none of these doctrines has carried the recognition of contingency to its most drastic conclusions.

In each case the equivocations of doctrine grew out of the hesitancy between the full-fledged acknowledgment of contingency and the attempt to hedge. The hedge may appeal to the ideal of an immanent moral rationality in history. It may presuppose the need for a choice among a small stock of forms of social life – a choice that gives rise to the "tragedy of ultimate values." Or it may attribute a half-transcendent weight to the intuitions and principles at work in a particular community or tradition. The real question becomes whether you can fully acknowledge the contingency of social worlds and complete the unfinished break with the spirit of classical social doctrine while nevertheless continuing to make normative claims. The hesitancy to make the break has surely been encouraged by the fear that the unrestrained recognition of contingency would disarm moral and political judgment.

Moving from the disputes of the theorists to a larger realm of public controversy, you discover another disturbing aspect of the same circumstance: two, closely connected features of the way people discuss the nature of ideal society.

Debates about political programs and schemes of social reconstruction have a perverse quality. If your proposals depart widely from immediate social reality, people dismiss them as utopian. If the proposals come closer to what exists, or if they distinguish several stages of improvement, they are denounced as apologetic and uninspiring. It is hard to avoid concluding either that people are just not serious about these debates or that the impoverishment of their transformative vision has undermined their capacity to invent and to judge social ideals.

The other, related feature of quarrels about the ideal is that the available visions of regenerate community seem largely unbelievable. Few may accept the domesticated romantic trope of the marriage as a community that could be equally free of hierarchy and of conflict. But fewer yet have devised any conception that might replace that trope. Similarly, many have ceased to believe – if they ever did – in the utopian socialist and communist ideas of a redeemed humanity (the collective historical counterpart to the romantic idea of marriage) without finding any alternative way to imagine a radically bettered society.

Such utopian ideals are unbelievable for two apparently contradictory reasons. On the one hand they represent an effortless reconstruction of established reality: the reimagination of society disconnected from any idea of constraint and, therefore, also from the sustaining and persuasive touch of reality. On the other hand, they lack authority for the superficially opposite reason: that, in seeming to escape established society they in fact return to it. The vision of the effortlessly reconstructed social order turns out, on closer inspection, to be only the reverse image of the established society. The mind that has failed to struggle with experienced or imagined constraint, and that lacks any scheme of transformative variation with which to work, can, in the end, only reproduce through inversion what it wants to abolish.

Thus, the sanctification of established society and the effortless denial of it represent two sides of the same circumstance. The unbelievability of the most radical ideals results, surprisingly, from their failure to be radical enough. The people who oscillate between a vague utopianism and a depressed tinkering feel unable to ground proposals for social reconstruction in views of social reality and possibility.

There are psychological, logical, and social-theoretical foundations to the link between transformative insight and ideal reflection. The analysis of these foundations reveals the wider significance of the circumstance I have begun to describe and thus provides still another point of departure for a revised understanding of society.

Take first the psychological connection. When people cannot imagine transformation (except as relentless, mysterious drift or catastrophic accident), any far-reaching ideal must seem like a utopian flight from established reality. At the same time, the lack of an ideal that remains in touch with a credible process of social change may persuade people that there is little worth fighting for.

The assent we give to the ruling ideas of a social world has a remarkable quality, which confirms the intimate psychological connections between the insight into transformative opportunity and the definition of the social ideal. So long as the fighting over the basic terms of social life remains in check, we talk and act as if the established institutions were natural, necessary, and even holy. But as soon as these institutions get shaken, the erstwhile devotees seem suddenly to abandon the beliefs which, just a while ago, they had upheld with such fervor. The tears of devotion are not yet dry when the glee of defiance begins to shine through them.

To an astonishing degree active belief in the pieties of a social world depends on the quiescence of that world. When actual social destabilization fails to occur, its role must be taken over by imaginative effort. The imagination remembers the fighting that is over and recognizes it as the opportunity for another round of struggle. Or it takes the petty conflicts of ordinary social life as localized experiments that might be reenacted on a vaster scale. The people whose conduct is inspired by a conception of transformative possibility may then undermine the established order enough to shake the pieties of the multitude of skeptics.

A particular variant of the psychological relation between imaginative vision and transformative experience has become especially important. Suppose that people stop believing in the naturalness or necessity of the existing social order. But imagine, as well, that they have a limited experience of transformative struggle: much of the social order seems immunized against collective struggle. Assume further that the ideas available to people about how to imagine actual transformation fail to illuminate the experience of constraint and freedom. The ideas may fail in several different ways. For example, they may consist in an analytic apparatus that goes to work only insofar as you supply it, from the outside, with empirical or normative assumptions. Or the ideas may appeal to a conception of a necessary sequence of forms of social organization, a conception that past and emergent experiences constantly discredit.

In such a circumstance people lack any ready way to imagine transformation. Their attitude toward the established vision of society is one of simultaneous belief and disbelief. They disbelieve in any particular attempt to justify the established social reality. But neither do they imagine or experience credible alternatives. Their minds continue to turn in the circle marked out by things as they are. They readily mistake their own situations for one of a small number of well-defined options that humanity must choose among. At the present time this experience of acquiescence without commitment has spread among large numbers of educated people throughout the world. Its basis and significance becomes clear only after other elements in the connection between transformative insight and the view of the ideal are understood.

Take now the logical or epistemological link between ideas about transformation and thinking about ideals. To grasp this link is to define, however tentatively, the nature of normative thought. An imperative of life appears in thought as a set of ideas whose descriptive and prescriptive elements we cannot clearly distinguish.

Whenever a view of the personal or the social ideal seems to keep propositions with prescriptive force separate from those with descriptive force (though acknowledging the way the prescriptive may imply the descriptive), it falls into contradiction or loses its persuasive authority. The moral philosopher may, for example, describe certain human emotions. But unless he means his descriptive account to bear, from the very start, a normative weight, he can never supply the foundations to an ideal. Other philosophers may seek this foundation in a conception of the nature of normative discourse. But they must then invent, and win acceptance for, a way of talking that overrides the supposed gap between factual claims and prescriptive contentions.

The deep reason for the need to combine description and prescription lies in the coexistence of two facts. The first fact is the impossibility of inferring an *ought* from an *is* (and the converse of this thesis), once the two have been cleanly separated. The second fact is the impossibility of grounding any ideal except in the vision of some reality, above or within ourselves. Whatever aspect of reality is chosen as a foundation to the ideal must, however, (because of the first fact), possess a normative force from the beginning. Otherwise, it will never generate that force at all. Even if you admit that normative claims must build an imperative of life into a vision of reality and must therefore include among their arguments and assumptions propositions that combine descriptive and prescriptive force, you may still wonder what, if anything, in our experience satisfies these criteria.

Religion is the exemplary instance. We cannot divide the central ideas of a religion into two columns: a set of propositions about what reality ultimately is and a series of doctrines about how people ought to live. The point is that the call to live in a certain way is felt to be the direct implication of the world's being a certain way. Yet it cannot be said that this conviction rests upon the fallacious inference of an *ought* from an *is*. For when we try to separate out descriptive and prescriptive ideas, we find, at the core of belief, that the attempt fails. It fails because ideas about, say, the relationship of human will to divine grace, represent, simultaneously and inseparably, visions of reality and imperatives of life.

The secular counterpart to this religious picture of ultimate and transcendent reality is always a view of personality, activity, or personal encounter. Only our most basic ideas about ourselves have this same character: that they express both a vision of who we really are and – if only by implication – a conception of how we ought to live.

Though not every such conception of personality may be given a larger religious context, every extended religious insight must include, explicitly or tacitly, such a picture of human nature, activity, or encounter. For the imperative of life, inseparable from the core religious vision, becomes intelligible only by making use of certain ideal and descriptive conceptions of ourselves. Such conceptions make visible the link between the imperative of life and the idea of ultimate reality.

These remarks hardly justify any particular conception of personality or society. Nor do they meet the arguments of the radical skeptic willing to bear the consequences of his radicalism by denying any truth value to all imaginative or practical activities that include the making of normative claims. Just how much activity and thought will have to be rejected as self-deceived to bear this skepticism out becomes clear only later in the argument.

The view of what is involved in thinking about the ideal that has just been sketched can now be combined with a conception of understanding – a conception worked out step by step and bit by bit throughout *Politics*. Its central tenet is the idea that to understand any part of reality is to conceive it from the standpoint of variation. You discover how this part of reality works by imagining it transformed. Imagination is just the term that describes the understanding conceived in this way.

A well-developed vision of a social or personal ideal must be, or must include, a descriptive as well as a prescriptive view of the person in society or of a form of social life. Its central prescriptions cannot be disengaged from understandings of reality. These understandings, in turn, imply a transformative perspective. The convergence of views about the imagination with views about the conditions of normative thought shows the deepest logical or epistemological connection between transformative insight and ideal vision.

Views of the ideals and insights into variation are connected politically as well as psychologically or logically and epistemologically. This political link gives content to the ideal imagination and refinement to transformative insight. It does so by showing how the content of certain recurrent elements in the vision of ideal society changes drastically under the influence of alternative ways of understanding the transformative opportunities, and therefore the inner workings, of social life.

Every developed vision of redeemed human society – the visionary imagination of human association – contains, in one form or another, at least two elements. Call one of them community and the other objectivity. By community in this setting I mean human association viewed as a set of relations desired for their own sake as well as for the independently defined wants that these relations may satisfy. One of the chief reasons for valuing association for its own sake is its occasional ability to provide people with a zone of heightened mutual vulnerability in which they can free themselves, partly, from the experience of a flat and insoluble conflict between self-assertion and attachment to other people. For this conflict unsoftened, unresolved, represents the exemplary loss of freedom. All our forms of self-assertion, from the most prosaic to the most spiritual, must work through forms of attachment, in systems of exchange and of discourse, in small and large associations. To the extent that self-assertion and attachment appear as forces that cancel each other out, to that extent self-assertion turns against itself. The entire social world then appears to be a machine for tearing the self apart. *Politics* argues that a conception of community that gives pride of place to heightened mutual vulnerability and to the partial reconciliation of self-affirmation and attachment can be justified more persuasively, and corresponds to more inclusive and radical concerns, than views of community that emphasize shared values or conflict-free harmony.

Another element in the vision of ideal society may be called objectivity. A social order possesses the quality of objectivity to the extent that it is not the result of force and fraud or of accidents of fortune. Consequently, these relations also do not arise from the arbitrary imposition of the interests and ideals of any one faction. The common denominator in all versions of the idea of objectivity is thus largely negative: a reprieve from what would otherwise be nightmarish violence, subjugation, and superstition.

The true relation between objectivity and community in the vision of the social ideal becomes evident only at the next step in the analysis. You need to see what happens to the vision of the social ideal as people's background assumptions about the transformability of society change. The differing degrees of acceptance or rejection of the naturalistic premise set a basic direction in which ideas about society and its transformations move. Accordingly, they also change the content of the elements of community and objectivity in the vision of the ideal.

Suppose that the naturalistic premise holds in its most extreme form. Society is perceived to have an immanent order of hierarchy and division. The maintenance of this order allegedly satisfies the deepest practical and spiritual needs of the collectivity and of its individual members. Guaranteed by a particular system of powers and rights, and imaginatively interpreted by a view of possible and desirable association, this canonical order is put forward as the true face of civilization. To realize the element of objectivity in the vision of the social ideal is to cling fast to this immanent structure and to avoid, at any cost, the confusion between it and the spurious hierarchies and divisions that would represent the takeover of the social world by force and fraud. What counts is not that there be more or less hierarchy and division but that there be the right kind of hierarchy and division. In the workplace, the family, and the state, some people may set terms to other people's activities. But this circumstance should not be confused – according to the view I am describing – with the one in which people pretend to what they are not entitled to and substitute a violent dominion for the right and proper structure of social roles and ranks. Only by avoiding this moral chaos can the collectivity flourish materially and spiritually. People can find themselves within their stations. (Remember the idea of work as an honorable calling.)

At the same time this real social order provides people with their best and most realistic chance for reconciling their wants as individuals with their social attachments. This reconciliation must be achieved through, rather than against, the established structures of society. For as soon as practical or spiritual self-assertion attempts to work outside or against this structure, it generates two parallel processes by which it undermines itself. On the one hand, it helps unleash the fraudulent and coercive struggles in which even the victories are precarious and bitter. On the other hand it disturbs the internal order of the emotions that sustains, and draws sustenance from, the rightful order of social life.

Consider what happens to the elements of community and objectivity when the naturalistic premise is decisively rejected: when you deny the existence of a natural structure of division and hierarchy. You can no longer distinguish clearly between two situations and say: Over here lies social order cleansed of force and fraud; over there, the world of treachery and violence. Power will be exercised and suffered. It can be criticized or justified. But all justifications are likely to be controversial precisely because there is no "natural" background picture of society on which to rely in formulating them.

The effort to escape from this predicament by finding decision procedures neutral with respect to clashing interests or ideals will never be more than partly successful. For the reasons earlier suggested it will be indeterminate to the extent that it remains neutral, and it will lose its neutrality as it gains determinacy. Moreover, each justification, once accepted, suffers a pressure toward overextension. The opportunity to exercise power will be taken beyond its original excuses unless countervailing guarantees are somehow built into the situation, no matter whether those guarantees rest on general justifications. Both the element of contestability and the dynamic of overextension point in the same direction. They require that the basic arrangements of the society, and the practical or conceptual activities by which those arrangements are reproduced, lay themselves open to revision in the midst of ordinary social life.

The idea of objectivity now acquires a new meaning. The struggle against arbitrariness, as violence and as deception, requires people to build a society that is less hostage to itself. No central aspect of its arrangements must be left invisible or immune to challenge in the normal course of our routines of conflict and exchange. Objectivity is achieved not by holding fast to a given structure, resolutely contrasted to the hell of force and fraud, but by rendering the structure insubstantial – by turning it, increasingly, into the structure of no structure. This is the realistic next best to the visionary ideal of a circumstance in which all hierarchies and divisions have fallen down forever. The next best consists in the circumstance in which these hierarchies and divisions are repeatedly dragged out into the light of struggle and revision. It is the political counterpart to an ideal of objectivity in science that relies not on the incorrigibility of self-evident propositions but on the universal and accelerated corrigibility of every feature of an explanatory practice, including the very conception of what it means to explain something. This comparison represents more than a vague parallel; it is, as a later stage of the argument shows, a precise and revealing convergence.

With the rejection of the naturalistic premise, the content of the idea of community changes in ways foreshadowed by the shift in the idea of objectivity. To the extent that any instrumental or passionate attachment incorporates an unjustified and unrevisable relationship of power – more generally, to the extent that it remains anchored in a structure of human association that has to be taken as given – to that extent self-assertion and attachment (or, rather, the twin enabling conditions of self-assertion) cannot be reconciled. The subordinates will remain torn between two impulses: the desire to reap the immediate material and spiritual benefits that come with accepting the established terms of association and the longing to achieve through some perilous struggle whatever material or spiritual gains can be won only by breaking those terms and putting others in their place. By remaining loyal they become dupes and servants. By breaking ranks they forgo the immediate advantages of an established form of collaboration or community in the name of an uncertain alternative. Even the superiors find that their self-assertion as people – citizens, specialists, lovers – remains circumscribed by its repeated and unavoidable confusion with their self-assertion as superiors – rulers, bosses, manipulators – and with all the stratagems of deception and self-deception, distance and closure, that the maintenance of their position requires.

But power still arises, no matter what, from the difference between what people are and do and from the endless contest over unavoidably contestable visions of collective opportunity and moral order. No particular experiment in association exists in a vacuum, apart from a larger structure of collective existence that, in some significant measure, is just there. In the idea of community as in the idea of objectivity, the line of advance passes through the effort to make the powers and the contexts maximally visible and vulnerable to strife.

For the fuller alliance of self-assertion and reconciliation depend on this visibility and vulnerability, and on the repeated liquefaction of entrenched structure they make possible.

The naturalistic premise has been shaken even though the consequences of its rejection have been only partly worked out. Perhaps precisely because it has not yet been fully rejected, no persuasive view of transformation had emerged to take its place. Because there is no believable idea of transformation, there is also no credible version of the visionary ideal. Each available version, disconnected as it is from a realistic sense of the breaking of constraints, oscillates between the reaffirmation of the existent and its easy denial. Thus, there arises a conviction destructive of normative thought and almost a kind of insanity. This conviction is the belief that the ideal ceases to be realistic insofar as it departs from existing reality, in any direction and by any means. The analysis of the psychological, logical, and social-theoretical connections between the vision of the ideal and the understanding of transformation helps us rediscover the roots of this predicament.

Here, then, is another way to understand the intentions of the social theoretical project that this critical analysis of the contemporary situation of social thought prepares and suggests. Philosophical disputes about the social ideal have increasingly come to turn on an unresolved ambivalence toward the naturalistic premise, an incomplete rebellion against it. The visionary imagination of our age has been both liberated and disoriented. It has been liberated by its discovery that social worlds are contingent in a more radical sense than people had supposed; liberated to disengage the ideas of community and objectivity from any fixed structure of dependence and dominion or even from any determinate shape of social life. It has also, however, been disoriented by a demoralizing oscillation between a trumped-up sanctification of existing society and would-be utopian flight that finds in the land of its fantasies the inverted image of the circumstance it had wanted to escape; disoriented by the failure to spell out what the rejection of the naturalistic view means for the vision of a regenerate society. The social theory we need must vindicate a modernist – that is to say, a nonnaturalistic – view of community and objectivity, and it must do so by connecting the imagination of the ideal with the insight into transformation.

5

The Constraints on Transformative Action

A Third Point of Departure

FACING FALSE NECESSITY

The Disappointments of Transformative Practice

Suppose, reader, that, moved by the idea of the transformative vocation and by a nonnaturalistic version of the social ideal, you threw yourself into some form of political action in the world of the late twentieth century. Imagine that your more concrete interpretation of the ideal included the attempt to relativize the contrast between the long periods of petty, routinized conflict and the interludes of expanded transformative struggle and to keep privileged factions of society from controlling the means to create the social future. All your particular programmatic aims referred back to the more general aim of cracking society open to politics: so that to every aspect of its established structure there might correspond some activity that made it vulnerable to collective conflict and deliberate revision.

The current ways of organizing the workplace, the economy, and the state appeared to you an imperfect realization of these objectives. You did not accept the notion that these available options were the only arrangements capable of satisfying insurmountable technical or psychological constraints. You did not believe that people had to choose between the kind of democracy that existed in the North Atlantic democracies of the day or the vanguardist dictatorships of the communist regimes; the kind of market that had arisen in the modern West or no market at all except as the tolerated appendage of central economic command; the kind of work organization associated with stereotypes of bureaucracy and assembly lines or no large-scale, efficient production.

In each instance, the available options appeared to combine an abstract, indeterminate idea – of democratic rule, market decentralization, or technical coordination – with a concrete set of institutions that developed the idea in some directions rather than in others. You could not accurately understand the emergence of these dominant institutional solutions as the inevitable result of practical constraints rooted in the facts of scarcity and efficiency, in the unyielding requirements of large-scale organization, and in the abiding truths of human nature. Much in these established institutional arrangements seemed capable of being explained only as the outcome of a highly particularistic and accidental history. Once you recognized this fact, you were much less likely to treat the available alternative forms of social and governmental organization as an exhaustive catalog from which humanity – at least contemporary humanity – had to select its future.

If, anywhere in the world, you entered politics with such ideals and understandings, you would soon be disappointed. Your disappointment would be all the harsher for resisting easy analysis. The constraints on action undertaken in this spirit could not be adequately understood with the help of the available social theories. On the contrary, these theories, representing as they did but a partial break from the naturalistic premise, were more part of the problem than part of the solution. They helped solidify the very constraints they pretended, but failed, to explain.

A Limiting Case of Social Closure

Consider first the circumstance of a society with the greatest conceivable degree of closure to politics – a society that remained as invulnerable as any society can to the struggle over the basic terms of its collective existence. One way to describe such a situation is to say that it is one in which the terms of people's material and moral access to one another find no counterweight in ordinary practical or conceptual activities that bring these terms into question or open them up to conflict and revision. Such is the characterization of closure developed at length later in *Politics*. For the moment, however, I adopt another more superficial, but essentially equivalent, description. The situation in which the terms of collective existence are most taken for granted can be described as the one in which society lives under the influence of three main constraints: the oligarchy, the identity, and the survival effects. Each of these entangles the pursuit of ordinary human aims in the perpetual regeneration of a social world with definite limits.

The Instruments of Closure: The Oligarchy Effect

Some groups have a privileged access to power and material surplus. The premise of this conception of privilege is the existence of a difference between relatively small leading groups and a vast majority: a mass of ordinary workers whose income is kept close to a socially defined subsistence level, whether or not they are legally free "property owners." These workers are denied a voice in running the government or the other central institutions of the society.

The powerful hesitate between two options. They may draw upon mass support in their internecine strife, as by raising a peasant army through agrarian protection rather than outright coercion. Alternatively they may resist the temptation to play to the common man even when they do not actively gang up against the people.

The first of these two paths is widely understood to be dangerous. If any faction of the powerful were to go too far in the recruitment of a mass following, it would risk being destroyed by the other factions or overwhelmed by its own supporters. The privileged – including the privileged turned demagogues – would face an ever starker choice between the need to impose a remorseless despotism in order to hold the agitated populace down and the radical opening up of access to advantage.

Each time the groups and rulers that clash at the summit of power step back from the gamble of drumming up active popular support, they renew the life of the established order. Thus, both the satisfaction of economic or military needs and the quarrels of the powerful are shaped by an ordinarily tacit but deeply felt constraint upon the alliances that can be struck between the higher-ups and the masses. This constraint is the oligarchy effect.

The Instruments of Closure: The Identity Effect

The practices of social life are inseparable from the conditions on which people are morally available to one another: the groups with an authoritative claim upon the individual's loyalties, the contexts in which heightened vulnerability becomes tolerable to him, and the terrain on which he can hope to be accepted by other people and to understand himself as a being with place. He cannot easily distinguish who he is and what his interests are from the groups to which he belongs. The multiple links between individual existence and group boundaries give rise to common identities.

Collective identities are entangled with distinctive, concrete forms of life. When countries fight, they struggle for the right to retain their identities, as defined by a settled order of practice and belief, as well as for wealth, power, and honor. Any overt and self-confessed assault upon the constitutive elements of the most inclusive identities is usually out of the question in normal politics, whether politics at the apex of government or politics in the recesses of a village community. This principle of exclusion is the identity effect. It operates with relative precision so long as the shared identity remains bound up with a richly defined tangle of customs. Even then, it may often be unclear just how much a group can change its way of life and still remain itself.

The confusion of shared identity with tangible custom emphasizes the distinctiveness of the collectivity by giving the distinction the semblance of a manifest difference rather than just a willed apartness. This prop seems to become the more important, the less the group identity can rely upon kinship or contiguity, though both contiguity and kinship are likely to be effects as well as causes of collective identities that have additional foundations. The same confusion offers sentiments and interests something they can readily grasp. It binds together the terms under which material needs are satisfied and group solidarities upheld: for both are implied by the detailed arrangements of power and exchange. It provides criteria that help evade the uncertainties of individual conscience or religious revelation and change habit into right. It lifts the burden of excluded and uncertain possibility that would otherwise weigh upon people's imagination of society and of themselves.

The Instruments of Closure: The Survival Effect

Each society's practical arrangements, including its dispositions of power and exchange, suspend the uncertainty and violence that prevail beyond the frontiers of a conditional world, and they determine the terms on which elementary material needs can be met. To attack these arrangements is to disorganize the means by which security is established and minimal needs are satisfied. Even when an alternative ordering is clearly in sight and ultimately successful, there will be a transitional period, of uncertain length, during which insecurity grows, many simple wants are denied, and the country is weakened in the contest with its rivals. When it is all over, everyone may still end up worse off than he was before. Such are the unavoidable risks of changing basic social arrangements, in the large or in the small. Though the fear of these risks is constantly exaggerated by oligarchic self-interest and by the collective commitment to a way of life, it has a basis that cannot be reduced to this self-interest or this commitment. The irreducible element is the survival effect.

The relationship of material needs to their established modes of satisfaction is like that of the passions to their conventional forms of expression. Though the conventions help shape the passions it is always possible for people to feel an ironic distance between an inchoate emotion and the language available to them for expressing it. They can even try to enter more fully into the denied possibility of emotion by changing the language. This enterprise is hazardous, and the measure of success uncertain: the nature of the passion changes as the means for its fulfillment are reformed. While the change takes place the difficulty of expression may increase rather than diminish. So, too, material needs get redefined as the means for their satisfaction are changing. In the interim, before these needs can be either reoriented or reaffirmed, they are threatened with frustration.

When the oligarchy, the survival, and the identity effects operate with full force, the limits of the possible in social life seem clearly and severely defined. For the facts to which these effects refer draw a relatively sharp distinction between what each social world incorporates and what it excludes. They circumscribe the range of normal conflict and the readiness with which a society can be willfully and deliberately altered, from above or below.

EMANCIPATION FROM FALSE NECESSITY

The larger historical setting of the ideas developed in this book was the experience of the partial breaking open of these different forms of closure. It was as if the denaturalization of society through conflict and insight had been unaccountably but unmistakably interrupted. In several different ways people all over the world had discovered that social orders could be remade and reimagined. The naturalistic premise had been shaken both as a basis for theoretical understanding and as a guide to practical action. But the different forms of closure had been broken in a way that maintained them in a loosened and less visible, but nevertheless intractable, fashion.

This partial freedom from false necessity was the common characteristic of the circumstances of mass politics, world history, and enlarged economic rationality. Each of these circumstances bore most directly on an aspect of social closure – mass politics on the oligarchy effect, world history on the identity effect, enlarged economic rationality on the survival effect. Nevertheless, each of them belonged to a single historical experience. Each shook all the devices by which the basic terms of social order became immune to the practical and spiritual conflicts of ordinary life.

The Sources of Emancipation: Mass Politics

Mass politics rattles oligarchy without tearing it apart. Its defining feature is a special pattern of opportunity and constraint in the capacity of ordinary people to remake, collectively, the conditions of their own existence. The result of this ambivalence is that the conditions under which people can win governmental power and use it to transform society become incorrigibly unclear.

In the age of mass politics all power in the state is ultimately justified by the will of the people, whether by the measured consent of an electoral system or by the virtual consent invoked by a party that claims to speak for a popular program. Moreover, this nod to the masses in the realm of words and apologies is confirmed, at a minimum, by a hard fact about the scramble for power: the individuals and cliques that can either enlist active mass support or count on tacit mass benevolence gain a decisive head start in the competition with their rivals. The weight of this advantage comes from a shared sense that there is no other ultimate basis of authority (save sheer technical necessity in the allegedly unpolitical areas of life). It results as well from the way in which popular loyalties give their beneficiaries a leg up on the successful management of the country's major business and military institutions. Faith in doctrines that justify the confiscation of power by elites is corroded by the discovery that this confiscation is at least unnecessary. You can run a country in a way that makes the working people something more than a favored mob, a desperate and unruly crowd, or an underling ally whose precarious rights are the reverse side of its duty to pay and to fight.

One way to describe the distinctive quality of mass politics is to consider its meaning for the relations between the leaders and the led, between those who stand within or near the circle of governmental power and the working people who neither participate directly in that power nor have the prerogative, the honor, or the wealth that might protect them from it. The spontaneous solidarity of the oligarchs that came from the fear of losing their condominium over the masses has been repeatedly thrown off balance; only laborious party discipline and propaganda can bring back, in tottering form, the oligarchic serenity that disbelief and discovery have taken away.

In all historical societies that never knew mass politics the hierarchical and communal–corporate divisions of the society set the terms on which the leaders could communicate with the laboring people and on which these people could make themselves heard in the state. The ruled understood that the rulers did not, in the end, belong to them. Even the most centralizing autocrat had reason to be frightened by the danger of playing too often for the favor of the rabble in the course of his run-ins with the oligarchs.

From this standpoint mass politics represents a special kind of confusion about the extent to which those who hold the chief offices of the state can appeal effectively to the simple populace over the head of the grandees and the intermediate powers – the capitalists, managers, bureaucrats, military officers, labor and party leaders, and other bigwigs with a lien on the economic surplus or on the guidance of the large-scale organizations of state and society. Though this confusion takes different forms in a representative democracy and in the one-party "people's democracy" it retains a recognizable identity.

Under mass politics the grandees and intermediate powers may be attacked at any moment from the very center of the state; the strengthened influence of the masses destroys the natural foundation of self-restraint in the internecine quarrels of the oligarchic power blocks. The point is not that these quarrels become any more violent or more crucial to the fate of the individual oligarch – they may in fact be deceptively gentle in style – but rather that the whole design and necessity of oligarchic power itself are brought more openly and thoroughly into question.

The paradox is that, no matter how important the leader's ability to win mass support may seem, he repeatedly finds himself captive to the grandees and the intermediate powers. Moment by moment, it is never quite clear, under mass politics, how seriously the transformative and antielitist uses of popular mobilization should be taken. The people in charge of central government may be able to go further in bypassing the powerful and the privileged, and the entrenched institutions at whose head they stand, than the rulers of past societies could ever have dreamt of. How far they can go at any one time or in any one country without destroying the basis of their own power is anyone's guess.

The intermediate powers can count on several resources in their efforts to limit the destabilizing effects of popular mobilization under the democratic or nondemocratic forms of mass politics. The first resource is their capacity to disrupt the workings of society and economy so seriously as to jeopardize the hold that the party, the coterie, or the leader in power exercises over popular sympathy. The second element is the special role of double agent that many of these organizational bosses and activists, entrepreneurs and bureaucrats, play in dealings between the successful politicians and the apprehensive masses. Consider, for example, the labor leaders in the parliamentary democracies or the party cadres and local managers in the communist states. At times they are the borrowed voice of central power cajoling and threatening the ordinary salaried worker and trying to rein in his supposedly unrealistic and shortsighted demands. At other times they are his confessed or covert representative. Often enough, they work both ways at the same time, and the key to their ordinary careerism is to learn when and how to play out the equivocation. The basis of this two-faced strategy lies in the ambiguity of the organizations themselves: in their tendency to superimpose the inchoate interests and ideals of a constituency and the prudence of an organizational elite in a manner that mixes the two up. The repeated opportunity for this mix-up is the constituency's need to have its claims translated into a language of pressure and persuasion that is intelligible and effective in the councils of the state. The third source of the influence exercised by the intermediate powers – and by far the most important and obscure – is the combination of forces that

shapes the large-scale business or bureaucratic institutions that provide these grandees with a power base, that ceaselessly re-create a
particular type of hierarchy within these organizations, and that make
it necessary for each organization to get governmental help in its
struggle against its enemies or the enemies of its leaders.

The same decisive paradox can be rephrased as a more impersonal
comment on pervasive hierarchies. The hierarchies that make mass
politics possible and that mass politics reproduces share the drive
toward abstraction marking collective identities in the age of world
history – the disengagement of collective identities from the maintenance of distinctive, elaborately defined ways of life. The abstraction results from the relative pluralism of multiple hierarchies of
advantage and of access to advantage, from the lack of a clear-cut
one-to-one relation between hierarchical position and the individual's
life outside the workplace, and from the bleeding together of criteria
of advancement based on inherited opportunity, formal certification,
and the putatively technical demands of the job. The more such a
hierarchy is set against the background of a shared culture of material
enjoyment or ambition and presented as the by-product of impersonal certification and practical need, the less it seems to exist in its
own right as a distinct and controversial aspect of society; the less,
also, are people able to grasp and alter these hierarchies in the routine
conflicts of official politics or everyday life.

The precise way by which mass politics nourishes this style of
hierarchy remains to be shown. But the suggestion can already be
made that the idea of society as a comprehensive hierarchical ordering
of ranks is both canceled and reaffirmed by mass politics, just as the
idea of mankind as a battleground of largely incommensurable and
incommunicable forms of life is both denied and reasserted by world
history. The social world is indeed cracked open for the will and the
imagination but, strangely, the crack seems to give a new resilience
and opacity to the order that remains.

The dictatorships that arise in an age of mass politics draw on a
small number of variations on the theme of oligarchy denied and
reestablished. Such dictatorial regimes may be efforts to enlist central
government in the defense of powers and hierarchies that cannot
stand on their own feet and that are jeopardized by the popular
agitation that mass politics facilitates and democracy protects. Or
they may be attempts to wage war on these hierarchies and powers
from a position at the center of society. In this event, however, they
will set up new screens between power and the masses unless they
can somehow change the deeper facts from which privilege continuously reemerges and gains immunity from politics. The success of
the dictator may also depend on his ability to persuade his petty
bourgeois or working-class constituency that he is engaged in a life-

and-death struggle with the privileged while, in fact, he is striking mutually beneficial deals with them. Or the dictatorship may commit itself to a vision of national power and unity against the background of an enforced social peace designed to close off possibilities that mass politics might otherwise make available.

Democracy, in turn, comes to both fulfillment and frustration in the conditions of mass politics. The defining elements of democratic practice are the organized competition for the control of governmental power, the appeal to a mass electorate as the final arbiter of this contest, and the sanctity of guarantees that allow the opponents of the people in office to associate and to propagandize. These traits pose a permanent threat to the domination of state power by a well-defined oligarchy, either as a hereditary class of rulers or as a loose cartel of privileged interests. They also establish an institutional device for undermining the identity effect from within: power is sought by the parties; the parties stand for programs; and the programs, however inconsequential and incoherent, make a portion of social life vulnerable to regular, overt conflict. Yet, as long as the oligarchy and the identity effects are disturbed rather than destroyed, democracy as an ideal has only a precarious hold on reality. Democratic party politics becomes a quarrel about forms of power and advantage whose real roots lie in aspects of society that party politics cannot ordinarily reach.

The Sources of Emancipation: World History

World history exists when all countries vie with one another for the same prizes and when their leaders are forced to recognize that no aspect of domestic practice and belief is safe from the demands imposed by the military, economic, and ideological rivalries of nation-states. A country's independence and the authority of its rulers depend on a proven capacity to deal with other states from a position of military, economic, or administrative strength. The brutal encounter with the demands of international conflict is accompanied by a discovery of the potential universality of practical thought and practical reform across the supposedly inviolable frontiers of distinct and hostile cultures. Everything that is tried out in one part of the world might in principle be tried out in another. If something really seems necessary to the cause of national power and prosperity, the rulers and bosses will understand that it must be used even if it jeopardizes aspects of life that had entered deeply into a people's sense of identity and even if it combines institutions in ways that had been regarded as impossible, bizarre, or wicked.

Again and again, governments, no matter how restorationist or revolutionary their intentions, find that the practical problems of production, administration, and warfare present themselves across national boundaries in recognizably similar ways; that in solving them it is dangerous to disregard any resource of analysis and technique available in the world, although the solutions must be suited to local conditions and described in a locally acceptable vocabulary; and that a sacrilege against the idols of collective identity will be forgiven more quickly than a practical failure as long as the profanation is delicate and its benefits unmistakable. The demands of common sense and ingenuity constantly liquefy the forms of social life and confuse them with one another. Ordinary prudence thus achieves, through a series of mundane questions and answers, desires and satisfactions, what the social iconoclasm of the world religions failed to accomplish with a frontal assault.

The need to produce the means of national prosperity and power overshadows the cult of martial valor, the ethos of pacificistic abnegation, and the effort to ennoble passion through ritual form. These elite ideals of civilization give way to the requirement of thinking matter-of-factly about a matter-of-fact world. Successful regimes must prove that they know how to fill stomachs, to win wars, and even to encourage the surprises of science and art.

The dominant moral alternatives that faced the ruling elites of so many past societies now appear archaic, and some of the atmosphere in which collective identities were championed or denounced lifts and blows away. No concrete set of traditions and beliefs is thought to define the necessary and sufficient conditions for holding on to a particular collective identity. Every custom and dogma may be changed through deliberate policy, under the shadow of foreign threat, or by mass conversion, at the touch of foreign example.

There was another reason for the inability to limit in advance the parts of social life susceptible to change under the influence of foreign teaching and example. The cracking open of society to politics was preceded, accompanied, and reinforced by the secular doctrines of emancipation, chiefly liberalism, socialism, and communism, that rejected the necessity and authority of the established hierarchical and communal divisions of society, the rigid contrasts among national traditions (though not among types or stages of social organization), and the accustomed ways of separating the practical from the utopian. These new doctrines denied that existing systems of social roles and hierarchies cut through to the marrow of humanity. These revolutionary ideas therefore implied the potential relevance of every social experience to every other one. They forced open the gates of universal spiritual seduction. They were aided in this effort by every feature of the situation that proved or suggested the transformability of society through politics.

For all these reasons collective identitites – at least at the national level – tend to become abstract: to consist more in a pure sense of apartness than in allegiance to a particular way of life. In this abstract condition they are excited as well as weakened. Though politics is allowed to roam over a broader area of existence and to transform the concrete practices that were revered as part of the shared identity, the will to maintain the life apart may become all the more intense. Besides, the fall into abstraction is softened: the awareness of the universality and toughness of practical problems does not wholly discredit the conviction that a people's distinctive existence is bound up with its commitment to a unique style of sociability.

National identities become concrete to the extent that they remain attached to tangible customary relations of production and exchange, division and hierarchy, and to intangible but distinctive preconceptions about the possible and desirable forms of human association. Several restraints on the evisceration of their concreteness are at work. The social forms and assumptions that embody a national identity become a "second nature" that resists manipulation. Or they survive to influence programs of thought and action that are meant to be universal but that bear the marks of their origin in the history of particular classes, communities, and nations. Or they get mixed up with the factional interests and self-images of an elite that knows how to turn a deaf ear to the requirements and opportunities of practical reform when they threaten its own position. Thus, despite the homogenizing effect of practice and of its organizational and technological instruments, the confrontation among peoples continues to take place in two dimensions: in one, where distrustful governments compete for similar advantages of wealth and power; in another, where the inability of nations and communities to accept one another's existence reflects an awareness, descending from the leaders to the led, that the things they stand for are irreconcilable.

Even as the national identity and the narrower group identities that have been formed as its corollaries or rivals lose their concrete content, they do not, in their abstraction, fall to pieces. For practical need or opportunity, which may be strong enough to rob a picture of collective life of all its substance, is not clear or inspiring enough to fill the vacuum it has created. The imperatives of running things fall short of establishing the basis of a true human unity, on a worldwide or even a more limited scale: the same objectives of power and prosperity can be achieved in too many different ways and with too much variation in the ideals, the interests, and the institutional arrangements capable of sustaining those aims.

By shaking the identity effect, the experience of world history makes the entire face of society more open to transformation through contests over power and moral truth. But, in its new remote and equivocal position, the collective identity also becomes harder to get at and to bring under the discipline of conscious will. Now that it is a worshiped idol without being a visible presence, people find it harder to discover its flaws and to resist its claims. Politics gains greater freedom to serve a more demanding and pretentious master.

What is true of the collective identities that are entangled with a state is also true of those that exist within the state or alongside the nation. For the characteristic mark of these identities (the oppressed nationality, the religion, the race) in an age of world history and mass politics is to represent experiences of community without a secure basis in a particular form of life or in an articulate organization. This willed and abstract solidarity remains at once seductive and obscure. There is no easy way to reach and redefine it through normal politics. In fact, the only group identity likely to depart much from this picture is one that is rooted in the immediate, shared material concerns of a relatively well-defined group, like an organized segment of the work force, that knows what it wants and is out to get it.

The Sources of Emancipation: Enlarged Economic Rationality

Enlarged economic rationality and quickened economic innovation complement the force of mass politics and world history. The key to economic rationality is the freedom to recombine and to renew. The advance of economic rationality always amounts to a greater facility to rearrange relationships, techniques, and organizations according to productive opportunity or economic reward. (A crucial, second-order sense of economic rationality is the avoidance of any non-self-correcting disparity between what must be done to maximize secure opportunity and to secure a profit that benefits and therefore motivates an economic action.) Positions in the production system must not be allowed to freeze into vested rights that narrow the range of further innovation.

The freedom to renew and recombine within the production system requires that social order not be so embracing and determinate in its orchestration of social relations as to deny economic innovators any open space on which to stage their experiments. At first this requirement may be satisfied by increasing the relative independence of the productive economy from the surrounding social order. But the more intense the pressure of economic innovation, the more likely it becomes that every feature of social life, within or outside the productive system, must be subject to the same relentless imperative of plasticity.

This logic of economic innovation can be exercised in two directions. It can be the work of a coercive will that shifts people and institutions around. Alternatively, it can operate by consensual de-

vices that keep claims to positions in the division of labor, or to
control over capital, from congealing into vested rights. However,
this distinction should not be mistaken for the contrast between
command and market economies as this contrast has come to be
understood. Thus, for example, current market institutions combine
coercive and consensual elements: they regularly generate social positions that enable some people to shape other people's activities,
through investment control, and thereby to gain a fix on the conditions of collective prosperity.

In the age of mass politics and world history the dissolving force
of innovation has advanced up to a certain point. Capital and labor
can be shifted around more freely, more constantly, and to greater
innovative effect than in most societies of the past. But many features
of the institutional context of productive activity remain excluded
from the range of revision. Some of the exclusions rest on formal
legal entitlements. Others result from established deals and traditional
expectations: the claims made by different segments of the work
force on places in the division of labor and on the active governmental
protection of their interests.

The limited quality of the progress of economic rationality is neatly
reflected in the vulgar notion of economic rationality: the ability
freely to combine factors of production. This vulgar notion can be
generalized into the idea of a free combination of the arrangements
that define the context of economic activity. Once generalized, it
draws attention to the differences among institutional systems in the
extent to which they facilitate experiment and diversity in the organizational settings of production and exchange.

The Quality of Partial Emancipation

The concepts of mass politics, world history, and enlarged economic
rationality describe an experience of the heightened availability of
social life to transformative action. At the same time, however, they
tell a story of incomplete freedom from the oligarchy, identity, and
survival effects.

As a setting for transformative action, animated by the visionary
ideal evoked earlier, the circumstance of mass politics, world history,
and enlarged economic rationality seems both mysterious and disappointing. The particular degree and manner of the dissolution of
these constraints resist any general analysis. The very same cumulative events that increasingly break society open to politics also
undermine the plausibility of the naturalistic premise and of its ac-
companying set of beliefs about societies and their transformations.
For belief in a preordained evolutionary sequence or in a well-defined
set of possible social worlds represents a lingering commitment to

the naturalistic premise and, for that very reason, a mystification of society and history.

It may seem that the oligarchy, identity, and survival effects can never be completely abolished. But why not more or less abolished than they have been in the age of mass politics, world politics, and accelerated economic rationality? Why abolished through some new forms of social organization rather than others?

The distinctive experience of society making in an age of mass politics, world history, and enlarged economic rationality has to be described more concretely before we can draw lessons from the frustrations of partial freedom from false necessity.

THE PUZZLES OF PARTIAL EMANCIPATION FROM FALSE NECESSITY

Toward the close of the twentieth century the paradoxical and revealing features of mass politics, world history, and enlarged economic rationality manifested themselves in two related experiences of puzzlement about the constraints on transformative political action.

Unexplained Routine

Throughout much of the world, the struggle over the uses of governmental power remained within narrow limits. Efforts at reform and retrenchment alternated in cycles whose content and scope changed only slowly. You might say that this was all you could expect: politics had always been like this, except for brief interludes of radical instability. You might add that political conflict would tend to become all the more routinized, once war – the horrible standard preface to drastic change – had ceased to be an easy recourse. But the more closely you tried to understand the limits on political conflict, the more quickly this appearance of self-evidence dissolved.

In the communist regimes moves toward governmental centralization that fell short of a terroristic campaign of the state against society were regularly followed by bouts of decentralization that rarely jeopardized the ruling party's mastery of government and the economy. In the rich Western countries halfhearted redistributive reforms and the imposition of selective public controls over accumulation alternated with periods of retrenchment in which disheartened or reactionary governments courted investor confidence and labor quiescence in the hope of rekindling economic growth.

The constriction of the ordinary political disputes in the advanced Western world became manifest in the position of the leftist parties that had committed themselves to a far-reaching reconstruction of society. To the extent that these parties remained faithful to a radical intention they found themselves pushed into electoral isolation. When they managed to capture a broad base of support they lost the reconstructive impulse. They narrowed their sights to a modest program of gradual redistribution and partial nationalization, with the basic structure of the state and the economy intact. In countries like the United States – where no major leftist parties existed – most of domestic party politics came down to a squabble among particular interests of big business or organized labor, clamoring for favors and backing up their threats by disinvestment or disruption. Disadvantaged groups demanded jobs, welfare, and reverse discrimination. A disheartened tax-paying citizenry, faced with unattractive choices by its politicians, tried, at least, to ward off fiscal pressure and economic decline. Whether or not leftist parties mattered, people easily lost the sense of living in history.

To explain the repetitive narrowness of political conflict in such settings, you have to identify the formative context of routine politics: the set of basic institutional arrangements and shared preconceptions that shaped conflicts over the mastery and uses of governmental power. To be counted as part of such a context, a practice, power, or right must meet two tests. First, it must not itself be frequently revised in the course of normal politics. It changes very slowly when it changes at all. Second, together with the other elements in the context, it helps explain the scope and content of the struggles over the uses of state power – and, more generally, over the basic terms of social existence. A formative context begins by determining the instruments and occasions of collective struggle. It ends by entering into people's most intangible ideas of interest, identity, and possibility.

The same arrangements and preconceptions that shape the scope and structure of routine politics and its reform cycles also create the social setting of production, innovation, and exchange. They determine the extent to which, and the sense in which, people can be shifted around and organizational practices revised.

Consider the rich Western countries. Their formative contexts of routine politics included a certain way of organizing democratic governments. This approach prevented any business oligarchy from exercising absolute control over the state. But it also helped fragment collective conflicts and separate the devices of electoral representation from the occasions for collective militancy. The formative contexts of routine politics in the Western democracies included, as well, an amalgam of legal entitlements, organizational styles, and hardened collective deals. This amalgam enabled small groups of businessmen to exercise a decisive influence over the basic flows of investment decisions. It divided the labor force into distinct segments, entrenched in different niches of the division of labor and benefiting from unequal degrees of collective organization.

Suppose that the state stopped being democratic at all, or that it became democratic enough to foment collective militancy and to subject centers of private power to public accountability. Imagine that the businessmen could have their way or that the government was sufficiently empowered to override their ability to affect, through disinvestment, the conditions of collective prosperity. Assume that none of the workers could organize or that all of them could and did. In any of these instances routine politics in the Western democracies would have changed. Its formative context would have been revised.

Once you define a formative context with enough detail to make it capable of explaining the actual nature of repetitious politics, you discover that the arrangements or assumptions that make up such a context are loosely connected. These components do not have to stand or fall together. They can be replaced piecemeal. And each such partial substitution changes the face of routine politics. So it was hardly surprising to find that the different elements of the formative context had distinct histories, only indirectly connected, like the elements themselves, with one another.

Here lies the mystery. How can these formative contexts be so tenacious – so impervious to the fierce ambitions of ordinary politics – when they are also so loosely held together? Given their looseness, how can you hope to gain any general understanding of their nature, genesis, and vicissitudes?

Interrupted Dissociation

The same experience of a constraint both enormous and elusive reappeared in another setting: the worldwide diffusion of technologies, organizations, institutional arrangements, and social ideals originally championed by the richest and strongest Western countries. These nations had once seemed on the verge of conquering the world militarily, economically, and spiritually. At first the non-Western peoples, or their ruling elites, had hoped to adopt the crucial technological innovations while leaving all else unchanged. Later, with more experience and with the further progress of Western technology itself, they felt themselves forced to choose between total acceptance or repudiation of the Western system: its machines and expertise, its way of organizing work, its governmental and social institutions, and even its ruling beliefs. Their conviction that they had to take or leave Western ways was reinforced by the leading Western social theories of the day. These doctrines also presented the triumphant way of life as an indissoluble whole, based on a coherent set of generative principles and corresponding to a distinct stage in the material and moral history of mankind.

But further experience told a different story. Governments and elites throughout the world found that levels of productive and destructive capability comparable to those of the advanced Western powers could be achieved within the setting of forms of work organization different from those that had taken hold in the intrusive Western societies. To a much more striking extent, styles of work organization taken from the West could be combined with unprecedented styles of social and governmental organization, different from both the Western example and the original indigenous practice. Politicians, propagandists, and entrepreneurs learned to dissociate formative contexts more boldly and deliberately: to incorporate elements from another society's formative context of power and production or its technology of production and destruction while rejecting other elements with which the incorporated ones were loosely linked in the foreign model.

There were real constraints on the dissociation of the initial version of industrial society. Some separations and combinations simply failed to work. But whatever the limits to dissociation, they could not be inferred from any of the available social theories that appealed to stage sequences in history or that relied on the idea of a strictly defined range of possible types of economic and governmental organization.

EXPERIENCES OF BLOCKAGE AND OPPORTUNITY

The Exemplary Instability of the Third World

In the late twentieth century, there were countries in the world in which the limits to the transformation of society through politics seemed far less tightly and clearly drawn than in the rich nations of the West. This vagueness of limits especially characterized those poorer countries, not under a communist regime, known as the third world. They included many rapidly rising powers. From events and efforts in these countries, you could learn something about the conditions under which society might, once again, be subject to far-reaching political experiment, democratic mass politics might regain its original impulse, and the visionary impulse in social life might find a fuller expression in the conflicts of social life. Whatever you might learn about the distinctive opportunities of contemporary politics would also reveal something of very general scope about the real and the possible in society: here history had supplied a new twist on the relation between freedom and constraint. The entire experience of practice and reflection in this less well-defined setting provided the most revealing example of the sense in which any episode of observed or lived turmoil can suggest general insights into society. To understand society deeply is always to see the settled from the angle of the unsettled. The settled is the region or the moment where relationships become fixed and, through their fixity, take on a specious aura of necessity. The unsettled is the experience that discloses the perilous, uncertain, malleable quality of society. By seeing the settled unsettled or by looking toward the disturbances that take place in its vicinity, we begin to understand how the settled really works and what it really is. The moment of escalated conflict, when nothing in society seems safe from politics, sets the outer limits to an understanding of the earlier or later times, when social peace returns and conflict appears to be about marginal though cumulative adjustments of advantage within an institutional and imaginative framework that is taken largely for granted. For those who already lived in an age of world history, the bolder experiments in the organization of power and production or in the imagination of society that went on in some countries revealed the deeper character of institutions and visions in those other places where the remaking of society seemed inconceivable outside catastrophic situations. The reference of the settled to the unsettled underlies my comparison of third world politics to the politics of the communist regimes and the Western democracies. It is a principle to which the main body of *Politics* gives a broader application.

All the third world countries of the time offered formidable obstacles to any effort to transform society through collective action. In these societies you found a clash between pretense and reality so relentless, uninterrupted, and unqualified that, in the end, the language of politics declined into an innocuous litany, and the most bitter cynicism appeared to be a redeeming form of sanity. These were also countries in which all organizations that depended on collective effort unrelated to the immediate attractions of the state, property, and the family were constantly falling apart. The weakness of voluntary associations that could not rely on some preexisting communal setting was the mark of societies in which almost everything that really mattered to people flowed through the same privileged hands, by the same means, and in which every attempt to work outside or against the established structure seemed, at first, like defiance of the way things had to be.

These obstacles to political invention were matched, however, by countervailing opportunities. For one thing, in many of these third world countries, the basic structure of group boundaries and group interests remained fluid. So, too, the operative rules about how governmental power could be conquered and about what could be done with it were ill defined. To each of the ways that people had of picturing the collective context of their activities or the limits of political possibility, there corresponded a different way of defining the aims of partisan political struggle.

For another thing, the third world countries could not reach even the levels of economic equality and prosperity or democratic participation that characterized the rich Western nations without achieving a much more intense degree of popular militancy than these nations had known in recent history. Militant grassroots organization had to combine with escalating conflict over the fundamentals of power in the state and the economy. Without both the organization and the conflict, there could be no mass involvement in politics capable of escaping the tutelage of caesaristic demagogues and fake revolutionary parties or of standing up effectively to attempts at outright repression. Once this higher level of popular collective action had been attained, it might serve to catapult these countries into ways of organizing government and the economy that would be more deeply egalitarian and democratic, because more exposed to transforming collective activity, than those of the contemporary rich Western societies. If only the unsettled nations could achieve the institutional forms that might transform a temporary struggle into a lasting structure they would become the testing ground on which society would be more thoroughly cracked open to politics.

The same counterpoint of aggravated constraint and heightened opportunity applied to people's imaginative ideas about society. In both the non-Western civilizations and the countries empty or emptied of an original civilization, men and women lacked the words with which to describe their experience of society. They knew that they lacked them. Slogans and ideas drawn from the most varied quarters were incongruously pasted together. People seemed even more confused than they usually are about the conditions under which they would be justified in revising their social beliefs. The brittle and half-baked quality of elite or popular political ideas seemed to be the imaginative counterpart of the strange mixture of churning and blockage in the practical life of the society.

The unformed and yet resistant quality of people's beliefs about social reality and possibility had an ambiguous significance for transformative democratic politics. It tended to bring all articulated schemes of association into dispute, to undermine the meaning of all the words by which individuals could explore their own experience and, whenever the high tide of ideological ardor and reconstructive ambition receded, to leave only a heartless and desperate materialism. But these circumstances also presented an opportunity. People's ideas about possible and desirable human association were not worked out into a set of detailed institutions and practices. The practices and the institutions did not seem to reveal any coherent though tacit picture of what society should be like in each domain of practical experience. The disconnection between images of society that lacked an institutional embodiment and practical experiences that lacked a ready-made interpretation released the imagination of the possible and desirable forms of human association from its traditional bounds. People could not match their received images of what their dealings with one another could and should look like in the different areas of social life with the practices and institutions they actually encountered. The combination of these anxieties of the imagination with the more tangible opportunities described earlier in this section made the third world countries at that time a privileged terrain for institutional invention.

These obstacles and opportunities came to life in national politics. All over the world, people who cared, and who could, anxiously followed the revolutionary experiments that took place in faraway countries, wondering what new light these initiatives would shed on the possibilities of mass politics and on the shattering of rigid structures of communal division or social hierarchy. But only when you were actually involved in a sustained political struggle was the full range of enigma and aspiration likely to come home to you. Only then did the inadequacy of the available ideas become bitterly clear.

A Brazilian Example

Imagine, reader, that you were involved in the politics of one of these countries, say Brazil, around 1985. It was then just haltingly emerging from a long episode of barely veiled military dictatorship. It combined huge dimensions, close prospects of rising to world power, and a breakdown in the ability of the political nation to distinguish clearly and confidently between the possible and the impossible in politics. In every decisive respect the Brazil of that time exemplified the way in which the unsettled social situation merely projects, in exaggerated form, the features of the settled one. The attempt at transformative action in this setting offered a distorted but revealing instance of what such an effort would be like in *any* setting.

The Brazilian state had gone through an oscillation typical of many third world countries of the period. It had moved between mock liberalism and controlled mobilization as devices by which to reconcile the self-defense of the elites with the partial introduction of the people to mass politics.

At times the elites had tried to run a state that imitated the institutional forms of the North Atlantic democracies. But the imported arrangements took on different uses when projected into a situation where a huge underemployed mass was only minimally incorporated into economic and political life. If at one moment liberal democratic institutions seemed to be a mere facade for the continuing tutelage of the working classes by an unreconstructed economic and governmental oligarchy, these institutions became, at the next moment, the vehicle of social demands more radical than those habitually pressed on the home ground of liberal democracy.

Controlled mobilization represented the half-deliberate, contradictory attempt to incorporate the masses into the life of the state while preventing much harm from being done to the advantages of the propertied and educated classes. The working people in town and country would have to be organized and flattered: organized from the top down, flattered by selective benefits and unselective promises. But the strategy of controlled mobilization required a shameless leader willing to play fast and loose with republican institutions. This leader would have to recruit to his service large numbers of minions who might end up as militants with ideas of their own. He would be imprudent to enrage the oligarchy or to offend the ideals and prejudices of the military and bureaucratic petty bourgeois. But neither could he afford to do too little for the propertyless. For his power depended on his influence over the people. Otherwise, what need would there have been of him in the first place? As a way to draw a bright line between concession and revolution, controlled mobilization always ran into trouble: it became, too quickly, uncontrolled.

When both mock liberalism and controlled mobilization failed as strategies of elite self-defense, the easiest solution might be an outright dictatorship that claimed to lay the basis on which both reformed democracy and national wealth and power might be established. The military had exercised such a rule since 1964 in a way that, involuntarily, kept access to alternative social futures open. The regime had repressed incipient working-class organizations. It had kept at bay any threat of attack on the fundamentals of power and privilege. But while protecting the wealth and safety of the privileged (which were never seriously endangered anyway), it had begun to undermine the basis of their power. Under military and technocratic rule, government, in precarious partnership with foreign capital, had consolidated a considerable measure of control over basic investment decisions. As a result, national investors and entrepreneurs had lost their ability to threaten the government with recession through disinvestment. They had become the well-kept clients of men they had foolishly expected to be a mere praetorian guard. Though the rulers had repressed the economic demands of almost every sector of the masses except the labor aristocracy employed in capital-intensive industry, they had also pursued the strategy of controlled mobilization by extending organization of the people through official, government-controlled unions. These unions could be taken over from within by militants committed to make them count.

The military regime had reinforced an economic system that artificially rewarded large-scale agriculture as opposed to family farms, that organized manufacturing cheifly around the consumption demands of the relatively privileged classes, and that used both its export revenues and the foreign loan capital and investment on which it had become increasingly dependent to keep this economic order going. But the government had increasingly to face a choice between two ways to keep the economy growing. Each alternative proved incompatible with the social alliances on which the regime had been founded, with the powers at its disposal, and even with its vision of itself. On the one hand, the government could attempt to break into the markets of the rich Western countries, compensating for tariff barriers and lower productivity by a massive and lasting repression of wage levels. On the other hand, it could try to redirect industry to mass-consumption goods, promote the agrarian reform necessary to reconcile economic growth with the economic and civic rise of the masses, and rigorously subordinate its export drives to the imperative of paying for the industrial inputs required by the program of internal reconstruction.

In the absence of either strategy the people in charge had to make ad hoc deals with the sectors of the entrepreneurial and working classes whose active or passive collaboration seemed most crucial to economic growth. In the face of economic slowdown the authoritarian regime discovered that it had to maneuver on a narrow ground in its attempt to coopt ever larger sectors of the population into acquiescence. During the final years of the military dictatorship, the central rulers retained the loyalty of local supporters and political machines so long as they had favors to distribute. But they had concentrated power within an ever smaller coterie at the cost of isolating themselves increasingly from the country at large, as well as from the main body of the officer corps.

Indefinition was the common denominator of all these features of the life of the state. No clear form of control over governmental power and therefore no definite link between the mastery of the state and the management of economic growth had been allowed to harden. This lack of definition presaged a weakening of the felt limits of political possibility. The impression was confirmed when you turned from affairs of state to the broader experience of the society. All this indefinition could be taken as both the voice of transformative opportunity and the sign of a paralyzing confusion. At one moment it seemed that new experiments in human association might be staged here; at the next, that nothing could come out of this disheartening and preposterous blend of structure, shiftlessness, and stagnation.

There were two especially striking features of the political ideas of the different social classes, in contrast to the attitudes most characteristic of the corresponding groups in the rich Western countries. The first fact was the spread of radical commitments among the middling classes of the society – smallholders and shopkeepers, the technical intelligentsia, the independent or bureaucratic professionals, the teeming multitudes of minor functionaries and paper pushers. Though many stood by conservative positions, a large number supported one or another stripe of leftism. Leftist party movements had failed to develop a program, a strategy, and a language responsive to the concerns of the petty bourgeoisie and of its technical or professional superiors. The left parties nevertheless found their main base among these classes rather than among the relatively small industrial proletariat (a veritable labor aristocracy) or the vast, underemployed mass of town and country. The other notable characteristic of the political nation was the lack of fixed divisions between the elite labor force employed in the most advanced sectors of industry and the unemployed and underemployed workers or between the rural and the urban masses.

These facts had a similar character and similar effects. In each instance, there seemed to be a departure from a logic of tangible material interests: the petty bourgeois and the industrial operatives, the rural and the urban masses, the labor aristocracy and the ordinary workers, failed to behave as if they had distinct and opposing interests. In each instance, the result was to generate political opportunities that had been all but foreclosed in the rich industrial democracies.

In these democracies the distinctions between the middle classes and the working classes and, within the working classes, between the relatively privileged, organized workers and the underclass, had consistently played a major role in the resistance of society to drastic transformation. The contest between the rural and urban masses had had a similar effect on nineteenth-century European history and continued to exercise a paralyzing influence on the weaker and poorer nations. The mere postponement of the hardening of these social distinctions, in the Brazil of that time as in other third world countries, broadened the range of available social futures.

In every society the hard logic of class or communal interests is only as solid and determinate as the undisturbed institutional and imaginative assumptions on which it rests. Here, as in all else, the Brazilian circumstance simply exaggerated features more or less common to all political experience. By examining the limits to this increased political availability, you might discover something very general about the nature of transformative opportunity in politics and the flaws in received ideas.

The middle classes of this society had alternated historically between passive service to an agrarian and commercial elite they could not dislodge from the heights of power and futile campaigns to reform the state and establish a regenerate democracy on the North American and Western European model. The military regime had done more for these groups than multiply opportunities of ascension to wealth and power through the officer corps and the civilian bureaucracy. It had provided them with an involuntary political education. It had taught them that politics was indeed fate. The newly manifest power of government to make or break the social order – the partial lifting of the blockage imposed on social life by the oligarchy – shook the sense that things could not be other than what they were. It converted people in the politically conscious but unpropertied classes to a deeper uncertainty about what would become of their social world.

As society came, increasingly, to be recognized as the artifact of politics and as alternative social orders began to seem realistic, class interests lost their self-evident content. The definition of class and communal interests began to depend more visibly on a range of unmistakably contestable views of social possibility and of social ideals rather than on ideas about the ideal and the possible inherent in a straitened, routinized conception of reality.

As a spur to the political availability of the intermediate sectors, this insight was combined with an illusion. But, strangely, the illusion only reinforced the effect of the insight. It was the mistake of people open to radical ideas whose destructive effects on their material habits and career expectations they failed to envisage. This illusion – the bastard child of political impotence and inexperience – weakened the contrasting tendency of class interests under the impact of escalating conflict, the impulse to grab on to the most tangible and immediate advantages.

Consider now the underlying reasons for the lack of clearly felt divisions between the rural and the urban masses, or between the labor aristocracy and the underemployed laborers. The analysis of these reasons elaborates the same picture of institutional and social indefinition. First, neither the privileged workers nor the rural smallholders were secure in their jobs or their properties. The skilled worker might suddenly be cast down into the ranks of the underemployed from which he may have recently emerged. The smallholder might find himself thrown into the landless peasantry. Second, in part because of this insecurity, the larger part of the mass was in constant movement from country to small town, from small town to metropolis, and from one social station to another. This sense of living in a seething and simmering world represented the characteristic experience of the breakdown of well-defined limits to the possible in modern politics. (Compare with, say, the years from the end of the New Economic Policy to the beginning of the civil war in Soviet Russia.) Each privileged worker might find himself supporting family dependents who had come from the countryside or who eked out a harsh existence in the big city. Third, the central government, caught in the uncertainties described earlier, failed to settle on a clear-cut relationship to the propertied or the privileged. The country's rulers hesitated between a policy of devolution to entrepreneurial, bureaucratic, or landowning elites and a counterpolicy of playing for broader popular support. Thus, the hesitancies of the state reinforced the anxieties that resulted from the material condition of the people. A fourth reason was the active choice by the emerging leaders of petty bourgeois, working-class, and underclass groups, or by the middle-class militants and priests who worked among them, of a political strategy that deliberately tried to avoid these divisions. This strategy emphasized a common struggle – vague but attractive – against the state, the bosses, and the foreigner.

The relative weakness of the felt divisions within the working-class and petty bourgeois mass – like the unusual availability of radicalized professionals and technical cadres – was no more than a fleeting opportunity. So are all opportunities in politics. The crucial question remained: What strategies, alliances, conceptions, and institutional structures created in this moment of openness could outlast the circumstance of indefinition and yet carry into the experience of normalcy something of the heightened availability to revision that society had achieved at this hour of uncertainty? Would the national entrepreneurial classes manage to regain their decisive control over the process of accumulation, or would they find themselves economically dependent on whoever managed to seize the central government? Would the left-leaning parties formulate a vision and a strategy that enabled them to connect a method of rapid economic accumulation with ways to deepen mass organization? Would they, at the same time, win over large parts of the petty bourgeois, professional, and technical groups while openly combating the business oligarchies and the large landowners? Or would they falsely imagine themselves forced to choose between a doomed "proletarian" struggle against everyone else or a paralyzing alliance with the national economic elites against the foreign investor (who was in fact far more willing than his domestic counterpart to bargain with any regime – since, unlike him, he planned for a profit rather than for a dynasty)?

The circumstance of indefinition was not limited to the activities of the state and to the relations among classes. It extended, as well, to people's basic ideas about human association. There, too, though more intangibly, a struggle was going on, rich with opportunity for remaking the society through politics.

The most striking fact about the social imagination of the elites was a particular incongruity between the spiritual ideals they had accepted as properly governing the life of the society and the vision of social life they in fact lived out in their relations to one another and to their subordinates. In their professed beliefs about state and society they had embraced a liberal view of social relations as well as of governmental organization. The correct understanding of social life – in this view – saw community, contract, and power as naturally distinct and even mutually repellent. Outside the family community, people should be bound together by the consensual ties of contract and citizenship. The official political dogmas of this ruling and possessing class enshrined the equality of right, the cult of consent, and the idea that power had to be ennobled by sentiment in the family, controlled by party conflict and legal rule in the state, and justified by voluntary agreement and impersonal technical necessity in the production system. If the Brazilian elites had some other view of human association, they failed to articulate it.

But their actual social life was another story. There they participated in social relations – in business, family, and political life – that combined the elements of community, exchange, and power, the very combination so thoroughly repudiated by their professed beliefs. There they treated each other as patrons and clients and traded in favors and dependencies. There they showed their almost complete disbelief in all institutions not founded on blood, property, or power. There they acted as if a moment of personal presence were worth a thousand promises and as if any exercise of power could be tolerated so long as the veil of sentiment covered it.

For many, the professed ideas may have been little more than a sonorous litany, deafening an experience – the real experience – that these ideas left voiceless. But for some, the professed ideas, combined with some larger vision of human solidarity, *were* the real thing. Those who felt this way were the counterelites – leftist and liberal, civilian, priestly, and military – who had tried to realize in society what the majority of the upper classes merely professed.

The indefinition of popular views of the possible and desirable forms of social life had a different character. To the extent that working people were taught any idea of human association it was precisely the idea that dominated elite life but found no place in elite belief. According to this gospel the best escape from an experience of pure subjection to untrammeled coercion was to treat the boss (the landowner, the proprietor, the supervisor, the doctor, and even the priest) as a patron. The poor man might at least expect to receive protection from the superior to whom he showed allegiance. The whole spiritual life of the working people, however, was an ongoing rebellion against this idea of association. Each segment of the people – the farm laborers and smallholders, the underemployed mass in the cities, the inhabitants of the small towns – discovered in its own way both the reality of coercion behind the pretense of contract or community and the possibility of other forms of association. People discovered such alternatives, in part, through their frequent movement from one social world to another – the worlds of the backward Northeast and the Southeast, of the dismal workplace and the entrancing soap opera; in part, by what they learned from the militants of the churches and the leftist movements.

The contest over the form and nature of association stood out most clearly in religious quarrels. People waged a fierce struggle over the idea of God. To each of these conceptions of God that they quarreled over, there corresponded a different view of salvation, society, and personality. To the believer the religious ideas served as more than metaphors for the secular realities. Each such conception of the relation between man and God implied, and was implied by, a view of the relations among people.

On one side worked those who saw salvation in withdrawal from the larger life of society into a community of the elect – a community that departed as much as it could from the moral characteristics of the surrounding society while continuing to work dutifully within it. The ennobled social island would stand as a denial of the despotic, mendacious, and shameful paternalism that tainted almost everything in Brazilian society. It would be, in effect, a small-scale realization of the liberal dream of autonomy, dignity, and self-respect. This religion worshiped a God whose work could be carried out in the world only through the slow, exemplary influence of purified hearts.

On the other side stood people who saw themselves caught up in a larger messianic and redemptive conflict. The God pictured by their religious vision was both more relentlessly transcendent and more completely engaged in history than the deity of the opposing vision. The contrast between his call and established social life was radical: it could not stop with liberal social relations. The redemptive commitment he required was total: it could not await the edifying influence of the elect. Such a Christian felt that the first and most terrible question he would have to answer when he met his God was: Where are the others? The individual soul and the mass of the people replaced the community of the purified as the key actors in this spiritual drama.

The spiritual vision that emphasized communities of the elect found its main champions in the pentecostal sects that were then making numerous conversions in the country. The other, more collective and messianic spirituality gained support from the Catholicism of the local priests and the radical theologians. The first seemed to have taken root most strongly among the petty bourgeoisie in town and country; the second appealed most readily to the social groups subject to the most violent economic and geographic dislocations. But neither message remained confined to a church or a class. These visions were alternative spiritual responses to a shared experience. They remained largely invisible to the educated elites, who were blinded by their pathetic mimicry of foreign ideas, their vulgar and heartless hedonism, and their prostrate, complacent faithlessness.

Every feature of the circumstance of indefinition whose presence in the life of state, class relations, and social visions I have discussed had its more subtle counterparts elsewhere in the world, even in the countries where the scope of the struggle over the uses of governmental power seemed narrowest. Even in those more tranquil polities the central government hesitated between different ways of dealing with the more privileged classes. Even there, opinion disturbed and transformed the play of tangible material interests. Even there, the occasional escalation of practical and imaginative conflict fragmented apparently shared material interests just as often as it unified them. Even there, people's vision of society served as a battleground between dominant, enacted ideas of association and countervailing experiences or longings.

Now imagine, reader, that you threw yourself into the Brazilian situation just described. Suppose that you were one of those many people who looked on politics as both an insider and an outsider. The contest for power mattered to you, but so did the vision of another society and the justification of your ideas about society. You lived out, among people who hardly cared, one of the only tragedies that the bourgeois world had to offer: the conflict between theoretical and practical activity, whose unity generations of radical thinkers had so unrealistically extolled. You took up partisan propaganda and intrigue, believing that grassroots popular movements were helpless unless they gained the means with which to participate in the struggle over governmental power. But you also tried to study the movements on their own terrain and to discover how they might be turned into a decisive force.

At this time in world history, an attitude once confined to great visionaries had become common among decent men and women. They could no longer participate in political struggle out of a simple mixture of personal ambition and devotion to the power and glory of the state. They also had to feel that they were sharing in an exemplary experiment in the remaking of society. A person who entered Brazilian politics in this spirit wanted his country to do more than rise to wealth and power as a variant of the societies and polities of the developed West. He wished it to become a testing ground for a way of organizing government and the economy that would enlarge the options available to mankind. He wanted to add alternatives that would advance a little further the radical project – the project of seeking individual and collective empowerment by creating institutions that weaken the hold of preestablished social divisions or hierarchies over our practical or passionate dealings with one another and impart to normal social life something of the heightened mastery over context that characterizes moments of revolutionary conflict or invention.

Such a person took seriously the view of grassroots organization as the indispensable device by which to break the vicious circle of mock liberalism, controlled mobilization, and outright dictatorship. He wished his country to establish a style of democracy that would ensure a higher level of civic militancy. Ultimately, every aspect of the established social structure would meet up with a collective activity of conflict or deliberation that might lay it open to challenge and revision. Economic growth would be achieved by a production system oriented toward popular goods, family farming sustained within state-supported cooperative, commercial or technical networks, and the combination of high-technology industry with decentralized, labor-intensive, and small-scale industrial or assembling centers.

To establish a different organization of the society and the economy, you had, at least, to recognize the situation for what it was. You could not see it as a stage in a preordained sequence or as the relentless working out of a set of objective class interests or as the application of determinate economic and technological constraints. You needed to develop a political practice that prefigured your most distant aims in your methods of mobilization and that allowed for the achievement of a series of transitional objectives. The tendency of means to generate their own ends remained the demon of politics: only the ends at least partly foreshadowed in the means had a chance of being realized in the world.

It was also vital to avoid the path toward isolation that had helped defeat or tame the European leftist parties and to renounce the preconceptions about feasible class alliances underlying that path. You could not, for example, assume that the only alternative to a politics of unremitting hostility to the petty bourgeoisie or the salaried middle classes was an alliance with the national entrepreneurs and landowners against the foreigner.

In all these respects a political practice meant to generate new variants in the forms of social and economic organization could not itself be inspired by ideas that relied upon belief in definite and irresistible historical tendencies. You had to envision political opportunity and constraint in a fashion that refused to treat emergent events as typecast from the start. You had to have a way to deal with the particular organizational form and institutional setting of an industrial system as up for grabs. And you also needed a view with sufficient generality and clarity to guide you and to place the immediate context of your action in a broader setting of worldwide experiments with the possible forms of society. When, committed to these aims, you turned to the people who had practical ideas about society, you were in for a surprise.

The high servants of the state adopted, for the most part, the culture of policy science and microeconomics. The more lucid and effective these officials were, the more clearly they understood that the intellectual techniques supplied by this culture lacked any substantive vision. These techniques might help you manage practical institutions and governmental policies, once the social practical circumstances had been specified from outside. At a stretch, they might even enable you to find a range of alternative feasible strategies of economic growth with different distributive consequences. But there the power of these ideas to elucidate social experience stopped. The top bureaucrats had no reasoned view of transformation from one social circumstance to another. They achieved the semblance of such a view only by smuggling into their analytic apparatus ideas about industrial evolution or about organizational constraints that the apparatus could not itself justify. Like most political managers of the contemporary world, they found themselves repeatedly forced to choose between agnosticism and prestidigitation.

The leftist militants, intellectuals, and oppositional politicians did have beliefs about institutional change. But these beliefs came closer to being parts of the problem than parts of the solution. David Hume had observed that: "Parties from principle, especially abstract speculative principle, are known only to modern times and are, perhaps, the most extraordinary and unaccountable phenomenon that has yet appeared in human affairs." The broader the experience of social possibility, the more overt the role of abstract ideas becomes. Aims and interests could no longer be defined on the basis of a tacit, uncontroversial picture of social reality and possibility. They depended upon choices among different visions of possible society and of the possible satisfaction and transformation of desire. By that very fact, practical actions became hostage to abstract ideas.

Ideas about personality and society never penetrate completely the experience for which they try to account. If, however, the ideas become too remote from the reality of the experience, they produce another, special disturbance. For people then act as if moved by two different springs: the spring of their residual, unilluminated, and untransformed experience and the spring of their newfangled ideas. Each interrupts the movements of the other. Such people have lost the spontaneous alacrity of the person whose beliefs remain implicit in his actions without gaining the reflective lucidity of the man whose thoughts self-consciously govern his conduct. The resulting situation becomes all the more dangerous and confusing when people's sporadic efforts to live out their ideas leads them to close down just those opportunities in their own undertheorized experience that might allow them to realize most fully their most serious intentions.

To the extent the best leftist militants and politicians had visionary ideas, these views remained both vague and unrelated to any transformative strategy. To the extent they had a conception of transformation, it relied upon social theories – Marxism preeminent among them – that had broken only incompletely with the naturalistic premise. These theories suggested an arbitrarily limited repertory of ideas about possible class alliances, stages of social evolution, and even the language of political controversy.

People fought for individual and factional advantage as they had always done. They also quarreled over speculative principles. But the sequences of social change to which the influential social theories referred bore so little resemblance to the immediate reality of the country that the theoretical slogans could be upheld only by being treated as metaphors for concerns they did not truly express. At any given moment the contestants could not tell for sure whether the vague ideological disagreements that seemed to divide them were simply the weapons of self-interested factional rivalries or whether, on the contrary, these rivalries were being disturbed and aggravated, rather than guided, by abstract ideas. They were like men wandering around in a daze: their doctrines were dreams. But when they tried to apply them – to take them literally rather than to manipulate them cavalierly as metaphors or pretexts – the results were even worse.

Try to understand, reader, by an act of imaginative empathy, the bitterness a person in such a circumstance might feel when he discovered that doctrines invented to emancipate and enlighten had now become instruments of confusion and surrender. To think correctly about society was not to guarantee successful action. Nobody could reasonably hope to ride to power on the crest of a wave of books or to reverse in the library defeats sustained in practical politics. But something had gone wrong if theories meant to reveal and enlarge opportunities were in fact constraining and masking them. When large numbers of potential militants slid back into an unjustifiably narrow view of possible social futures or sank into an impenetrable confusion between personal antagonisms and ideological claims, you began to feel toward the inherited radical theories a little as Machiavelli had felt toward Christianity. Ideas had spoiled the contest for power. These ideas disoriented the leaders who rose from the people as well as the middle-class radicals who agitated among workers. The influence of Christianity, however, had been exercised in the name of a higher reality, and it had proved a continuing source of inspiration to those committed to demystifying society. Radical social theory had no such excuse. It was an instance of illusion passing into prejudice. You wanted to write a book to set things straight.

6

The Circumstance of Social Theory

A Fourth Point of Departure

SOCIETY AS MADE AND IMAGINED

EACH of the points of departure discussed in Chapters 3–5 can carry us forward to the beginnings of a social theory that extends the conception of society as artifact. A criticism of the current situation of social and historical thought can reach similar results more directly. It can reach them quite apart from the effort to make sense of the idea of a transformative vocation, or to reimagine the social ideal, or to reflect on the constraints and opportunities of practical action.

I begin with a loose comparison of the history of our modern ideas about mind and society with the history of certain modern views of nature. This comparison lays the basis for the more detailed discussion that follows. It also connects the analysis of the internal problems of social theory with the picture of human activity presented at the start of the book.

The Broader Intellectual Context: The Rejection of Self-Evident and Unconditional Knowledge

The whole body of established ideas about nature was once viewed as a system of propositions ultimately deducible from axioms that were both true and self-evident. Self-evidence implies incorrigibility, truths that need never be revised. Incorrigibility and self-evidence together testify to truth. A particular theory of the physical world may have been discovered under the impulse of tortuous reasonings and carefully analyzed observations. Once formulated, however, its basis could be seen to lie in self-evident and incorrigible axioms.

This Euclidean view of science never recovered from the blow it suffered when Newton's mechanics turned out to be less than the last word on nature. The philosophical understanding of science sought refuge in a variety of fallback positions. People discovered that self-evidence was no touchstone of truth: no one picture of the physical world remained safe against rejection or demotion to the category of a special case. Nevertheless, scientists and philosophers continued to hope that certain features of a way of doing science or certain ideas within the changing body of scientific theories might remain above the flux. Sometimes this device of immunity was found in certain privileged representations, like the concepts of space and time. These representations supposedly described a pretheoretical experience whose core content remained stable as the substance of scientific theories changed. Sometimes the invariant guarantee of objectivity became a conception of the scientific method, including criteria of validity, verification, and sense. So long as claims could be justified by the appeal to a preestablished and unchanging canon of explanation, all was well. Thus, the idea of a theoretical system that gained self-evidence through its axioms was swept aside. It gave way to the chastened program of a science that based its hope of objectivity on the continuing deployment of a few immutable elements: its basic ideas or methods.

But the fallback positions from the Euclidean idea of science proved temporary reprieves. All candidates for the role of foundational conceptions, including the geometrical ideas that had originally supplied the model for absolute certainty in science, remained vulnerable to changes in the content of scientific theories. As the content of scientific theories changed, so, albeit more slowly, did fundamental scientific ideas and conceptions of scientific method.

The criteria for objectivity and progression in science had to be found elsewhere: in the self-correcting qualities of science or in the demonstrated bearing of this endless work of self-revision on the advancement of certain practical interests. Such interests defined a relation to the world more basic than knowledge. The major disputes about science became the controversies among ways – from the realist to the skeptical – to understand the intellectual situation resulting from the abandonment of views that tried to rescue part of the old ideal of incorrigibility.

To push the rejection of that ideal far enough, however, is to discover an alternative basis for objectivity. In its capacity to discover truth – to reason in new ways or to have incongruous perceptions – the mind is never entirely imprisoned by its current beliefs. It can achieve insights that it may not be able to verify, validate, or even make sense of within the established criteria of validity, verification, or sense. All past and present modes of discourse put together do not exhaust our faculties of understanding. If objectivity cannot consist in the attachment to unrevisable and self-authenticating elements in thought, then it may lie in the negative capability not to imprison insight in any particular structure of thought. It is even possible that science may progress through the development of ideas and practices that accelerate the process of self-correction. Thus, the wheel would come full circle: objectivity through maximum corrigibility.

The Failure to Rescue the Ideal of Unconditional Knowledge

The movement away from an ideal of incorrigible knowledge undermines belief in the quest for unconditional or absolute knowledge described at the start of this book. Unconditional knowledge is the knowledge whose basic structure of explanation and criteria of validity, verification, and sense are compatible with the discovery of any truth, or with the making of any defensible claim, about the world. Knowledge, in this view, can be incomplete and nevertheless unconditional so long as it can grow without subverting its own basic methods and assumptions. The decisive quality of unconditional claims is the definitive, all-inclusive character of the framework of standards of sense, validity, and verification on which these claims rely. For knowledge to be unconditional these assumptions must be both significant (that is, they must provide effective guidance) and sufficient (that is, they must accommodate all true or defensible claims). Once the ideal of unconditional knowledge is defined in this way, it no longer seems able to survive the repudiation of self-evidence as a criterion of truth. What is abandoned with the rejection of the Euclidean and Cartesian ideal of self-evidence is not simply a criterion of assent. It is also the ideal of unchallengeable assumptions.

Nor can we hope to rescue from the wreck of the idea of an absolute frame of reference, interpreted as a body of indisputable truths, the related notion of a type of knowledge whose guarantee of objectivity is its ability to account for all other more local representations of the world and for itself. Either we cannot tell a complete story about our experience, or about any part of our experience, or we can tell it only on terms that guarantee the availability of many different complete stories. The resulting need to choose among alternative complete stories severs the link between completeness and absolute knowledge. Moreover, the objectivity we are actually interested in has little to do with the completeness of the stories we can tell. A complete story would not stop with facts about non-human nature that lend themselves more or less successfully to explanation by reference to closed systems or random process. It would have to account for the mental and social activities that are not governed by any lawlike list of structures of thought or of social life. It would have to be a higher-order view capable of dealing with both the most structure-dependent and the most structure-breaking phenomena. But where are we to look for such a metaview? As it becomes more complete, it would probably also become more controversial and provisional. For that very reason, it would suggest alternative complete stories.

The same point can be restated more loosely and intuitively. Any complete story about nature and society lacks the compelling character of the most compelling local narratives. We cannot retell the interesting parts of such a story in the language of natural science: many if not all the things that matter most to us about society and consciousness slip through the net of natural-scientific explanation. Or they demand an immeasurably large and fine net: a theory that can never finish the statement of intermediate links between ultimate physical causes and immediate social or mental experiences in time to explain anything at all.

Many of the most influential modern thinkers tried to reestablish the idea of an absolute frame of reference. Yet in each instance their doctrines turn out to be compatible with the critique I have rehearsed. Consider the examples of two very different philosophers: Peirce and Hegel. For Peirce the basis of objectivity in science became the gradual convergence of scientific opinion toward a final opinion, "independent not indeed of thought but of all that is arbitrary and individual in thought." It hardly violates his central insight to interpret independence from what is arbitrary and individual as a heightened autonomy from confining presuppositions. This autonomy may in turn be seen less as an outcome, completed once and for all, within the history of thought, than as a continuing process and a regulative ideal governing this process. You can say the same, though with less assurance, of Hegel's idea of absolute insight. For, though we can interpret this idea as completed and unconditional knowledge, we can also read it as an ideal limit, never actually reached. It is the affirmative mirror image of the negative, cumulative practice of context smashing that plays so large a role in Hegel's detailed studies of mind and society.

So the history of our views of nature suggests that the ideal of unconditional knowledge cannot survive the rejection of self-evidence as a criterion of truth; that we can no more hope for unconditional knowledge as a complete story about all stories than for unconditional knowledge as incorrigible insight; that the abandonment of the search for an absolute frame of reference in either of these two senses does not prejudice the possibility of cumulative insight but supplies us instead with a more modest and realistic version of objectivity – the assurance of not being definitively and completely imprisoned by whatever basic assumptions we happen to have inherited; that objectivity so understood implies corrigibility rather than its opposite; and that this entire view, though leaving open all options in the philosophy of science short of extreme skepticism or dogmatism, can be reconciled with some of the famous philosophical doctrines that seem to antagonize it.

From the Rejection of the Ideal of Unconditional Knowledge to
the Abandonment of the Naturalistic View of Society

The naturalistic premise dominated the most influential forms of social thought in much of world history. Whether or not the ruling doctrines invoked divine sanction, they portrayed a mode of social life meant to represent the natural form of civilization. The core form of society could undergo corruption or regeneration. But it could never be fundamentally remade or reimagined.

These doctrines had both a social and a personal message. Each transmuted a particular ordering of human life into a universal image of human possibility. In forming this image each treated a particular collective tradition as defining the universe of collective opportunities. But because each conceded that the social order might be corrupted it could also denounce contemporary social practices as departures from the canon of desirable human relations. The correct social order helped form the emotions in right and beneficial ways. These emotions, in turn, renewed the life of the canonical social scheme. When all went well, the just order of division and hierarchy in society would sustain, and be sustained by, a hierarchy of faculties in the soul.

These beliefs form a close counterpart to the Euclidean idea of science. They appeal to self-evidence as a test of truth. More generally, they provide an absolute frame of reference: the image of a social order that, though richly defined, provides an unconditional measure of human value and possibility. No wonder the gradual abandonment of the naturalistic premise in natural science offers so many parallels to the subversion of the naturalistic premise in social theory.

The history of all that is great and powerful in modern social thought is in large part the history of the rejection of this naturalistic view of society, each new movement of thought attacking its predecessor for the naturalistic residues it continued to harbor. Much in our modern ideas about society represents the relentless development of the principle contained in Vico's statement that man can understand the social world because he made it. But even today this idea has still not been carried to the extreme point. At the height of its struggle against the naturalistic view of society, the Vicoan principle came under the spell of alien conceptions and concerns. Thus, a series of compromises with the naturalistic theory emerged. In the character, and even in the motives, of their relation to earlier, more purely naturalistic doctrines, these compromises resembled the initial fallback positions from the Euclidean idea of science. They all made social and historical explanation depend upon a reference to deep-seated economic, organizational, or psychological constraints, often thought to generate a list of types or stages of social organization. To the extent that this concealed guiding plan failed to determine historical events or social facts, you had to resort to weaker, contextualized explanations.

The first example of this strategy of compromise with the naturalistic view had been the idea of a science of human nature or of morals that would lay bare the basic laws of mind and behavior (e.g., Mill's idea of a foundational science of ethology). Particular societies could then be portrayed as variations on the central themes described by this foundational science. For this idea to work, you had to believe that this science could explain the most important matters in history and society. The rest would be detail or development. The romantic movement in historiography, magnified by later anthropological and literary discoveries, posed the essential challenge to this project. There were just too many ways to be human. The differences among them went to the heart rather than to the details.

The second major compromise form of the naturalistic idea of society to appear in the history of modern Western social thought was the idea of a set of constraints rooted in practical social needs to produce, to organize, and to exchange. The convergence of this second compromise idea with the first one gave rise to classical political economy. The main objection to the second compromise was the looseness of the relation between the practical imperatives and the actual forms of society that these imperatives were alleged to shape. There always seemed to be too many social routes to the execution of the same practical tasks.

A third compromise appeared when people began to think that these transformative constraints had a certain cumulative direction of their own. Social worlds, in this view, fall into a natural sequence, each of them an indissoluble system of institutional traits. In the nineteenth-century heyday of Western world conquest, this belief found support in the impression that a mode of life and belief, originally championed by the conquering Western powers, lay on the verge of taking over the world.

The combination of this third compromise idea with the previous one inspired many of the great social theories of the late nineteenth and the early twentieth centuries. These are the views discussed in greater detail in the following sections of this book as deep-structure or deep-logic theories of society. Marxism is the most important example. History just did not happen as these deep-structure theories required. Events kept breaking out of the correct transformative sequence and producing social worlds that fitted none of the stages or alternatives through which mankind supposedly had to pass and from which it supposedly had to choose.

These compromises survive today in the form of an essentially simple intellectual predicament. The adherents to the deep-logic social theories oscillate between a reality-denying commitment to the hard-core versions of doctrines like Marxism and an attempt to absorb resistant fact by dissolving these doctrines into a morass of metaphor and suggestion. The mainstream of economics has abandoned the goal of combining a science of mind with a science of material and organizational constraints. Instead, it has taken refuge in a strategy of analytic neutrality toward substantive empirical or normative controversies about social life. The earlier, classical ambition survives only in the preconceptions and shibboleths of ruling elites (who nevertheless regard themselves as free from theoretical prejudice) and in the handy stratagems of macroeconomics. Finally, the idea of a foundational science of mind and morals reappears occasionally in the major traditions of individual psychology and psychiatry. In them, however, it connects only tenuously with the understanding of society. A multitude of self-contented researchers practice an empirical social science, confident of their freedom from the arbitrary and constraining assumptions made by the other, more high-flown brands of social theory. But their practice of explanation has proved to be less an alternative way of imagining personality or society than the more or less confused and unpremeditated combination of the fallback positions described later in this chapter.

Another way to understand the point of this book is to read it as an effort to take the antinaturalistic idea of society to the extreme. The argument anticipates a view that refuses to hedge on the conception of society as artifact. Such a theoretical project would just keep going from where all the incomplete realizations of the view of society as artifact – all the halfway departures from the naturalistic approach – leave off. Once the naturalistic premise had been conclusively rejected, the view of personality, the analysis of practical constraints, and the recognition of cumulative transformative influences might all be reintroduced, purged of the residues of the naturalistic idea. Social and historical explanations would no longer rely on lawlike conceptions claiming to define the limits of possible social worlds or to determine the necessary sequence of actual social orders.

To understand society in such a spirit represents the counterpart, in social thought, of the full-fledged abandonment of the Euclidean idea of science, with its appeal to incorrigibility as a test of truth and its search for an absolute frame of reference. People once feared that to abandon the Euclidean idea of science would be to lay down all defenses of skepticism. Only later did they discover that the rejection of objectivity as incorrigibility enabled them to recover objectivity as an extreme corrigibility. So, too, it may seem today that to sever all remaining connections with the naturalistic premise would leave us without a way to imagine society or to formulate the social ideal. We ordinarily admit into our thoughts only that measure of seemingly disordered reality to which we can give an active response. To limit the perception of reality is the natural strategy of intellectual survival: the mind fears being overwhelmed by more than it can imaginatively order. But unless we occasionally move at the edge of our imaginative capabilities we cannot hope to extend our vision of reality and to refine our conception of how things may be ordered.

Social theory today must choose between two directions. It can stick to its compromises with the naturalistic premise, continuing to imagine society from the standpoint of a vision of compulsive sequence or of possible social worlds. When we choose this path we become entangled in an ever denser web of intellectual equivocation and aimlessness whose character the next few sections of this book describe. Alternatively, we can reject all compromise, pursue the initial, antinaturalistic route of modern social thought to its outermost limits, and see what happens.

The following pages set out in detail the circumstance of social theory at the close of the twentieth century. They then show how the effort to respond to this circumstance in different fields of thought about society suggests a point of departure for the remaking of social theory – a point of departure that is most constructive precisely where it seems most nihilistic. Just as you can reach similar concerns and ideas from other, more practical beginnings, so, within theory itself, you can also start from the internal problems of different disciplines and arrive at convergent conclusions.

DEEP-STRUCTURE SOCIAL THEORY

Two partial dissolutions and partial reinstatements of the naturalistic view of society dominate the history of modern social thought. One of them is the practice of deep-structure or deep-logic social theory, which has taken ever more diluted and equivocal forms. The other is conventional, empiricist, or positivist social science, whose theoretical agenda, methods, and self-conception have been shaped in large part by the perceived failures of the deep-logic tradition. The crucial difference between deep-structure social analysis and conventional social science turns on their respective attitudes toward the existence of institutional and imaginative frameworks that stand apart from the routines of social life and shape these routines.

In this section I examine the distinctive characteristics of deep-structure analysis. Marxism serves here as its most richly developed and influential example. But many other famous modern social theories also illustrate deep-logic methods and principles. Thus, Durkheim's theory of society, especially as stated in *The Division of Labor in Society*, might well replace Marxism as my primary example even though its distinctive explanations and political intentions differ strikingly from Marx's. Moreover, it should be clear from the outset that much in the writings of Marx and his followers not only resists assimilation to the tenets of deep-structure analysis but provides tools for attacking those tenets. The next section studies the lessons to be learned from the evolution of Marxism. For the moment the discussion focuses on an approach that no theorist has ever fully accepted but that many theorists have implicitly treated as the bedrock of generalization about society and history.

Deep-structure social analysis is defined by its devotion to three recurrent theoretical moves. These moves are not reducible to one another. Together, they represent a specific approach toward social and historical explanation. Despite the many difficulties to which it gives rise, this approach deserves study not only because of its remarkable influence but because of the continuing failure to construct an alternative at a comparable level of theoretical generality and ambition.

The Distinction Between Routines and Frameworks

The first distinctive mental operation of deep-structure social theory is the attempt to distinguish in every historical circumstance a formative context, structure, or framework from the routine activities this context helps reproduce. The most important of these routines are the repetitious practices of conflict and compromise that perpetually create the social future within the social present. These practices include the methods of normative controversy (legal, moral, or theological) as well as the methods for exchanging commodities and labor and for winning and using governmental power. To portray them is to describe the habitual disposition of the major resources of society making: economic capital, state power, practical knowledge, and accepted moral and social ideals.

The deep-structure analyst emphasizes the distinction between these routines and a framework of social life. This framework is distinctive, but, as we shall soon see, it is never unique. For deep-logic theory repudiates from the beginning the naturalistic commitment to a single, canonical ordering of human life. It prides itself on its ability to recognize the discontinuity among social worlds created in history, seeing in each of these worlds a genuinely unique solution to the problems of mankind.

Each of these formative contexts is defined by its ability to help generate and sustain a richly developed set of practical and imaginative routines and by its corresponding tendency to resist disturbance. The framework is not vulnerable to the effects of the low-level conflicts and compromises it shapes. A sharp contrast therefore exists between these everyday disputes or combinations and the revolutionary transformations that replace one basic structure with another. And a special theory is required to explain how such transformations come about.

A formative context may consist in imaginative assumptions about the possible and desirable forms of human association as well as in institutional arrangements or noninstitutionalized social practices. Each deep-logic theory pictures frameworks and the relative influence of the elements that compose them in its own way. This picture already implies an account of how such frameworks get made and remade.

In Marx's theory of history the formative contexts are the modes of production. The most important constituents of each mode of production, given Marx's theory of historical change, are the legally defined institutional arrangements that govern the regimes of labor and capital and, more specifically, the relation of each class to the productive resources of society. The most significant routines are the daily forms of production and exchange, especially the repeated transactions by which some classes (i.e., the occupants of standard positions in the social division of labor) gain control over the labor of other classes and over the product of that labor. But the mode of production exercises an influence over social life that goes far beyond the organization of production and influences even the most intimate and intangible aspects of social life.

It may seem strange to cite the distinction between the defining institutions and the resulting routines of a mode of production without immediately relating this distinction to the explanatory conjectures that loom so large in Marx's system: the ideas that a mode of production is eventually succeeded by another when it begins to hinder the maximum development of the productive forces of society and that it generates within itself a class with the interest and the ability to lead the transition to the next mode of production. But these ideas represent the specifically functionalist aspect of Marx's theory. They explain the emergence of a mode of production as a consequence of the contribution which that mode makes to the fullest development of the forces of production. They use class interest and class conflict to show how the consequence can operate as a cause. I want to show, however, that even within Marxism the deep-structure moves are more fundamental than the functionalist story.

Particular Frameworks as Instances of General Types

The second mental operation that distinguishes deep-structure theory is the effort to represent the framework identified in a particular circumstance as an example of a repeatable and indivisible type of social organization such as capitalism. There are two main variants of deep-structure social theory: one evolutionary, the other nonevolutionary. Each of them casts in a distinct light the types that particular frameworks exemplify. The nonevolutionary version sees a closed list of possible frameworks, not ordered in any necessary sequence. The evolutionary version believes in a compulsive, world-historical sequence of stages of social organization, with each stage a type.

In the nonevolutionary version the repeatable character of the type is unmistakable. In the right circumstances a form of social organization can recur. But repeatability also holds good in the evolutionary variant of this style of analysis. Even when the theory argues for an irreversible historical sequence it is likely to recognize that different countries may pass through the necessary stages at different times. This recognition represents more than a concession to historical plausibility; it also lends support to an explanatory approach that refuses to treat a framework as merely the singular outcome of a singular history.

Indivisibility is the other quality a framework must possess in order to play the explanatory role that deep-structure analysis demands of it. A formative context must stand or fall as a single piece. If it lacked this atomic quality the idea of a closed list of possible types of social organization or of a compulsive sequence of stages of social organization would be hard to maintain; there would simply be too many possible social worlds and evolutionary trajectories.

Much of Marx's theory of history can be understood as an evolutionary version of deep-structure analysis. The modes of production fall into a sequence, a sequence determined by the fit between sets of institutional arrangements and levels in the development of the productive forces of society. Capitalism is supposed to be capitalism in China as much as in England or Italy. Familiar controversies internal to Marxism, such as the debate about the "Asiatic mode of production," already suggest the difficulties that history places in the way of this theory; and the attempt to understand the worldwide hierarchical relations among supposedly capitalist national economies complicates matters further. The thesis that each mode of production represents a general and repeatable type is greatly strengthened if each such mode can be shown to arise by independent origin as well as by diffusion from a single source. But whatever importance may be given to independent origins, the deep-structure style of analysis requires that nothing vital about capitalism, for example, turn on its original European source.

A mode of production is also indivisible. Some of its elements may come under attack before others. But once the attack begins, either it must be temporarily suppressed or it must result in the replacement of one predefined stage or mode by another. One corollary is that there is a fundamental difference between the disputes and reforms that leave a system of relations of production intact and the revolutionary struggles and discoveries (discoveries rather than inventions) that usher in the next mode of production. Another corollary is that mixed modes of production turn out to be either unstable, transitional forms or satellites of another, dominant mode of production. An example that plays an important role later in *Politics* is petty commodity production: the would-be system of independent producers who neither work for others nor control (nonreciprocally) any considerable pool of dependent wage labor.

General Types as Subjects of Lawlike Explanations

The third characteristic move of deep-structure social analysis is the appeal to the deep-seated constraints and the developmental laws that can generate a closed list or a compulsive sequence of repeatable and indivisible frameworks. A view of the internal composition of these frameworks and a theory of their making and transformation complement each other.

The nonevolutionary deep-structure analyst must appeal to underlying constraints that set the limits to the list of possible social orders and that, by excluding many combined forms, determine the composition of the list. These constraints may be economic, organizational, or even psychological. The more interesting the theory, the tighter and more richly defined the mediating causal links that connect these ultimate constraints to observable features of particular social worlds and the more likely the theory is to define as possible certain forms of social life that have not yet been established while excluding as impossible others that people have vainly sought to inaugurate. If the theorist of possible social worlds is especially ambitious he may even explain why a possible form of organization becomes actual in a given circumstance. But these explanations may be particularistic or fragmentary, and they are in any event less important to this theoretical endeavor than the ideas that account for the configuration of the possible.

The evolutionary deep-structure analyst must deploy lawlike explanations that generate a particular sequence of particular frameworks. The purpose of the account must be to present what actually happened as a murky, unfinished procession of specific frameworks of social life and to credit this procession to a developmental logic of unfolding capabilities and insights or of cumulative causal influ-

ences. Marx provided such an account. There will be more to say
about its character when the discussion turns to the relation between
deep-structure analysis and functional explanation.

Both the evolutionary and nonevolutionary variants of deep-structure analysis must appeal to laws and constraints far removed from
the intentions and understandings of historical agents. People may ex-
ceptionally will a new structure of social life into existence or grasp
the relation between the invention of a new framework and the development of certain faculties or interests. But even then they are not
conscious of standing on a single cumulative trajectory or do not agree
on its definition. And the goals and consequences are likely to have at
best a troubled relation to each other. When deep-logic theory is interesting, when it does more than lend a spurious semblance of necessity to
established arrangements, it is also secret knowledge, and it requires a
wrenching out from the perspective of commonsense experience.

The second and third moves of deep-structure social theory – the
subsumption of a particular framework under a repeatable and indivisible type and the appeal to deep-seated laws and constraints – are
closely linked. Without both of them the deep-structure theorist sees
no way to combine explanatory generalization with respect for the
distinction between the shaping structures and the shaped routines of
social life. He would, he believes, be driven to a style of generalizing
explanation that disregards, one way or another, the importance of
the difference between change of a framework and change within a
framework. He would therefore also lose the means with which to
describe and understand the discontinuities among frameworks and
among the whole forms of life, thought, and sensibility they help sustain. One outcome of this attempt to free generalizing explanation
from the framework–routine distinction might be the return to the
old project of a unified science of mind and behavior that can explain
the diversity of customs. Another result might be to settle for much
more modest explanations in the fashion of the positivist social science and the naive historiography discussed later in this book. Whatever its specified form, the abandonment of the contrast between the
formative and the formed threatens our ability to acknowledge the
radical differences among past frameworks of social life. It therefore
also undermines our sense of our power radically to remake our own
society. Without imagination of structural variety, the stakes go
down in practical politics as well as in theoretical controversy.

The Limits of Deep-Structure Analysis

Much of the discussion in the following sections of this book is meant
to show that deep-logic social theory purchases this conception of
structural diversity at too high a cost. Part of the cost is a loss of
descriptive and explanatory plausibility; the facts simply do not fit.

Another part of the cost, however, has to do with the constraint that deep-structure analysis imposes on the imagination of structural diversity itself. It relies on the notion of a closed list of structures. It makes generalizing explanation depend on a script that towers over conscious actions and works through them. It fails to see that the character, as well as the content, of formative contexts is put up for grabs in history: there are major variations in the extent to which the institutional and imaginative orders of social life reduce us to passivity or, on the contrary, make themselves available to us for challenge and revision. In all these ways the deep-structure tradition hedges on the repudiation of the naturalistic premise and sacrifices to its scientistic apparatus much of its vision of social order as made and imagined rather than as given.

A major aim of *Politics* is to develop and illustrate an explanatory practice that preserves the first move of deep-structure social theory – the distinction between framework and routine – while replacing the other two moves with an alternative style of generalization. A great deal more than theoretical correctness depends on whether we can carry out such a reorientation. From its beginnings deep-logic social theory has been the chief theoretical instrument of what might be called the radical project or the enterprise of the modernist visionary: the effort to seek our individual and collective empowerment through the progressive dissolution of rigid social division and hierarchy and stereotyped social roles. The explanatory failures of deep-structure social theory jeopardize the advancement of that project. For, as my discussion of transformative practice has already suggested, these failures encourage prejudices and tactics that obstruct the realization of the leftist and modernist program.

The most serious dangers that deep-structure analysis poses to the endeavor of the modernist visionary are precisely the dangers that arise from its truncation of our insight into structural diversity: the closure imposed on the sense of historical possibility, the reliance on an explanatory script and, most importantly, the inability to grasp how and why the relation between the formative and the formed, between social structure and human agency, may change. Deep-structure social theory disorients political strategy and impoverishes programmatic thought by making both of them subsidiary to a ready-made list or sequence of social orders. Nowhere are these perils clearer than in the reliance of leftist movements, the major bearers of the radical project, on Marxism, the most developed version of deep-structure social theory.

Deep-Structure Analysis and Functional Explanation

The problem of functional explanation can now be related to the discussion of deep-logic social analysis. The tradition I have been calling deep-structural is often associated with functional explana-tion. The association is so constant and the difficulties of functional explanation so familiar that the criticism of functional accounts reg-ularly overshadows the critique of the deep-structure moves.

Functional explanations account for the emergence or the perpe-tuation of a state of affairs by the consequences that the state of affairs produces. The consequence operates as a cause. When action is inten-tional the mechanism by which the consequence acquires causative power is straightforward: the consequence, intended by the agent, serves as a motive to action, and the agent's control over his envi-ronment enables him to carry out his intentions. But the further away we move in social and historical study from the paradigm instance of intentionality, the more controversial the use of functional explanation becomes: if there ceases to be a well-defined individual or collective agent, or if the agent's control over his environment weakens, or if the sheer length and complexity of the causal sequence disrupt the translation of intentions into consequences. Once any link with intentional action disappears, the justification for functional explanation in social or historical study may depend on the availabil-ity of a social counterpart to natural selection.

The form of functionalist explanation that fits most easily with deep-structure social analysis combines three ideas. Once again, Marx's theory of history provides the clearest illustration. The first idea is a test of reality or success. Read, in Marxism, the maximum development of the forces of production. The second key concept is that of a response: a state of affairs capable of ensuring that the test is met. Read the mode of production: the relations among people, centered on the organization of labor and the exchange of the prod-ucts of labor, but implicating, in ever wider nets of influence, an entire way of life. The main weight of the system is borne by a third idea: a story that tells how over a period of time the states of affairs adjust so as to meet the test of reality or success.

A mode of production exhibits a given set of class relations. Even-tually this set of class relations begins to hinder the further devel-opment of the productive forces of society. A new class emerges whose particular interest in the overthrow of the existing mode of production coincides with the universal human interest in the de-velopment of mankind's productive capabilities.

This story is functionalist because it is a consequence of contrib-uting to the maximum expansion of the productive forces of society at a given level of their development that ultimately explains not only the rise and persistence of each mode of production but the world-historical sequence that all the modes follow. But in Marxism, as in many of the other most influential social theories, the func-tionalist story hinges on deep-structure assumptions. The deep-structure moves, not the functionalist quality of the explanation, are responsible for the thesis that only indivisible and repeatable frameworks – the modes of production – rather than, say, discrete institutional arrangements, can bring about the explanatory consequence – the fullest development of the productive forces. Many of the most familiar functionalist claims in Marx's theory depend on such implicit deep-structure premises.

Notice also that the most obvious and formidable objection to a functionalist narrative like the story about the productive forces and the modes of production has more to do with the deep-structural backdrop to the tale than with the functionalist's traditional conundrum of how the consequence serves as a cause. Any given set and level of practical capabilities can characteristically be realized by alternative sets of institutional arrangements, not just by a unique set. Many nonconvergent institutional pathways can therefore also lead to the development of similar practical abilities. The aspects of Marx's theory that stand in the way of recognizing such possibilities are the deep-structural tenets, not the functionalist style.

Suppose that we could successfully reform Marx's theory of history so as to make it consistent with the idea that alternative modes of production and alternative sequences of such modes can serve to realize a similar level of development of productive forces. Then, the traditional puzzle of functional explanation – the difficulty of explaining how the consequence acts as a cause – would be aggravated rather than solved. We would need to show why one trajectory prevails over another. We could not explain this prevalence functionally, for in our revised view the explanatory consequence (the development of the forces of production) can be achieved by more than one route. A nonfunctional explanation would be required. But once we had this explanation, functional explanation might well become superfluous. In explaining the triumph of one evolutionary route over another, we would also have explained the evolutionary route itself; no work would be left over for the functional account to do. The revisionist deep-structure analyst might well say of functional explanation what Laplace said of God: "I have no need of this hypothesis." Thus, when we try to expand deep-structure analysis to avoid the additional difficulties it creates for functional explanation we unwittingly intensify the functionalist's most traditional problem of linking final and efficient causes. We obscure rather than clarify the relevance of an analysis of the distant consequences of a state of affairs to an understanding of its occurrence. This problem, it seems, cannot be solved unless we sever the link between deep-structure analysis and functional explanation and abandon either one or the other.

A deep-structure social theory can dispense with functional explanations. Consider, for example, Durkheim's emphasis, in *The Divi-*

sion of Labor, on sheer demographic pressure as a cause of the passage from mechanical to organic solidarity. Conversely, functionalist explanation may be deployed in theories that reject the deep-logic style of explanation. But deep structure without functionalism is likely to result in an aggressively mechanical and superdeterministic theory, portraying historical agents as caught in structures whose built-in tendencies dwarf conscious human interests and intentions. On the other hand, a theory that makes functional explanations independent of deep-structural assumptions must either reject the distinction between the formative context and the formed routines or find a way to make this distinction independent of the other two moves of deep-structure theory. These considerations go a long way toward explaining why deep-logic analysis and functional explanation appear so regularly conjoined despite the severability of their connection.

The criticism of the comprehensive social theories of the modern age has traditionally focused more on their functionalist aspects than on their deep-structure characteristics. The discussion here of the predicament of social thought reflects a belief that this emphasis is misplaced. For in these theories functional explanations characteristically achieve their power only when combined with deep-structure principles, and it is these tenets that bring us closest to the core intentions of the theories that are functionalist as well as deep-structural. More importantly, the primacy accorded to the critique of functionalism is misdirected because the substitution of the deep-structure moves can generate far more surprising and illuminating results than the abandonment or demotion of functionalist analysis. Once we do the right thing to the deep-structure tradition, the problems of functional explanation may very largely take care of themselves. As the argument of *Politics* passes from criticism to construction it makes good on these claims.

MARXISM AS AN EVOLUTIONARY
DEEP-STRUCTURE SOCIAL THEORY

The Two-Sided Relation of Marxism to Deep-Structure Analysis

Marx's theory of history is the most richly developed and influential example of deep-structure social theory. As such, it has provided the radical project with its most important theoretical weapon. Yet in Marx's writings we may also find many ideas that not only resist assimilation to deep-structure views but also provide means with which to criticize and reconstruct those views. Three of these countervailing themes stand out. They are mentioned here less out of a desire to do justice to the historical Marx (who cares about that?)

than because of the role that each, once revised, plays in the constructive social theory to which this critical diagnosis leads.

First and most important, consider the radically antinaturalistic animus that inspires much of Marx's work and that appears most unequivocally in his critique of English political economy. For Marx, the cardinal sin of political economy was its habitual mistaking of the constraints and regularities of a specific type of economy and society for the inherent laws of economic life – a confusion tempered only by the passing acknowledgment that these laws may not have fully applied to more primitive or despotic societies. The entirety of Marx's social theory can be understood as an attempt to criticize our commonsense or theoretical views of society in the spirit of his criticism of economics.

A second theme in Marx that stands in tension with deep-structure analysis relates to the idea that the sequence of modes of production advances toward the eventual breakdown of social division and hierarchy and the revelation or development of the unitary, creative, negating quality of human labor. This is certainly the aspect of Marx's ideas most closely connected with the project of the modernist visionary: the reach for individual and collective empowerment through the invention of institutions and ideas that dissolve the rankings and contrasts of society. The thesis of the unitary character of human labor suggests that organized frameworks of social life may differ in the extent to which they impose a predetermined structure upon our practical and passionate dealings. To be sure, Marx believed that only with the twofold end of scarcity and class conflict would mankind come out from under its domination by the reified and hierarchical social orders it had created; thus domination would have to increase (the loss of primitive communism and the succession of historical modes of production) before it could be overcome (the inauguration of true communism). But we can dispense with this simple contrast between acting under the compulsion of a framework before communism and acting freely from such compulsions, though not from other causal influences, after communism has been established. We can work toward a social theory that represents the structure-bound and structure-free situations Marx imagines to be radically discontinuous as in fact coexisting throughout history. We can go on to recognize that the institutional and imaginative frameworks of social life differ, among other things, in the extent to which they respect and develop the framework-transforming capabilities of the agents who inhabit them. And we can ask what style of social thought could turn these apparent obstacles to generalizing explanation into explanatory opportunities.

A third theme of Marx's theories that falls outside deep-structure analysis and provides a clue to its correction can be found chiefly in his more concrete political and historical writings. This theme contains the kernel of an entire theory of politics. The key idea here is the conception of a two-way connection between the place a community or class (say, the French peasantry under the Second Empire) occupies in society and its distinctive posture of prostration or resistance: the degree and the way in which the group either takes things for granted or treats them as up for grabs.

Given Marx's own ambivalence toward the deep-structure moves, it is not surprising to find that the tradition of Marxism, like much of the tradition of classical social theory as a whole, can be understood in two different ways. On the one hand, it can be seen as the entropic history of deep-structure theory: a gradual discovery of its deficiencies and consequences, limited only by the fear that a frank recognition of failure would result in theoretical nihilism and encourage political defeatism. On the other hand, however, the tradition of Marxism can also be studied as a series of loosely related critical and constructive explorations, one of which is the attempt to reform deep-structure analysis from within. The dimly perceived objective of this particular line of exploration is the attempt to preserve the first deep-structure move – the contrast between the formative framework and the formed routines – while replacing the other two moves with an alternative approach to the understanding of society. Though much in the following pages may seem responsive to the first of these two readings of the Marxist tradition, even this seemingly negative perspective is meant to contribute toward the reconstruction of deep-structure analysis.

Marxist Theory and Leftist Parties

The decision to single out Marxist deep structuralism for a relatively detailed discussion is justified not only by the hope of enlisting the critical results in a constructive effort but also by the extraordinary influence Marxist theory has exercised on the beliefs and the practice of leftist movements.

Popular movements in Europe in the late nineteenth and early twentieth centuries seized on the doctrines of Marx and his followers and made them an official creed. Their startling decision officially to commit themselves to the beliefs of a philosopher was then repeated on a larger scale and, with a greater show of success, in the non-European world. Power over mighty nations was there exercised in the name of these ideas, though the men who knew how to stay in power also knew how to take the theories at a heavy discount. In other places the doctrines vaporized into a haze of vague conceptions and catchwords. Sometimes, these fighting phrases served tightly organized parties, bent on capturing the state. Sometimes, they were just the favored slogans of large numbers of indignant and half-educated people, determined to side with the poor and the powerless.

In these latter-day apparitions the ideas lost their rigor. No longer able to work as living and critical thought, they nevertheless remained to confuse the commitment to political aims and movements with the belief in a dead man's doctrines. All over the world thousands of clever and bookish militants, who saw themselves as friends of the people, anguished and haggled over the limits of orthodoxy. Experiments in thought and action were stifled by the fear that they might be viewed as an apostasy from cherished beliefs and from the practical habits those beliefs justified.

The European parties pioneered in championing this theoretical system as a guide to political practice and a source of political vision. These parties had, on the whole, ended in failure. The political strategies of hopeless compromise they pursued, and the understandings of society they entertained, had helped get them into trouble. To the extent that they kept faith with their revolutionary transformative intentions, they became isolated from the majorities and excluded from power. When they broke out of this marginality, they did so by abandoning or diluting their transformative commitments.

The particular ideas and strategies adopted by the more radical European parties were not the only plausible ones to be derived from Marx's doctrines. Moreover, the same strategies and ideas might have been made to rest on entirely different theoretical traditions. But intellectuals and militants have regularly persuaded themselves that the theory and the practice are tightly connected; after all, the tightness of the connection was part of the theory itself. The adoption by the European left of this somewhat arbitrary mix of abstract conceptions and concrete beliefs gave the amalgam enormous influence. The influence extended to other parts of the world, where political movements of great promise anxiously emulated the language and the stratagems of a European failure.

Having radical transformative aims, believing in some reformed version of Karl Marx's doctrines, and even accepting some canonical interpretation of how these theories ought to be translated into a political movement – were all seriously taken as part of the same package. As a model for the kind of relation of theory to practice that democrats and revolutionaries should hope to achieve, this was a willful closure to the surprises of politics. Thus, it is, after all, important to show both that something is wrong with the ideas and that the ideas provide clues to their own correction.

The Core Problem of Indeterminacy

My discussion of Marxism focuses on an inclusive set of problems: problems that result from the difficulties of applying Marx's synthesis of deep-structure moves and functional explanation to the particulars of historical study and contemporary political experience. It is tempting to conclude that the difficulties arise merely from excessive theoretical ambition and that similar problems would plague any social theory of comparable generality. But there is something important to be learned from tracing whatever in these difficulties can be attributed to the specific features of Marx's synthesis of deep-structure argument and functionalism and then asking what a social theory would have to be like in order to solve these problems.

On the functionalist side, the crucial problem is the lack of a one-to-one correspondence between modes of production and levels of development of the productive forces of society. At any moment and in every circumstance there turn out to be alternative sets of institutional arrangements that can serve as a basis for the further development of any particular productive or destructive capability. There is no sure way to tell which of these alternatives has the best long-run potential. Though some alternatives are either more promising or more accessible than others, there is no good way to define the class of possible alternatives or evolutionary trajectories, even for a particular society at a particular moment in its history.

When we turn to the distinctively deep-structure elements of Marx's view, the major difficulties result from the attempt to carry through the second and third moves of deep-structure analysis. The sets of institutional arrangements that represent the most plausible candidates for the mode of production called capitalism do not in fact exhibit the qualities that a mode of production is supposed to have. They do not behave as a repeatable and indivisible type, marking a stage in a world-historical sequence. Nor can they be plausibly explained on the basis of the kinds of laws, tendencies, or constraints that would be capable of producing such a sequence. Moreover, the strategies of adjustment and revision that have been used to rescue the theory from these difficulties prove to be inadequate until they become points of departure for a more basic reform of deep-structure analysis along the lines I have already suggested and shall further develop.

The following argument moves forward in three steps. First, I discuss the difficulties of giving content to the key concept of capitalism. These difficulties anticipate, on the plane of mere description, the major objections to Marx's combination of deep-logic analysis and functional explanation. The second step of the argument shows how the most familiar stratagems for defending Marx's theory against these objections are tenable only as preliminaries to a more basic reconstruction of the approach they are employed to defend. The third step of the argument works out some implications of these theoretical controversies for transformative political practice.

The Troubles of the Concept of Capitalism

We can often infer the shortcomings of an explanatory theory from the difficulties we encounter in the use of its key concepts. For the explanatory view implies an interpreted description of its subject matter. The conundrums that beset the explanation can be counted on to reappear in the interpreted description. So it is in Marx's theory of history with the idea of capitalism.

The concept of capitalism in Marx's system is the paradigm for all other modes of production. In fact, the whole sequence of modes and the science that claims to account for this sequence were devised in large part as an effort to understand the realities to which the idea of capitalism refers. At the same time the concept of capitalism designates the framework within which the lawlike processes detailed in *Capital* hold good. The description of that framework implies, and is implied by, a view of these processes. To dilute the sense in which capitalism represents an indivisible type of social organization feasible in different societies at different times is to alter or diminish the sense in which the economies and societies we describe as capitalist do indeed operate according to laws.

When put to use, the concept of capitalism turned out to be both too universal and too particular. Whenever the concept was defined in a loose and general way, it proved to apply to a large range of historical situations. Many of the societies to which an inclusive concept of capitalism seemed to apply were not industrialized. In fact, many of these situations arose in societies utterly different – in their forms of state power, their types of social hierarchy and division, and their ruling beliefs – from the North Atlantic countries that led the worldwide industrial revolution. Even if, left to their own devices, these other "capitalisms" had eventually industrialized, it seems plausible to expect that they would have done so in social forms utterly different from the ones people had in mind when they spoke of capitalism.

To deal with these embarrassments of overinclusion, you were driven to make your definition of capitalism more concrete: to read into it a more particular set of institutional arrangements. These arrangements might define, for example, the rights and powers that governed the claims on other people's labor and the crucial savings–investments decisions that helped drive accumulation forward. In the setting of a particular theory such as Marxism, you might even define capitalism genetically and sequentially as well as structurally and descriptively. Capitalism then follows certain defined stages and precedes others. In this view, there *is* a sequence of types of social organization. If capitalism seems to occur out of order, look closer, and you will see that it is not really capitalism. Or else you must have the wrong theory.

As the concept of capitalism is made more concrete in the effort to escape overinclusion, it runs into a characteristic dilemma. On the one hand, until it has been totally locked into a stage-theoretical sequence and laden with all sorts of institutional details, it is still not exclusive enough. There are still too many examples of societies and circumstances that seem to meet the definition but are not really what you were thinking of nor anything that could have been counted on eventually to bring about what you had in mind. By the time you have finished parrying all the problems of overextension you seem to have ended up describing a very particular society and a very particular series of events. At the same time, you have passed your ad hoc descriptions off as a theoretical category ready to figure in general theoretical explanations.

On the other hand, long before the concept of capitalism has been compelled to play a set role within a foreordained historical description or taken on the characteristics of an ad hoc description, it has become too exclusive. There are too many examples of transition to an industrial economy even within the core North Atlantic zone, that seem to jar with the elements of your more detailed definition. Yet you would find it strange to say that these many deviant cases were not cases of capitalist industrialization. For capitalism would then have to describe a special, exemplary core case. And how would you choose this exemplary instance? Would it be the country that industrialized first? But what if its immediate successors and rivals followed a quite different route to industrialization? Or should the controlling case be the most common one? But what if no plausible candidate can be found to perform this role?

The point about this dilemma of abstraction and concreteness can be put another way. When you make the concept of capitalism more textured, you do so with the hope that the more concrete traits will reveal what is most significant about the more general and abstract traits you began with. You also expect them to single out the historically decisive cases of capitalist breakthrough. If deviations exist, they can be treated as variations on the central theme. It would weaken and even undermine the force of your argument if the more detailed definition turned out to describe situations and events that seemed no more faithful to the more abstract and general elements in the concept of capitalism than all the historical situations your more precise definition excluded. It would be equally disappointing if the excluded cases were at least as important historically as the included instances.

So far I have given only the disembodied analytic structure of a criticism of the concept of capitalism. Now let me give this structure content. The most promising basis for an abstract and general definition of capitalism lies in the combination of a structural trait with a dynamic orientation. The structural trait is the predominance of wage labor as opposed to all forms of coerced or communitarian work. The mass of ordinary people need to work. They lack, either individually or collectively, the means of production with which to produce on their own initiative or to sell the products of their labor for their own account. Another class, in control of the means of production, buys their labor. The dynamic orientation that complements this structural characteristic is the struggle for profit. The people in charge of the means of production compete with one another. They must try to move ahead in order not to fall behind, expanding and reinvesting their profits. Production must serve the accumulation of capital. The decisive majority of producers are free laborers dependent in fact on the resources supplied to them, in exchange for their labor, by the class that controls the chief means of production. (The technical refinements that these ideas gained in Marx's system may be put aside. My aim now is to explore the usefulness of the concept of capitalism even when you disengage it from the more detailed and distinctive segments of Marxist doctrine or indeed from any brand of Marxism at all).

In fact, however, economic orders with just these characteristics have existed at many moments in history. The North Atlantic countries seem to have been only a subset of the societies that meet this general definition. They stand apart by the fact that, for reasons not even hinted at by this definition of capitalism, they pioneered in the industrialization of society. In almost all the agrarian empires and in many city-state republics, there were long periods during which coercive or communitarian forms of labor played only a subsidiary role; a large class of legally free though economically dependent workers sold their labor in town and country, and rural and urban markets became thoroughly money-based.

Often the legal regime of free labor differed in its institutional details from the arrangements that emerged in late medieval and early modern Europe. But this difference is beside the point, unless the specific legal structure of European free labor is incorporated into the definition of capitalism. Often, in these non-European societies, free individual labor shaded into various sorts of communitarian work regimes. But the same could be said of Western Europe until quite late in the day and on the very eve of industrialization. Often the independent smallholder and the petty trader or manufacturer played just as prominent a role in the economy as the propertyless laborer. But so did they in several variants of the European experience. In the crucial area of agriculture, they continued to play this role even after manufacturing had moved toward mass-production industry and agriculture had passed through succeeding stages of mechanization (e.g., the development of North American agriculture).

Many of the non-European societies that met the structural criterion in this definition of capitalism – the prominence of free labor – also satisfied the dynamic criterion – the commitment to accumulation. Both outside or within Europe, the labor buyer's search for profit blended with his interest in prestige and power. Governments treated their concern with the enrichment of the country as an integral part of their struggle against domestic and foreign enemies. If there are finer distinctions to be made between the types of profit orientation that do and do not exemplify capitalism, the definition I have been discussing fails to suggest them.

Consider the example, such as China during the Sung Dynasty, of a society that seems to have gone far in meeting both the structural and dynamic elements of the definition of capitalism. It is possible to parry the disconcerting overextension of the concept of capitalism by two familiar techniques. One tactic is to say that the apparent example was really not capitalism at all because it lacked certain other essential traits of a capitalist order. On one variant of this tactic you claim that major aspects of society and culture altered the effect and changed the sense of what we are at first tempted to describe as capitalism. But this solution pushes the concept in the direction of increasing concreteness, with consequences that soon prove embarrassing. The other stratagem is to treat these troublesome analogies as cases of "seeds" of capitalism, developments that proved to be abortive because of independent supervening events. But, then, once all these cases of blocked development are cataloged, the concept of capitalism will be found to have been undermined. The case of successful capitalist development turns out to be an aberrational success story standing out against the background of a much longer list of relative failures. The first definition of capitalism, on its face, denotes the many instances of eventual failure as well as the few eventual successes. It seems unlikely to perform the decisive role in a theoretical explanation that distinguishes failures from successes.

So let us try again with a different though similarly abstract and general definition of capitalism. This second formulation can be viewed as either an alternative or a complement to the first. Like the first, it attempts to define capitalism with enough generality to keep the definition from being a label for a unique historical situation. In this second statement, the distinctive feature of capitalism becomes a shift in the relation between commercial–industrial capital and agriculture, with a corresponding transformation in the dealings between town and country. Capitalism, you might say, exists if, and only if, the accumulation of commercial and industrial capital, guided by the profit motive, gains a large measure of independence from the manipulations of the agrarian surplus and the exploitation of peasant labor. The town becomes a major center of commerce and production in its own right rather than just a place of residence for predatory officials and absentee landowners who, though served by a local urban population, remain primarily dependent upon the agrarian production and the cash flow it generates. These transformed cities witness the development of forms of technology and organization that end up revolutionizing agriculture itself.

Like its counterpart, however, this alternative approach to the definition of capitalism says both too much and too little. It says too much because, for all but the smallest countries with a highly specialized role within the world economy, agriculture has continued to impose an independent check on the pace and nature of urban industrialization. It imposes this check even in the economies that are held up as prime instances of capitalism by the historians and theorists most anxious to use the concept of capitalism as a major tool of analysis. At the same time, the alternative definition says too little. There are an indefinite number of ways in which commercial-industrial capital has in fact increased – or might one day increase – its margin of independence from the ups and downs of the agrarian economy: more or less state control; greater or smaller class disparities; and even more or less differentiation between town and country. Industry may, after all, be largely country-based. It may be dominated, for example, by a mixture of small-scale private or communal proprietorship and large-scale governmental initiative.

In fact, when you subject the second definition of capitalism to the same type of comparative application and analysis to which I earlier submitted the first definition, you come up with the same sorts of embarrassing results. Once again, you find many periods in the history of each of the major agrarian empires when commercial-industrial capital gained a certain measure of independence and the cities became centers of considerable trade and manufacturing. In some of these situations, there were even technical breakthroughs that raised the productivity of agriculture (per field size) to a level comparable to that of Western European agriculture before the industrial revolution. On the whole, these were the same periods in which small-scale proprietors and legally free but economically dependent laborers achieved a presence in the economy and its work force. Sung China is as spectacular an example of one set of changes as it is of the other. So were many periods in the history of other agrarian–bureaucratic societies.

These extended periods of commercialization, of flourishing independent wage labor and small-scale proprietorship, and of changed relations between agrarian surplus and commercial–manufacturing capital or between country and town did not lead into an industrial revolution. Instead, they were usually reversed. The typical reversal included the decommercialization and demonetization of the economy against a background of governmental decline or collapse, the rise of coerced, dependent labor and large-scale estates, and the waning of urban vitality. The non-European societies that stood the best chance of initiating an industrial revolution of their own before being overtaken by Europe were those that, for reasons examined in *Plasticity into Power*, had done best at postponing or imitating these periods of reversion.

The two abstract and general definitions of capitalism discussed in the preceding pages offer little help with these problems. Both definitions fail to mark out the exceptional successful case from all the analogous situations that nevertheless had utterly different outcomes. Either of them is therefore unsuited to play the key part in an explanation of the European breakthrough and of the spread of industrial techniques and organizations throughout the world. Neither of them marks out with adequate distinction what the devotees of the term really seem to have in mind when they talk of capitalism.

Now suppose that, in order to deal with the difficulties of these abstract definitions, you try to make the concept of capitalism more concrete. You may do this by simply adding further elements to the definition of capitalism. Or you may do it as well by specifying the sequence of social and economic orders of which you expect capitalism to be a stage. In either case, an explicit or tacit theory tells you why all these traits go together or why these stages follow upon one another as they do.

A more detailed definition of capitalism may, for example, focus on the initial stages of agricultural transformation. Capitalism, in this view, is the system that emerges from a process including the replacement of small-scale family farms, the triumph of the large, relatively non-labor-intensive estate, and a sequel of massive migration of the country population to the cities. But there were many Western European countries that underwent a very different kind of agrarian transformation and that preserved the small family farm as the basic agrarian unit throughout their experience of industrialization. It is hard to show that the European countries that preferred this alternative were backward *on that account* if they were backward at all.

For example, the Dutch failure to anticipate England in passing from "commercial capitalism" to industrialization had at best a complex and indirect relation to the Dutch pattern of family-size holdings. On the other hand, the beneficial effect of this agrarian style on the early economic success of the Dutch Republic was unmistakable. Even French fidelity to the family farm had ambiguous consequences. If agricultural productivity per man may have been lower in France than in England during much of the nineteenth century, English industrial productivity seems to have been correspondingly lower than its French counterpart in the same period. France was also helped by its agrarian option to avoid social dislocations that might have hindered its industrial progress at a later moment in its history and might have caused immense suffering.

So this addition to the concept of capitalism makes the concept too exclusive to describe the range of societies and situations to which it is traditionally applied by Marxists and non-Marxists alike. Yet, paradoxically, the addition also seems to leave the definition not exclusive enough. For throughout the history of agrarian empires, we find periods when the small agrarian property was squeezed out by the large estate. Though these estates might start out as active participants in a commercialized market economy, their rise was often an episode in, or a prelude to, a period of collapse. Markets and manufacturing would be set back. Surely the concept of capitalism is not meant to describe a step in a process of agrarian concentration that repeatedly led to economic regression and decommercialization – the reverse of the standard historical connotations of the concept.

Suppose you exclude the inconvenient analogies by making the definition even more textured. For example, you include the existence of a protective barrier between government and large-scale capital. For capitalism to exist, you say, the large property owners and investors must be protected from arbitrary governmental expropriation. The hands of the central government authorities must be tied enough to enable the crucial investing and innovating groups to act on their own. But everyone knows that German industrialization, for instance, was carried out with a degree of overtness and exuberance in the partnership of government with large-scale capital that, from an English vantage point, seems to border on capitalist heresy. Yet to say that this state-guided or state-led industrialization was simply a secondary distortion caused by the need to catch up quickly is to misconceive both its extent and its origin. For Wilhelmine Germany as for many of the countries that began to industrialize only in the twentieth century, the role assumed by the state had more to do with particular social conflicts, governmental opportunities, and authoritative ideas than with any inherent dynamic of the world economy and capital accumulation. Moreover, even in England itself, government undertook important preparatory, protective, and entrepreneurial tasks. It is not obvious from the more detailed definition how the "capitalist" forms of this governmental sponsorship differ from the noncapitalist ones.

Here, too, overinclusion is as troublesome as underinclusion. For there were many times in the history of the agrarian empires when the holders of central state power lost the capacity to intervene effectively in the control of resources or even to exact the minimum of taxes and recruits needed to uphold the state in foreign and domestic strife. Even at the zenith of their power, the rulers ran up against harsh factual if not legal constraints on their ability to intervene in the allocation of resources or the organization of work. The cause of decentralized economic decision making could rely on the recurrent weakness of governmental power even when it could not count on a fixed order of individual and collective entitlements.

We can go even further in tightening the comparison between the supposedly capitalist European situations and the periods of commercial and manufacturing vitality in many non-European societies before the industrial revolution. In these non-European societies, the legal structure of contract and property was sometimes utterly different from what it came to be in early modern Western Europe. But it was often just as effective in multiplying the sources of decision over the use and investment of resources and the control of labor and in circumscribing the reach of governmental power.

The effort at greater concreteness in the definition of capitalism can take yet a third route. This solution builds on the first abstract definition of a capitalist order: the prevalence of legally free but economically dependent wage labor, combined with the commitment to accumulation. In this view, for capitalism to exist, great numbers of independent earners must work side by side. Free labor and economic dependence must be combined with the disciplined organization of large pools of workers under the command of those who own the major means of production or who act as the owners' agents. These owners or agents must not be simply the direct rulers of the state even though the rulers may be drawn largely from their ranks or suffer their preponderant influence. It all adds up to something like the European factory and industrial system.

Once again, however, the more detailed conception remains both underinclusive and overinclusive. As applied to the West, it pushes the definition of capitalism to a relatively late stage of Western economic history, after industrialization was already in full swing. It disregards the fact that large-scale plants have never employed more than a minority of the active work force in any of the situations traditionally labeled capitalist. It fails to explain why the concentration of large numbers of workers in productive units as opposed to their dispersion in smaller but technologically advanced organizations should be singled out as indispensable or why this concentration is particularly connected to the features emphasized in the abstract definition of capitalism.

Moreover, outside Europe there were periods and societies in which hired labor, combined with different kinds of tenancy arrangements, often tilled large agricultural estates. The labor force did not work in mechanized factories because these societies had not yet been industrialized. It did not usually work in factories at all because the factory system pays off most in the setting of mechanization.

Every attempt to make the definition of capitalism more concrete comes up against the same hurdles. Every addition to the list of defining traits produces a category that seems to include both too much and too little and to have an arbitrary relationship to the more abstract conceptions of capitalism. If you go far enough, you no longer have a concept at all but the summary description of particular developments that took place in particular countries, with the particular outcomes that resulted from time to time.

The Sources of Difficulty

Why are attempts to deploy the concept of capitalism so troublesome? One source of trouble relates directly to the use of functional explanation. The idea of capitalism is meant to perform two different roles within Marx's theory. These roles cannot be reconciled because history just does not happen in the way required by the Marxist style of functional explanation.

On the one hand, the term capitalism is supposed to describe the necessary institutional basis (the relations of production) for a certain level in the development of the productive forces: the level at which machinery combined with the physical congregation of large numbers of workers multiplies the productivity of labor and at which surplus becomes enormous without vanquishing scarcity. To perform this role adequately the concept of capitalism can never be inclusive enough. The more we learn about history, the greater the variety we discover in the institutional contexts of any given measure of development of productive capabilities. Even in modern Western history the more familiar sets of institutional arrangements turn out to have coexisted with deviant and repressed alternatives. The containment of these alternatives can be credited more persuasively to a particular history of political victories and defeats, insights and illusions, than to their inherent practical limitations. The experience of institutional experimentation in an age of world history confirms and extends the conclusions of historical study. States constantly discover new ways to combine modern Western productive capability with forms of work organization without close Western counterparts, or Western modes of work organization with economic and governmental institutions more closely suited to the experiences, interests, and intentions of the indigenous elite. The ever widening range of variation that we encounter in our past and present suggests other variations that might have occurred or that might yet be introduced and that are not in any event precluded by deep-seated economic, organizational, or psychological constraints. The hunt for the institutional conditions that make possible a particular level of economic growth begins to seem futile.

In Marx's style of functional explanation, the concept of capitalism also performs another role. In this role it can never be exclusive enough. It describes a unique historical reality whose outward manifestations were familiar to Marx's readers: the realities of certain modern European institutions and ways of life. Like other classical social theories, Marxism saw global significance in the history and transformation of these institutions. In this second role, the concept of capitalism does not apply to the similar institutional arrangements of other societies or other epochs that failed to produce these revolutionary results.

A second source of trouble with the concept of capitalism has to do with the deep-structural rather than the functionalist aspects of Marxist theory. Here too the idea of capitalism performs two different roles. Here too the character of historical experience makes these roles irreconcilable.

On the one hand, the concept must describe an indivisible and repeatable type of social organization: indivisible in the sense that its elements cannot be disaggregated and recombined with other elements; repeatable in the sense that it does not merely designate, retrospectively, a unique state of affairs capable of being realized only once and in one place. To perform this role adequately the concept of capitalism can never be abstract enough. As soon as you begin to define it more richly and concretely, you see that its components have in fact been dissociated and rearranged in many ways. You lack good reasons to exclude the possibility of any number of analogous disaggregations and recombinations that never actually took place.

At the same time, however, the concept of capitalism must perform the role of designating a framework defined precisely enough to account for a complex set of repetitious, even lawlike economic and social processes. But once you define capitalism with the concreteness necessary to justify its formative role, you undermine the plausibility of its representation as an indivisible and repeatable type. You make it look, instead, like the name for a unique state of affairs, or a unique series of events, that must be understood as the outcome of a unique constellation of causes. The term capitalism then loses, together with its generality, its clarity and punch. It becomes a shorthand way of referring to a loosely connected series of events that happened in the North Atlantic world at a certain time. But which events exactly?

The two sets of difficulties – the functionalist and the deep-structural – overlap. Once again, the problems that result from the deep-structure assumptions are more basic than the difficulties that arise from the functionalist premises. You may be tempted to resolve the functionalist dilemma by affirming the existence of multiple institutional contexts for any given level of development of the productive forces and therefore also of multiple pathways of institutional change. But where a single type of organization and a single evolutionary sequence fail to do the job, it seems that several could not work either. For each type or sequence must still be defined richly enough to justify its shaping influence on a world of practical routines. To define a set of institutional arrangements with enough detail to show how they can exercise this formative influence is to undermine the plausibility of the attempt to represent such arrangements as examples of an indivisible and repeatable type or stage of social organization. There may indeed be constraints on the disaggregation and recombination of the elements that constitute such formative institutional orders. But it is a big step from recognizing such constraints to showing that they can generate a closed list or a compulsive sequence of institutional systems.

Concepts like capitalism continue to be used in historical and social-science writing and in ideological debates by people who would deny subscribing to functional or deep-structural assumptions but whose use of such concepts belies the denial. Without having found a substitute for deep-structure analysis they insist on speaking as if concepts like capitalism could be used as more than allusions to a historically unique and uniquely located state of affairs. They talk as if such concepts could designate indivisible and repeatable types of social organization, at once abstract and richly defined. They enact in their imagination and in their discourse a way of thinking they will not or cannot defend. Their equivocation is symptomatic of the troubled relation of current views of society and history to the deep-logic tradition. When we reach toward general explanation, we often lapse back into the deep-structure moves. But we do so fitfully and half-consciously because our discoveries and our experiences have deprived those moves of their legitimacy.

Two factors have brought to the surface these weaknesses in the use of the central categories of descriptive and explanatory social theory. One is an enlargement of the available knowledge about the past; the other, a change in the apparent lessons of contemporary history. Ignorance can protect against the former. Only obtuseness and indifference can conceal the latter.

In the mid- and late twentieth century, it has become possible to study the history of most past societies with what – by comparison to previous conditions of scholarship – is a fabulous glitter of secondary and primary sources. You can spend endless days and nights in a fever of exultant discovery learning the languages, studying the records, and reading the historians of these remote countries or epochs. The further you go, the more problems you find for the sequences of the Marxist theory and even for the attempt to analyze in its categories the experience of those societies it considered capitalist. The history of the great agrarian empires of antiquity or of the non-Western world, until recently the most numerous and productive societies of history, cannot be understood in its most astonishing and instructive aspects if forced into the straitjacket of its relation to the story about the rise of capitalism. To handle the historical material you have to loosen the theory until it vanishes into a cloud of words and intentions. Or else, following Marx's own example in some of his more historical writings, you have to open an ever larger gap between your theoretical professions and your actual explanations.

The other source of disturbance and enlightenment is the course of contemporary events. At the time Marx and the other great theorists of the late nineteenth and early twentieth century were developing their ideas, the intellectuals and thinkers of the pioneering countries lived their romance of practical reason. Much in the experience of the time suggested that a single pattern of social life was spreading out from Europe to the entire world. This pattern might be organized around the arrangements of production and power. But it also dragged along with it a whole system of hierarchy, habit, and belief. Other countries, in other parts of the globe, had to take it or leave it. If they wanted to survive in the worldwide contest, they needed to take it.

Social theories differed on how this practical convergence was connected with social conflict and the rise of the masses and on whether it prefigured a further, decisive transformation in society. Whatever the connection, the clash of nations, of spiritual visions, and of armed force – everything that was most unruly in history – seemed to have been revealed, once and for all, as a by-product of more prosaic and fundamental constraints.

Many among the rulers of the present world and their apologetic toadies or despondent subjects still seem to believe some version of this picture of things. A contemporary industrialized society, they say, is very complicated. It consists in large-scale organizations and delicate relationships. By the time you have done everything you have to do to keep these institutions running and to stop things from getting too bad, there is very little room left over for maneuver – which is to say, for politics and philosophizing. The rest is all daydreaming.

I have already referred to the aspects of contemporary history that have made it hard to believe in the romance of practical reason, in either its early, militant and theoretical, or its later, dumb and cringing, mode. The poorer, non-Western countries have long since begun to combine features of rich Western-style technology with non-Western varieties of work organization or Western types of work organization with different ways of organizing society. This practice of institutional invention has never gone as far as democrats and revolutionaries would have liked; but it has already gone far enough to make unclear the limits to this process of dissociation of advanced practical capabilities from their original institutional basis. In fact, neither the failure to dissociate more, nor the surprise of dissociating so much, seem to have any simple perspicuous relation to the Marxist account of the rise of capitalism or to any other account that combines functionalist and deep-structure tenets. Nor can either be easily explained by vague references to the requirements of industrialism.

A time has come in the world when hopeful democrats everywhere follow closely any sign of a social experiment, any place on earth, hoping that it may reveal something about the unexplored opportunities for the advancement of the radical project. To view these experiments, and these failures to experiment, as fumblings toward a vaguely foreordained conclusion or as sidelights upon an already disclosed truth is to miss the point. It is to trade citizenship of the age for membership in a sect.

Playing Up Politics:
The Failure to Rescue the Theory from Within

The history of Marxist theory since Marx's own time is in large part the history of attempts to deal with the difficulties of functional and deep-structure argument that the troubles of the concept of capitalism illustrate. But these would-be rescue operations never seem to go far enough: the weaker, looser version of the theory remains open to a variant of the same objections leveled against the stronger, tighter version. These successive disappointments may be more than merely destructive in their results. They may help create the means for a more fundamental reconstruction of deep-logic theory.

One familiar defensive measure is to downplay the parts of the mature Marx's view that present a comprehensive theory of the evolution of modes of production and to place the emphasis instead on the internal analysis of capital, the subject of his major work. But this distinction cannot be maintained. The core of Marx's study of capitalism is an account of the characteristic laws of the capitalist modes of production. Some of these laws specify repetitious processes; others, developmental tendencies. The claim that such laws exist and the specification of the sense in which they are laws depend on assumptions about the existence, nature, and history of a mode of production. For the mode of production represents the framework within which those laws apply. The theory of modes of production does not merely trace the domains within which each set of laws operates; it shows why there can be laws and what kinds of laws they are.

Empirical observation may persuade us that the laws of motion Marx describes do not in fact hold. We may be tempted to reformulate them and to blame the inaccuracy of the original theory on unforeseeable developments or on disregarded factors. But the critique of the concept of capitalism, summarizing as it does a broader range of empirical studies, suggests that the search for laws of this kind is basically misguided. Even if we could correctly specify a set of repetitious processes and developmental tendencies, we would not be justified in interpreting them as the inherent laws of an indivisible and repeatable type of social organization. They might be merely the routines and trends encouraged by a unique and divisible complex of institutional arrangements. Their stability, rather than reflecting deeply rooted constraints or evolutionary laws, might be merely the expression of a redeemable failure to recommence practical and imaginative conflict over the basic terms of social life. The implications for theoretical understanding and political practice would be very different from a mere recognition that we had settled on the wrong laws of motion.

Of all efforts to save the initial theory, the most familiar and rewarding has been the attempt to emphasize the importance of traditions of belief, collective action, and governmental policy in determining the history and even the content of modes of production. Revisionists have shown how the evolution and variations of what they continue to call capitalism reflects the influence of varying degrees and varieties of grassroots collective organization, the multiple forms of class consciousness and class formation, the different possible ways in which governmental power can link up with social privilege, the ideas people have about themselves and society, and the many loose relations among all these subjects.

The effect this emphasis has on the peculiarly functionalist aspects of Marxist theory is to loosen the ties between the explanatory functional advantage (the development of the productive forces) and the institutional arrangements this advantage allegedly requires and helps explain (the mode of production). Thus, this revisionism goes in search of a theory of multiple evolutionary trajectories. Alongside the rigid functional account of the emergence of a mode of production it places nonfunctional explanations, mired in particularity, explanations that speak of the influence of distinct traditions of militancy and belief on the grand succession of social worlds.

The problems the detailed explanatory stories of the revisionist are meant to solve and the new problems they pose merely highlight insoluble difficulties in any social theory that deploys functional explanations against the background of deep-structure assumptions. The less detailed the story about how the functional advantage (in Marxism, the maximum development of the forces of production) becomes a cause of its own achievement, the harder it is to relate the story to historical learning and ordinary experience. On the other hand, the further the revisionist goes in providing an independent explanatory narrative of institutional, technological, or ideological change – a narrative concerned with the different circumstances of different groups in different societies – the less he finds himself referring to the functional advantage. The advantage begins to seem a by-product of independently caused events and independently intelligible processes. Thus, the overarching functional story (e.g., about forces of production driving changes in modes of production) starts to look superfluous. The revisionist turned skeptic can undermine functional explanation by leaving it without a job of its own. Particularistic, noncausal accounts take over.

Of course, this dilemma might be solved by positing complex and controversial connections between the operative functional consequence and the visible events of history or the conscious intentions of historical agents. After all, just such connections support functional explanation in natural science. But the question remains: Can we actually supply the missing links without either hedging on the large-scale functional account or blinking many recalcitrant facts? Because there are never enough links available to close the gap, each dose of revision seems to require a further dose – or a lapse back into historical dogmatism.

The impact of this revisionist analysis on the deep-structural aspects of the theory is just as subversive as its effect on the properly functionalist parts of the doctrine. The revisionist tendency restricts the influence that a formative structure (i.e., a mode of production) exercises on the deeds and thoughts of historical agents. It appeals to particularistic or multiple explanations of their remaking, explanations that undermine confidence in the existence of evolutionary laws. And it plays up the causal importance of the differences among otherwise similar modes of production: the role that each mode allows to government, for example, or to the collective organization of peasants and workers.

Whether we look to the implications for deep-structure argument or to the effects on functional explanation, the problem remains the same: there is no good place to stop, no defensible line against further attacks on the distinctive explanatory style that arises from the combination of functionalist and deep-logic methods. If, for example, three alternative trajectories can be discovered where the hard-core version of Marxist theory required only one, why not say that thirteen were possible? If non-functional and particularistic explanations can account for many features of a mode of production, or of its genesis, who can be sure that more explanations of the same kind might not account for all its interesting characteristics? If factors left out of the initial definition of a mode of production are nevertheless crucial to the transformation of institutional arrangements and to the fate of social divisions and hierarchies, why not include them in the definition of the mode? And, having incorporated those factors into the definition, how can we hope to keep up the pretense that a mode of production is an indivisible and repeatable type?

Consider, for example, a characteristic disagreement in contemporary Marxist historiography: the role that collective peasant organization in Western Europe performed in opening the way to capitalism. Someone argues that a certain weakening of grassroots communal organization by the peasants is important to capitalism because it allows the formation of large capitalist-type estates by entrepreneurial landlords and tenants. This argument is meant to score points against historians who analyze developments in primarily demographic or technological terms and to underline the role of politics in the evolution of modes of production. At the same time, the argument is designed to uphold the idea of a sequence of steps toward capitalism. These steps necessarily pass, at a crucial stage, through the destruction of small-scale family farming and cooperative forms of peasant activity. Then someone claims that in Eastern Europe and Russia the defeat of the peasants was part of a tale of avoidance of capitalism. So further refinements have to be introduced about the role of the state (in Russia) or of a unified and unchecked landholding nobility (in Eastern Europe) in stamping out the early possibilities of capitalist development. Then someone else shows that in many of the most enterprising centers of late medieval and early modern Western Europe the maintenance of customary rights by peasant collectives and the continued prosperity of small- and middle-scale farming turned out to favor transformations that might be also described as beginnings of successful capitalist development. There was no necessary passageway through the large-scale agrarian enterprise built up at the peasants' expense. So on and on it goes. The point is not just that historians disagree – even historians who believe that they are working within the same theoretical tradition. It is that the historiographic debates undermine confidence in the strength or necessity of the connections among the traits that define each mode of production or in the forces that lead from one mode to the next. They wreak havoc with the story the theory is supposed to tell.

As he discovers the inadequacies of prior revisionist efforts, the Marxist (or the adherent to any other deep-structure theory) can try to hold the line. But will he – even in his own eyes – succeed? He may even attempt an alliance of convenience with the prostrate social scientists or historians who attribute the embarrassments to the inherent inadequacies of theory. He may then console himself with the thought that his procrusteanism is the price of intellectual and political faith. Alternatively, he may carry the revisionist campaign further. Then he finds that each successive dilution of the inherited theory is never enough and always too much. It is never enough to prevent the same kind of objection from being raised again. It is always too much to preserve a coherent version of the theory, a version that does not play fast and loose with the deep-structure moves. In the end, the super-revisionist finds that he has turned the theory into a list of fighting words and obsessive concerns and embarked on Noah's ark without Noah.

If, however, you could work through and beyond the deep-logic approach by replacing its second and third moves while retaining its first move, these successive moments of disillusionment would appear in a different light. The seemingly negative insights they produced might be extended and generalized and shown to be compatible with an alternative style of generalizing explanation. Then, those cumulative acts of revision would no longer seem makeshift compromises along a line of retreat but approaches to another, stronger position.

The Practical Significance of Theoretical Error

The preceding discussion of Marxism as an instance of deep-structure analysis may seem to be of merely theoretical interest. Yet the implications are as relevant to the present as they are to the past and as important to political issues as to theoretical concerns. My earlier example of the confusions of engagement in Brazilian politics suggested, by anticipation, the perverse effect of deep-structure ideas on political practice. Now, that suggestion can be developed and exemplified in a North Atlantic setting.

To the extent that you pursued the revision of deep-structure theory to an ever more nihilistic conclusion, you jeopardized your ability to imagine past, present, or future frameworks, to contrast them with the routines they shape, and to talk about their history and transformation. You therefore lost the only readily available tool with which to resist the claim that existing routines were the inevitable products of organizational, economic, and psychological constraints or of the clash among numerous interests coexisting in tension with one another. If you acknowledged the influence of a formative institutional and imaginative context at all, you treated the components of this context as merely higher-order routines, time-tested collective rules of thumb. You slid into the shadowy, one-dimensional world of positivist social science and naive historiography described in a later section.

But suppose you tried to hold the line, as a Marxist or any other style of deep-structure analyst, against the extremes of revisionism. The results were damaging to both the programmatic inspiration and the strategic unity of transformative, leftist movements.

The chief consequence for programmatic ideas was to make it appear that no middle level existed between reformist tinkering, which helps a set of basic institutional arrangements and social preconceptions to survive in the face of changing circumstance, and all-out revolution, which replaces an entire framework of social life. Thus, programmatic thinking turned away from the effort to imagine detailed institutional alternatives and transitional forms. Such proposals as were occasionally produced lacked support in any credible view of transformation.

Suppose, for example, that as a Marxist in a late twentieth century Western democracy you found yourself engaged in debates about efforts to reform the capitalist economy from within. The spirit of your theoretical system encouraged you to distinguish as sharply as possible reforms that were merely attempts to stave off crises predicted by the laws of motion from fundamental changes in the mode of production and the class system, with their corresponding or preparatory shifts in the control of the state. Take, for example, a governmental commitment to underwrite mass consumer demand during economic depressions as well as to make costly basic investments and difficult social accommodations. Such a commitment might be needed to keep the economy running and to stop the poor from disrupting it. But it would not necessarily alter the laws of motion (if they operated in the first place) nor redirect the basic aims of the workers' movement.

But what if the aim of the reforms was to alter the institutional structure of democracy and the market? It might be a matter of bringing the basic flows of investment decisions under political control. Or it might have to do with redesigning the constitutional organization of government so as to promote, rather than replace and avoid, repeated mass mobilization. Were these aims worth fighting for as an alternative to capitalism? Or were they just like those defensive reforms that contain crisis and conflict without transforming the basic reality that generated them? At what point would the implementation of such reforms render obsolete the concepts and laws of the analysis of capitalist economies?

The implications of a hardened version of deep-structure theory were no less dangerous to strategic thinking about social transformation. A formative structure of social life restricts and interrupts conflict over the basic terms of our availability to one another. It thereby produces and sustains a plan of division and hierarchy, held fast against the depredations of ordinary practical and imaginative fighting. (How much hierarchy, as opposed to division, this structure generates may depend on the extent to which groups are mobilizing economic or cultural resources on a societywide basis when the moment of stabilization occurs.) The more indivisible and deeply rooted in general imperatives or in an evolutionary logic we believe such a structure of social roles and ranks to be, the greater the clarity we attribute to the system of class and communal interests each such structure generates. The person who sees society through the lens of deep-logic theory expects escalating conflict to make these interests more transparent. But in fact it muddies them by disturbing people's assumptions about social possibilities and group identities and by dissolving classes and communities into parties of opinion. The unreconstructed deep-structure theorist believes, for the same reasons, that certain class alliances or antagonisms are unavoidable and that each emergent type of social organization has its predetermined champions. But he is mistaken. The lines of alliance and antagonism are in fact fluid, both because the next step in context revision always remains uncertain and controversial and because fighting breaks down the very structure within which group interests seemed to be certain. The theoretical illusions exact their toll in practice, blinding people to many opportunities, providing them with alibis for inaction, and strengthening the animosities that they claimed faithfully to recognize.

Thus, many of the more ambitious labor and socialist parties of late twentieth century North Atlantic countries remained committed to ideas that represented the organized working class, headquartered in the declining mass-production industries, as the major force for social transformation. These parties continued to speak a language unresponsive to the concerns of the old petty bourgeoisie, of the independent professionals, of the new technical cadres, and even of the unorganized and suffering underclass. From this self-imposed isolation they escaped only into a program of marginal economic redistribution, welfare-statism, and administrative modernization. Sometimes they combined the worst of both worlds and continued to rehearse the language of proletarian challenge long after settling down to the routines of conflict management and redistributive compromise.

The preconceptions of Marxist deep-structuralist theory have contributed to the drastic understatement of the variety of institutional arrangements that accompanied European industrialization. In particular the biases of theory have obscured the leading role of artisans, skilled workers, and small-scale producers and professionals and of the advocates of small-scale and cooperative enterprises in challenging the emergent dominant order of the modern West. The aims of these publicists might have remained attached solely to a vision of petty proprietorship and decentralized authority. In this guise, their program would indeed have been fatally unstable and regressive in just the sense described by Marx's critique of petty commodity production: the transitional or subsidiary mode of production constituted by the existence of large numbers of independent, small-scale, and relatively equal producers. But their vision might also have served as a point of departure for the development of institutional proposals that met those criticisms.

Such proposals – a major theme in *Politics* – might have shown how access to capital and to governmental power could be made both more freely and equally available and more compatible with economies of scale and with effective governmental policy than it can be within the current institutional forms of markets and democracies. In these alternatives, the leftist parties might have found, and may yet find, a way to break out of their isolation without giving up their radical transformative ambitions. But Marxism and other deep-structure theories have come to stand in the way of this reformulation of vision and strategy. Vitiated by a retrospective sense of triumph – by an identification of dominant institutional systems with inevitable historical transitions – adherents of these theoretical traditions have turned a blind eye to less familiar historical transitions and anomalous institutional solutions. And they have failed to recognize that the most common form of social invention is the effort to turn deviations into models.

ECONOMICS AS A NONEVOLUTIONARY DEEP-STRUCTURE SOCIAL THEORY

In some of its early statements classical political economy offered a rudimentary version of an evolutionary deep-structure social theory. Adam Smith, for example, building on the work of his Scottish predecessors and contemporaries, distinguished stages of social evolution marked by turning points in economic development. Though he held a dynamic of self-interest and of productive opportunities responsible for the entire forward movement, the laws set out in *The*

Wealth of Nations were meant to apply solely to the commercial economy, the final stage of evolution. That stage alone saw the final triumph of market institutions, by which Smith, like his predecessors, referred to a particular market order, complete with built-in rules of contract and property.

But economics soon turned aside from this style of theorizing. Instead, it took a direction that might have enabled it to serve as the model for a nonevolutionary version of deep-logic analysis. Such an account would have focused on the constraints that the satisfaction of material needs or ambitions imposes on social organization. In its most developed form it would have consisted in a theory of possible social worlds, specifying the alternative institutional systems that might satisfy those constraints. It might even have explained why any one of these alternatives became actual at a given time and place. For some time political economy bid fair to become just such a doctrine. Nevertheless, its work not only failed to produce this theory but demonstrated why any such theory would have to fail, just as the history of Marxism brought out the inadequacy of an evolutionary version of deep-logic theorizing.

The following discussion has a more general aim than to show the self-subversion of one more type of deep-structure analysis. This self-subversion was not followed by the development of an alternative way of thinking about the relation between economic activity and the institutional or imaginative framework within which this activity takes place. The undermining of the nonevolutionary form of deep-logic theory encouraged, instead, a dismissal of the very problem of the framework: the problem of understanding the relation of routine economic activity to the institutional and imaginative context within which it takes place.

If you were to give these events in intellectual history a clarity of purpose they in fact lacked, you might say that the rejection of the second and third moves of deep-structure argument led to a downplaying, if not a repudiation, of the first move: the basic contrast between a formative context and the routines it shapes. Thus, classical political economy shared its origins with the evolutionary variant of deep-structure theory. It went on to show by example the untenability of such a nonevolutionary view. But it ended up as the most rigorous model for a positivist social science distinguished by its indifference to the task of understanding the making and the influence of the institutional and imaginative contexts of social life. The next section discusses the momentous intellectual and political consequences of this indifference.

Classical political economy, as it developed in Western Europe from the seventeenth to the mid-nineteenth century, was a theory about the causal relations among the social activities most closely connected with the production and distribution of wealth. For good and ill, it lacked the special deep-logic structure of Marx's doctrine. Because the concerns that animated it were so explicitly tied to the statecraft of the day, it formulated some of its central problems in ways that more or less deliberately crossed the lines between an explanatory project and a political polemic. Hence, its favorite questions: What is the true basis of "value"? Which activities and classes contribute most to national wealth? Under what systems of rights and forms of government does a people grow richer?

The central tradition of political economy suffered the pressure of an effort to escape from the endless and largely sterile conundrums of value theory and to answer the old question of how use values could become prices. Through an analysis of the price system, free from all philosophizing about value, economists set out to discover universal coefficients of transformation in the economy: to show how exchange values, then consumer prices, and finally all aspects of a price system depended on one another. (Unlike their counterparts in physics, these coefficients were not natural constants.) The market economy, in which a large number of independent agents bargain on their own initiative and for their own account, could be represented as an ordered cosmos. A precise and narrow analytic meaning could be assigned to the idea of maximum efficiency in the allocation of a set of resources, given certain definitions of scarcity and wants. A large number of problems in economic analysis could be redefined in a way that made them amenable to mathematical formulation.

The other source of pressure for the transformation of classical economic theory was the desire to disengage the core of economics from contestable descriptive or normative commitments. Faced with socialist attacks on political economy and escalating social-theoretical debates about how society worked, the new marginalist market theory simply withdrew from the contested terrain. It relocated on what it believed to be a higher or, at least, a more general ground. The emerging analysis could do its limited work regardless of the positions people took on most of the disputed normative or empirical issues.

The marginalist general equilibrium theory, conclusively formulated by Walras, represented the influential answer to these two sources of pressure. The result was a theory that differed in its explanatory aims, as well as in its content and scope, from the tradition it displaced. The keynote of the new economics was the effort to achieve generality and certainty by putting to one side the explanatory and normative controversies that had beset political economy.

The new marginalist economics, however, failed to achieve complete immunity to factual or normative challenge. Even taking for granted the redefined explanatory aims of the theory, three closely related points of weakness remained. The effort to deal with them – an effort that has not yet been carried through to its final implications – kept up the pressure on economics. The pressure presented a choice: either to extend still further the break with classical political economy by making economics yet more general in scope and formal in purpose or to change course altogether.

The first point of weakness was the issue of whether equilibrium, in the marginalist sense, would in fact be spontaneously generated in a market economy. It was possible to argue that there was an inherent possibility, repeatedly realized, of persistent disequilibrium or of equilibrium at low levels of employment (it did not really matter much which description you preferred). Such an occurrence might be attributed to underinvestment and underconsumption: the hoarding of money. Or it might also be imputed to market failures: even in the absence of monopoly, wages and prices might prove systematically unresponsive to the signals that would clear markets and restore equilibrium at the highest level of resource employment. This stickiness of wages and prices might be ascribed to the differential organization of distinct segments of the work force, the infusion of wage or price relations by customary standards of fairness, the struggle of risk-averse managers to maintain relative financial autonomy and a stable relation to their core markets and labor force, or any number of other plausible factors. Finally, failure of self-correcting equilibrium might result from the distance that separated the marginalist picture of rational choice from the decision-making procedures used by managers, workers, and consumers, in conditions of ignorance and uncertainty. The distance was often great enough to take away much of the explanatory and prescriptive value of that picture. Everything interesting seemed to be in the behavioral and institutional facts that marginalist analysis had to take as givens rather than as topics for analysis and explanation.

The point about all these possible sources of constraint on spontaneous equilibrium is that they could not plausibly be disregarded by a market theory as either noneconomic or incidental. They seemed to be very deeply built into the market economies that in fact exist.

A second embarrassment to the marginalist theory has played a much smaller role in the development of mainstream economics, though its theoretical implications are just as important. It is the relation of the marginalist doctrine to the idea of a market rather than to the recurrence of disequilibrium. Analytically, the theory evoked the background image of a market as if that image were straightforward and determinate. The evocation of a seemingly uncontroversial view of what a market is in turn favored the polemical conception that markets – whatever they were – represented the naturally efficient framework for the allocation of resources. Here two problems arose.

For one thing the indeterminacy of the market concept becomes clear as soon as you begin to think of the concrete legal–institutional forms that markets can take. The rights and powers that make up the conventional categories of property and contract can be reshaped and reallocated in any number of ways. Each of these detailed institutional interpretations of the idea of a market has very different consequences for the social arrangements of power and production. Yet there is no way to tell, just by analyzing the market concept, which of these rival interpretations is most truly a market, even in the trivial sense of promoting the greatest amount of decentralized competition. Such questions are empirical and demand empirical answers. Any particular market picture already presupposes a prior commitment to one of the open-ended number of possible interpretations of the market idea. The commitment is justified by the claim that this is the right kind of market to have or that it is the peculiar kind that in fact exists in some economy that you are talking about.

For another thing, economists soon diacovered that the analytic structure of marginalist theory – with all its rich connotations of effectiveness in getting things done – could easily be applied to a centralized command economy. Right-wing economists living at the first flush of marginalist triumph – von Wieser, Pareto, Barone – showed that there was no insuperable analytic obstacle. They demonstrated that a command economy could be described through a system of equations with a uniquely determined set of solutions, graced with all the properties that hold for the equations of the market economy. Decisions about distribution or other matters are simply made beforehand by the centralized socialist agency. To be sure, this planned economy might prove less productive. The nonmarket signals might function less effectively. The state administration of the production system might be inept. The command system might also undermine an independently justified program of civic freedom. But these arguments were hardly at the same level as those that attempt to justify the confinement of marginalist analysis to market economies.

The third point of weakness in marginalism had to do with the polemical uses of the concepts of efficiency or "Pareto optimality." Just as the new analysis had to be disentangled from the idea of self-sustaining equilibrium and from any determinate picture of the market, so it had to be separated out from all specific conceptions about the economic arrangements that would either cause growth or guarantee a maximum satisfaction to the individual participants in the economy. Late nineteenth century economists like Alfred Marshall already understood the consequences. One consequence was the downplaying by marginalism of all considerations of distribution among individuals, classes, or generations; the distributive state of affairs was simply taken for granted. The other consequence was the lack of a dynamic perspective: the investments and innovations needed to generate repeated breakthroughs in productive capacity would not necessarily coincide with the relation of prices and quantities under any interpretation of equilibrium. Later argument, which showed the idea of aggregate satisfaction (the "collective welfare function") to be incoherent anyway, simply carried the point one step further. Marginalist efficiency could just not be taken as an effective guide to the making of collective wealth or welfare. What is still less widely recognized is that these limitations result directly from the lack of a way to deal with the relation between routine economic activity and the institutional and imaginative framework in which it takes place.

The three sources of trouble in marginalist theory share the same general character. There are two ways to deal with them. One tactic is to explicate and exaggerate still further the line of development that began with the marginalist break with classical political economy. Disengage the theory from self-adjusting equilibrium, determinate market institutions, or strongly defined efficiency. Make it into a general but narrowly defined theory of maximizing choice. Transform it, once and for all, into a pure analysis neither descriptive nor normative, although it may serve as a powerful tool in descriptive or normative theories built on other foundations. The alternative solution is to reverse direction and plunge back into all the contested empirical and normative issues that marginalist economics was partly designed to avoid.

By the close of the twentieth century, the leading economists in the mainstream marginalist tradition (so inaptly dubbed neoclassical) thought they were using both these strategies effectively. Actually, however, they had been much more successful at the first than at the second, partly because they failed to grasp the incongruity between this second aim and the explanatory methods that had emerged from the marginalist transformation of economics.

The two responses to the trouble are incompatible. The generalizing, agnostic solution amounts to an extension and clarification of what was most novel and coherent in early marginalism. To be successful, this textured empirical and normative approach would require a different kind of analysis rather than more and better of the same. It would demand a style of economic explanation focused on the interplay between production or exchange and the institutional and imaginative framework in which they occur. And it would therefore call for a solution to the very problems that deep-structure social analysis, in its evolutionary or nonevolutionary forms, have been unable to solve.

To understand the force of these last remarks, consider the relation between marginalism, in its final, most general development, and the causes that explain why self-adjusting equilibrium fails to occur. What these causes actually were or how they influenced one another and other forces was not something that pure economic analysis itself purported to describe and explain. They were conjectures and observations that had to be made outside the central explanatory structure rather than presented, and tested, as derivations from it. Sometimes you incorporated them by relaxing assumptions and sometimes you included them as values for the coefficients of variables in the equations. But you did not, within the core analysis itself, develop a theory of cause and effect relations between any extensive aspect of the material life of society.

Pure economic analysis and particular discoveries and conjectures about the actual workings of actual economies remained largely independent of one another. The former became little more than a language in which to formalize the latter. The latter never upset the former. As a result, the general parts of the analysis provided no pattern for such conjectures and discoveries. Either these empirical findings accumulated ad hoc, or they had to be ordered by a pattern derived from some other discipline.

For the same reasons, the uncovering of new facts need never lead to a change in the basic marginalist analysis of the economy. Once the theory was defined with sufficient care, and duly purged of unwarranted assumptions about self-adjusting equilibrium, about the determinacy and necessity of the market framework, and about the aggressive senses of the efficiency concept, it became neutral as between different empirical or normative positions on all these more concrete issues. If, however, it failed to achieve this neutrality, it lay itself open to all the objections that could be brought against the earlier, less general and coherent versions of marginalism. There had to be something wrong with any theory that was true by definition once you defined its terms carefully enough.

Mainstream economists shrugged their shoulders. With mock humility and sincere self-contentment they claimed to be doing science in the only way that it could be done: by piecemeal observation and gradual revision. They were mistaken in their understanding of both science and their own practice. This practice was not science in the sense of a strong account of possible worlds, with auxiliary hypotheses about the operation or genesis of an actual world, the manner of some branches of physics. Nor was it a science, like neo-Darwinian evolutionary theory, that presented a causal explanation of the workings and history of one particular world and of why and how a given state of affairs passed into some neighboring state of affairs. In this marginalist economics, mathematics, though extravagantly used, was less a storehouse of imaginative schemata that might or might not describe the world – which is what it had become in physics since Galileo – than a pure instrument of inference and calculation and the nearly empty analysis of a small number of simple ideas. Purists saw the core of this style of economics as an analytical apparatus, free of surprising and controversial hypotheses, except when coupled with observations whose accuracy and causes had to be determined outside the discipline. The intellectual consequences of this merely tangential connection between economic analysis and empirical discovery were far-reaching.

First, such an economics lacked the means for cumulative and continuous progression. It had no prospect of revolutionary pressure against its own assumptions and no organizing imagination with which to investigate relations in the world. When the theorist withdrew to the heartland of the analysis he had little to say about the surprising features of real economies. When he turned to these facts, his analysis left him more or less at sea. His surprises – a thinker's treasure – were wasted on ideas that nothing could surprise. The formal virtuosity of his general analysis was but the silver lining of its substantive sterility.

The second implication was that, driven by the desire to take a position on the empirical and normative disputes of the day, economists easily fell back into the assumptions of early marginalism, though not all of them played with the same double entendres at the same time. Sometimes, the trouble was the obscuring of the degree to which certain strong claims actually still depended on the hypothesis of self-adjusting, optimal equilibrium; sometimes the equivocal picture of the market as a more or less institutionally determinate idea, with the system of property and contract rights (though part of the definition of a market) taken for granted; and sometimes the unwarranted expansion of the efficiency idea to justify a particular distributive scheme or growth strategy. So the widely held belief that marginalist economics was apologetic by vocation – a belief so offensive to professional economists – had a large element of truth. The criticism was often confused, but not as much as the theory it indicted.

A third consequence for economics was the way in which the formulation of crucial debates in macroeconomics developed. A crisis in economic policy generated a response. The response reflected certain limited political aims and empirical conjectures peculiar to the intentions of its authors and the circumstances of its time. Later on, this relativity was forgotten, and the more or less successful stratagem was treated as a pattern for a general theory – given that general theories could not be derived from marginalist microeconomics. All this can be seen in the episode of Keynesianism, one of the strangest interludes in the history of economics.

The one organizing theoretical element in Keynes's mature doctrine was the development of the argument for the possibility of permanent disequilibrium or of equilibrium without the optimal properties of Walras's "special case." Faced with what he recognized as an underconsumption crisis and with the illusions of the doctrine of sound finance, Keynes offered a solution. His solution was keyed to an intention, a situation, and a narrow set of conjectures.

Keynes reckoned that it was politically easier to sustain aggregate demand by public spending than to socialize major investment decisions, though he recognized that either route might have provided a way out. He was dealing with circumstances in which the characteristic double limit of post–World War II economic policy had not yet become clear. Popularly elected governments were not yet faced with the contrasting impulse not to give in completely to either the investors (because underconsumption and unemployment would create social unrest and impoverish the nation) or to the working and consuming populace (because failure of investment confidence would produce economic crisis, with or without inflation). At the time of Keynes's campaigns, sound-finance doctrine still saw to it that the first pressure counted for more than the second. Finally, Keynes found himself in a situation in which the stimulus of economic activities could count on a large amount of unused capacity. The focus of concern was not yet on the ways in which a noninnovative, risk-averse managerial class, a segmented labor movement preoccupied with self-defense, and a paralyzed state worked to block continuous enlargements of output and productivity. When the last two sets of facts changed, Keynes's judgment about the first set of facts no longer held. Many of the crucial issues of redistribution and growth in the rich Western economies could be dealt with only by gaining political control over the basic flows of investment decisions.

Such controversies and positions never added up to a theory of any kind. To pretend they did and do is to depoliticize politics and to dehistoricize history. They have the same status, and many of the same themes, as the debates between the Soviet economic schools led by Bukharin and Preobrazhensky during the 1920s. When the American economists began to speak of microeconomics and macroeconomics as two mutually referring theoretical systems, they were doubly mistaken. Neither amounted to a theoretical system, though each fell short in its own way. One was a formal analytic of choice; the other, an exercise in statecraft, based on limited causal judgments whose validity could hardly outlast their occasions.

A FIRST STATEMENT OF THE PROBLEM

By the late twentieth century, then, the core areas of theoretically ambitious social thought had undergone a dual development.

On the one hand, the theories that invoked the idea of a deep logic of transformation – Marxism first among them – were in an advanced state of disintegration. To accommodate their central ideas to historical reality and contemporary practical experience it was necessary to dilute them more and more. Each succeeding dose of dilution turned out to be insufficient. You had to withdraw back into the theoretical system and do violence to unblinkable facts. Or you could let the system fall apart into a series of slogans and concerns without cohesive explanatory force. The root of the problem seemed to be the reach and nature of contingency in history. Practical or visionary conflict could transform every aspect of material or spiritual life. Whatever existed in society depended on a foreclosure of fighting. No master logic governed the making or the abandonment of basic institutional arrangements.

On the other hand, marginalist economics and its sequels had taken refuge in analytic neutrality. To the extent that this economic theory remained coherent with its own premises and program, it could not hope to be more than ancillary to some other body of substantive explanatory or normative ideas. It could not itself become these ideas. To the extent that it tried to make large explanatory or normative claims of its own, it had to smuggle in empirical or evaluative premises, to treat them as generated within economic analysis, rather than as stipulated on the basis of independent views and observations.

A key element in the decline of these two traditions of explanatory ideas was the failure of dogmatic assumptions about the limits to possible combinations of institutional arrangements. At times these preconceptions took the form of claims attributing a built-in, uncontroversial content to abstract institutional projects, such as a market economy or a representative democracy. At other times, as in the synthesis of deep-structure views and functional explanation, the constraint was represented by the belief that only one combination of institutions can sustain the development of the practical productive capabilities of society. Either way, the restrictive dogmas implied that institutional systems are indivisible wholes.

In the face of such prejudices the task of social theory became to grasp the extent to which the apparently lawlike routines and regularities of social life depend for their force on distinctive, fragile groups of institutional arrangements and enacted beliefs. To avoid the errors charted in the preceding pages, you had to understand the history and the internal composition of these shaping institutional orders without repeating the second and third moves of deep-stucture social theory: the appeal to the idea of indivisible types of social organization and the invocation of the developmental laws or the deeply rooted constraints that supposedly account for the content, the realization, and even the sequence of such types. Easier said than done. The effort to work out such an approach required change in the preception of the basic alternatives open to students of society – another way of seeing and talking.

Much more was at stake in this intellectual reconstruction than a point of theoretical clarity. The adherents to the modern ideologies of emancipation and equality, whether liberal or socialist, had to fight to prevent their transformative proposals from being discredited together with the understandings and explanations that informed these proposals. Either the inherited emancipatory programs would survive as frozen statements of commitment, without a vital link to views of social reality and possibility, or they would emerge, remade, from the reconstruction of explanatory ideas.

POSITIVIST SOCIAL SCIENCE AND NAIVE HISTORIOGRAPHY

The Avoidance of Context

The discussion so far has focused on deep-logic social analysis: the disintegration of its evolutionary version in the course of the history of Marxism and the failure of political economy to provide it with a persuasive nonevolutionary statement. But deep-structure social analysis is no longer the only or even the most common style of social and historical analysis. A retrenchment of theoretical ambition, wrapped in the garb of scientific method, has produced the style of positivist, empiricist, or conventional social science. And though the method of positivist social science might seem in many respects to be the very opposite of narrative history writing, it converged with naive historiography on the crucial point of its attitude toward institutional and imaginative structures. The choice between deep-structure analysis and conventional social science has come to define the predicament of social thought, though a sufficiently diluted version of the former merges imperceptibly into the latter.

A decisive feature of positivist social science is its refusal to take the distinction between the formative context and the formed routines, or between structure-preserving and structure-transforming conflict, as central to the practice of social and historical explanation. The positivist social scientist sees in society and history an endless series of episodes of problem solving or interest accommodation. What the deep-logic theorist presents as a specific institutional and imaginative framework, context, or structure of social life, exemplifying an indivisible and repeatable type of social organization, the positivist social scientist may see, when he sees them at all, as merely a series of more influential routines, the hardened residues of past episodes of interest accommodation or problem solving.

A corollary of this attempt to discount the significance of the contrast between the structure and the structured is the downplaying of discontinuity among structures. The positivist social scientist and the naive historiographer understand history as the experience of similar people struggling with similar problems in changing circumstances rather than as the creation of radically distinct social worlds, each of them supportive of a specific set of practical and passionate dealings, each of them a different way of being human. The one-dimensional and gradualistic quality of positivist social science and naive historiography is a direct result of their implied repudiation of the contrast between context and routine.

This style of analysis draws much of its seduction from the discomfiture of deep-structure explanation. The second and third characteristic moves of deep-structure theory – the subsumption of a framework under an indivisible and repeatable type of social organization and the invocation of constraints capable of generating a closed list or sequence of such types – have been shown to produce results increasingly hard to reconcile with research and experience. So long as no way is found to separate the first move from the other two, the former appears discredited by the failures of the latter.

In the social sciences, additional support comes from the ideology of science. The framework-denying mode of analysis is supposed to be scientific, in its avoidance of uncorroborated speculation and in its commitment to the gradual discovery of verifiable correlations among particular events and influences. Yet it contrasts with post-Galilean natural science in its repeated failure to reach counterintuitive results. For the most part it resembles instead an Aristotelian science of the social world, organizing and reinforcing familiar beliefs and commonsense perceptions. The rejection of the context–routine distinction, when combined with a preference for narrowly focused investigations, leads social scientists to study routines of conflict and compromise at a particular time and place. These routines depend in fact on the stability of a particular institutional and imaginative framework. Nevertheless, so long as the stability persists, the influence of the framework can be forgotten. The routines can be attributed to inherent economic, organizational, and psychological constraints or to a logic of interest accommodation and problem solving, carried on within a framework that is itself uncontroversial if only because it results from previous accommodations and solutions. Thus, despite his claim to detachment, the positivist social scientist sees society with the eyes of a resigned insider, who takes the fundamentals for granted and shares his subjects' sense of reality

and possibility even when he has claimed indifference to their interests and ideals. No wonder the results of his studies so often tally
with their beliefs.

Consider an example drawn from political science. The study of
voting and legislative behavior is a typical topic. Why do voters
prefer some parties or candidates to others? Why do they switch
party allegiances? And why do their elected representatives in turn
vote as they do? A characteristic line of answers to such questions
attempts to develop correlations between electoral decisions and the
places that voters occupy in the system of group divisions: the contrast of classes, communities, ethnic or religious groups, generations,
and regions. Then each correlation can be glossed with the help of
other, similar correlations to bring out the latent rationality of the
voter's choice. To explain this vote is to trace it back to a series of
social stations and to the material or ideal interests these stations
generate. The point of successful electoral campaigns is to combine
credibility with coalition building. Legislative behavior can in turn
be explained by a series of approximations to the norm: get yourself
reelected – reelected, that is, by voters who decide in the manner
described by the studies of voting behavior.

This style of inquiry can successfully map and even predict outcomes so long as politically active groups continue to avoid escalating
conflict over the fundamentals – the formative institutional and imaginative structure of social life – and concentrate instead on
redistributive quarrels or spiritual crusades that take this structure
for granted. But as soon as such controversy does begin to develop
– and it can never be more than slightly below the surface – the
platitudes of these electoral studies cease to hold good. You then
need ideas about frameworks, about how they get remade, and about
the relation of disputes concerning them to quarrels within them.

For one thing, escalating conflict never turns out to mean merely
the more intense pursuit of the same interests that carried the day
during the earlier period of quiescence. The search for preemptive
security and for immediate material advantage may redouble under
the influence of broader and more intense fighting. But the preexisting logic of group interests also starts to dissolve as the assumptions
about the possible and about the necessity or authority of group
divisions begin to lose their basis in an unshaken institutional and
imaginative order of social life. You need a way to understand the
inhabitants of such a dissolving world other than by presenting them
as puppets of a structure they have helped break down.

For another thing, to develop a view of events and attitudes in
situations of framework-disturbing politics, you need independently
supported beliefs about the transformability of these frameworks.
Do the people engaged in these more basic conflicts remain in the

thrall of unjustifiably restrictive assumptions about feasible alternatives to their current arrangements? Or are they, on the contrary, disoriented by voluntarist fantasies and subject to constraints they fail to appreciate?

The political scientist may try to extend his methods to the circumstance of escalating conflict. Alternatively, he may frankly acknowledge that his science has dealt only with the relatively stable, normal situations; beyond a certain level of disturbance, all bets are off. But the implications of the acknowledgment are not easy to contain. If the routines of voting or legislative behavior studied by the political scientist depend on the stability of a framework whose emergence, content, and persistence he cannot explain, if this framework cannot in turn be explained by any higher-order necessity, and if in fact we have no formed ideas about the composition or reproduction of the framework, how can we do anything but describe the routines of this quiescent world and express what it feels like to inhabit it? If we lack insight into how or when conflicts within a structure turn into struggles about that structure, how can we have confidence in the claim that a given social circumstance will continue to provoke a given political response?

Techniques of Avoidance

The problem of the framework is so pervasive that it can hardly be overlooked in many forms of social and historical study; but a number of intellectual techniques have been developed to minimize its impact on social analysis. Positivist social science and naive historiography consist in these intellectual stratagems as well as in the framework-denying view these devices help protect.

There are three main techniques of avoidance. Each is exemplified by a distinct style of economics. As its chances of providing a basis for a nonevolutionary version of deep-structure social theory faded, economics became a model for several variants of positivist social science, each distinguished by the technique of avoidance it emphasized. The methodological rigor and self-consciousness of economics may account for the comparatively prominent role these methods of containment have played within it.

The first method is the technique of the disclaimer. You make no claims about the significance or insignificance of frameworks, or about their nature and transformation. You present your discipline as an analytic apparatus, empirically and normatively agnostic. You offer it as a limited though powerful tool to be employed by some other discipline able to supply descriptive data and explanatory hypotheses.

The most rigorous and generalized forms of microeconomics and econometrics prefer the technique of the disclaimer. One problem is the transfer of responsibility: the tactic charges another science with the task. But where is that discipline? Only deep-structure social theory has a developed view of context change, and that view has been discredited. Another problem is the difficulty of keeping up agnostic innocence and of resisting the temptation to smuggle in unconfessed empirical assumptions.

A second route to avoidance is the technique of idealization. You acknowledge the framework but you explain and justify it (justification and explanation being inseparable in this mode of thought) as the optimal solution to a problem of institutional design: namely, the problem of establishing the framework within which first-order problems can be most effectively solved or independent interests and viewpoints most freely accommodated. In other words, you treat the attempt to find an optimal answer to the choice of a framework by analogy to the effort to find optimal solutions within such a framework.

The more aggressively ideological forms of market economics (and the related historiography of modernization) illustrate this option. The market, by which the proponents of this view mean a highly particular set of economic institutions and private rights, supposedly represents the tangible form of economic rationality, the one structure within which all other resource-allocating decisions can approach maximum efficiency. But the internal evolution of economic and legal thought has shown not only that a pure logic of maximizing choice is neutral among market and nonmarket systems but that a market order itself can assume an indefinitely wide range of alternative institutional forms, some of them far removed from the arrangements that right-wing economists hope to justify. The lesson of this evolution may be generalized. There is no way to get from principles of choice within a richly defined system of assumptions to principles of choice among such systems.

The third and most interesting method of avoidance is the technique of hollow concession. It consists in granting that, yes, in principle everything depends on the framework, at the same time continuing to describe and to explain situations as if this proviso were largely irrelevant. If the framework is disturbed, its disturbance can be counted on to be temporary; once a revised framework gets stabilized, the framework-disregarding analysis can begin all over again.

For an example, look to the "macroeconomics" practiced by American Keynesians. Faced with criticisms like those presented in the preceding pages, they had a dismissive and evasive response. Of course, they said, we know that the correlations we study – between inflation and the level of employment, for example – depend on particular institutional conditions. They recognized that these conditions included many detailed arrangements such as the form and reach of unionization and the accepted relation of government to the economy. Yes, of course, they added, but let's get back to business. Business consisted in relating large-scale economic aggregates, like the levels of inflation and employment, directly to one another, against the assumed background of institutional arrangements.

There are two objections to be made to this response. First, the sense in which we affirm such economic regularities changes radically when we attribute them to quiescence over distinctive institutional arrangements rather than to, say, the intractable problems and built-in constraints of an advanced industrial society. Second, if we take seriously the influence of the institutional and imaginative framework of economic activity and if we think of the components of this framework as unique and pliable, the relation of economic phenomena to such institutional and imaginative structures has to become the central topic of economics. We cannot hope correctly to describe or to explain routine activities unless we have a way to think about this relation.

A SECOND STATEMENT OF THE PROBLEM: HISTORY WITHOUT A SCRIPT

Trouble with the Script: The Shared Embarrassments of Deep-Structure Social Theory and Positivist Social Science

Reconsider now the situation of social and historical studies from the vantage point offered by the preceding criticism of deep-structure social theory and positivist social science. The key idea to have come under assault is the belief that the history of society has a ready-made script. Must social and historical analysts respond to this assault only by limiting their sense of what the script contains and by retrenching their explanatory ambitions? Or can they avoid the appeal to the script altogether and find an alternative basis for generalization?

The core of this idea of the script, shared by deep-structure social theory and positivist social science, is a belief that our practical and imaginative fighting over the terms of social life is not entirely in earnest. The fighting is not in earnest in the sense that the conflicts over the formative contexts of social life or over the procedures for social problem solving and interest accommodation take place under the controlling influence of forces the contenders cannot master and do not even fully understand. The fighting may also not be in earnest in the sense that whatever the intentions of the disputants, only a narrow range of possible outcomes can stand the test of practical reality. Inflexible economic, technological, or psychological imperatives determine which forms of governmental or economic organization can and cannot work.

The idea that history has a script assumes different forms in the varied traditions of social theory. In deep-structure social theory the script appears as a set of practical and psychological constraints or of overpowering developmental tendencies. In the nonevolutionary variant of deep-logic analysis, deeply rooted constraints generate a list of possible social worlds and even specify subsidiary conditions that determine when each of these worlds becomes actual. In the evolutionary variant of deep-structure social theory, the script consists in the developmental tendencies that specify an actual compulsive sequence of types of social organization.

That positivist social science accepts the idea of the script is a good deal less obvious. But this mode of social analysis embraces the notion of a preestablished plot to social and historical life in the form of a belief in the existence of a relatively uncontroversial setting for problem solving and interest accommodation. The techniques of avoidance that play so prominent a role in positivist social science make it possible to treat particular, accidental arrangements as if these arrangements represented a better or worse approximation to a procedural scheme for rational social choice. Thus, for example, a historically distinct set of market institutions may be treated as a more flawed or less flawed embodiment of the one true and necessary form of market order. It may suffer from too much oligopoly or governmental regulation. It may allow too many economic agents to escape paying for the harms their activities inflict on others. But its basic generative principle – the use of property claims that are nearly absolute in both scope of usage and temporal succession – is supposed to be the sole basis on which a market can rest. The view of actual institutions as better or worse approximations to a relatively uncontroversial standard of rationality represents a version of the idea of the script because it drastically restricts what is understood to be at stake in the fighting that goes on in history.

My entire discussion of the contemporary situation of social thought can be read as commentary on the problems produced by the appeal to a script. The growing awareness of these problems and the devices employed in order to resolve them form a major part of the contemporary situation of social and historical thought. In the tradition of deep-structure social theory the sign of this self-critical advance is the increasing dilution of the necessitarian assumptions with which the contrast between frameworks and routines has traditionally been associated. This dilution becomes evident, for example, in the varieties of Marxism that play up the relative autonomy of class conflict from social structure. In positivist social science, on the other hand, the main sign of concern with the difficulties of the script is the increasing importance accorded to what I earlier called the techniques of avoidance. It has become increasingly clear that not one of these social sciences can solve its key explanatory problems without referring to the institutional and imaginative contexts that overshadow the routine activities of social life and set the terms on which social conflicts or exchanges take place. Thus, the particular social sciences have become ever more absorbed in efforts to allude to these frameworks and to recognize their importance without breaking with a style of description and explanation in which the distinction between formative contexts and formed routines has no secure place. These efforts, I have argued, cannot succeed. Either the reference to formative context must remain empty of significant consequence or the habits of conventional social science must be drastically reformed. The problem is nowhere clearer than in the particular method of avoidance labeled earlier the technique of the hollow concession. The social scientist who embraces this solution acknowledges in principle the importance and the uniqueness of particular institutional settings. But he then returns to his normal practice of description and explanation as if this concession hardly mattered.

In both the major traditions of contemporary social analysis those who try to hold on to the part of their inherited explanatory practices that relies on the idea of the script find themselves locked into increasingly self-defensive and implausible positions. They confront a mounting tide of inconvenient facts and persuasive objections. But those who seek to rid their disciplines of everything that depends on the neonaturalistic idea that society and history are scripted seem to deprive themselves of the sole basis for explaining social facts and historical events. At least, they seem to forswear all explanations that go beyond the most narrowly focused and causally agnostic correlations and the least probing historical narratives. Skepticism about the script seems, inevitably, to result in skepticism *tout court*. The effort to prevent the complete disintegration of the naturalistic element shared by deep-structure explanation and positivist social science appears inseparable from the attempt to uphold the very possibility of social explanation. Conversely, the relentless insistence on freeing contemporary social thought from its residual attachments to the naturalistic view of society begins to seem a desperate surrender to nihilism. No wonder the same social theorists, social scientists, and historians often oscillate between the narrower, more orthodox and the looser, more skeptical strands in their traditions. For if the former commits them to necessitarian illusions, the latter appears to lead them into nihilistic impotence.

The great inspiring idea of the most successful efforts of modern social thought has been the idea of emancipation from false necessity. At any given time, the existing forms of social life may seem more or less the ones that have to be: at most, the corrupt or deviant forms of a small stock of possibilities. This impression is likely to apply with special strength to the most central aspects of society: the formative relations of power and production and the ideas, embodied or implied by institutions, about the possible and proper ways that people can and should associate in the different areas of social life.

Before the emergence of modern social theory the most influential social doctrines in and outside the West had disregarded or downplayed the collective power to create an unprecedented social world rather than just to regenerate a corrupt one. Modern European social thought did not limit itself to proving that history could innovate rather than merely ring the changes on a small number of associative options. It also showed that the understanding of any dense social reality had to begin in the discovery of a history of accomplished or failed transformations and a set of variational possibilities. You grasped the relations among different elements in social reality by seeing how they might be recombined or replaced and by discovering that some recombinations or substitutions were easier to come by than others. The facts most resistant to willed transformation were the most fundamental.

Marx stated the relation between enlightenment and emancipation from false necessity in the most powerful and uncompromising way. The social world was not a natural order, but a domain of collective struggle, constraint, and acceptance. The material relations of society were real relationships of domination and dependence among people. The whole structure of society was the expression of temporary constraints and particular contests rather than part of the inherent nature of things. Economic growth, which had once required oppression, would soon make it superfluous. The role of social thought, as an accomplice of emancipatory social practice, was to demystify society and to reveal it to itself.

This core conception reappeared, in more limited ways, in other bodies of social thought. It came up, for example, in the idea of the progressive economic innovations that would be possible if people were free to combine the factors of production for themselves, free from coercion and privilege and from the illusions of necessity or sanctity that supported these restraints. Or, the ideal reemerged far afield, as in Freud's view of the way that true self-understanding, worked out in relation to another person, would liberate the patient from a rigidified pattern of conduct and perception that made him helpless in the face of his own unconscious and of life's sufferings.

Nevertheless, in all these branches of social thought, the liberating intention was dragged down by the theoretical instruments with which it armed itself. The history of modern social thought can be written as a history of the paradoxical relations between the idea of emancipation from false necessity and the theoretical strategies and concepts through which this idea was worked out.

Here are some examples of the way the execution compromised the purpose. Sometimes, through the sacrifice of an acknowledgment of contingency to the search for fake laws and the imitation of some preconceived notion – modeled on the physics or the biology of the day – of what respectable science had to look like. Sometimes, through the substitution of politics by social structure: the belief in a natural history of forms of social life, propelled forward by social classes that had natural boundaries and whose only two options were either to understand their own true interests and identities, or to fail to understand them, thereby slowing down the history machine. Sometimes, by the reification of concepts that described a contingent historical reality, as when the different elements that went into someone's working definition of capitalism were treated as naturally connected with one another or the abstract idea of a market was confused with some tacit picture of property and contract rights. Sometimes through physicalist models in psychiatry and psychology, the image of forces working against each other and maintaining a perilous balance of energy and control.

By the 1980s social theory, imprisoned in discredited orthodoxy or dissolved into flaccid eclecticism and mock scientism, had failed to adjust its theoretical instruments to its original aim. It had simply forgotten about the aim. It continued to use, in more fragmentary fashion, all the conceptual strategies that betrayed thought to false necessity. Because these strategies no longer belonged to a cohesive and deliberate theoretical project, they stopped being mistakes, and became superstitions.

The Modest Eclectic Response

What should our attitude to this situation be? The most common response can be called modest eclecticism. Modest eclecticism blends into the more diluted versions of positivist and deep-structure practice. Only its heightened self-awareness of a shared predicament and its self-conscious attempt to make the best of a bad situation mark it out for special treatment.

The modest eclectic dilutes and combines the traditional claims of positivist social science and deep-structure social analysis. He believes that the appeal to a script can be made plausible only if the constraints and tendencies that form the script are recognized to leave open a broad range of variation. He therefore also advises that explanatory claims in social and historical studies must be drastically deflated if they are to be supported. But though he wants to limit the scope of his explanations he does not want to change their character. For the modest eclectic accepts the assumption that only by referring to a script can we explain social situations and historical transformations. His message is: Abandon heroic pretenses, but do not go too far. Even excessive skepticsm can be dangerous.

If the modest eclectic comes out of a Marxist tradition he may insist that there is something to the story about forces and relations of production. But he treats the story as highly exaggerated and simplistic because, for example, it fails to recognize that there are many pathways from one mode of production to another and because it drastically understates the autonomy of class conflict from economic circumstance. This modest eclectic typically continues to employ the term capitalism even though he may refuse to swear by the assumptions that would entitle him to use a category like this one as more than a label for a historically unique constellation of arrangements.

If the modest eclectic comes out of the positivist tradition he will be attentive to the importance of the institutional arrangements that define the setting for the ordinary deals and disputes of social life. He will not go so far as to claim that the organizing principles of modern Western market economies represent an approximation to an ideal scheme for rational economic choice. But he will nevertheless be quick to emphasize the facts of convergence among institutional systems of constraint upon institutional invention. He may, for example, claim that any advanced industrial economy is bound to end up with something like the mass-production style of industrial organization; that any market order in similar conditions is sure to look something like the regulated market orders of the contemporary Western democracies; and that any representative democracy in a populous and pluralistic society will probably be something like the democracies that have in fact been bequeathed to us by nineteenth-century North Atlantic states. The vagueness of the "something like" in these views is crucial to the beliefs of the modest eclectic. He reminds us that the constraints which produce these convergences allow for a wide, even an indefinitely wide range of variation. But he is also convinced that drastic reconstructive proposals will shatter against limits more unyielding than a mere accumulation of institutional and imaginative biases.

Like any richly defined diagnosis of an intellectual situation, modest eclecticism suggests a therapy. It sees hope for intellectual progress in an incremental, inductive clarification of the respective roles of determining constraint and undetermined freedom. It treats the distinctive procedures of the major traditions of social and historical analysis cavalierly and jumbles them together, because it is unwilling to abide by the stricter necessitarian assumptions with which these methods have been associated. It sees no unavoidable discontinuity between its incremental and inductivist program and the weakened versions of positivist and deep-structure accounts, for it identifies the difficulties faced by these accounts with the problems that any adequate practice of social and historical explanation must confront.

Notice that the modest-eclectic agenda usually goes hand in hand with a nonradical attitude toward the present formative contexts of social life. Even the modest eclectic whose heritage is Marxist finds himself tempering his faith in the redemptive power of the dialectic, extending his appreciation of the resiliency of "capitalism," and refining his awareness of the many disasters and perversions threatening all societies that attempt to break out from capitalist arrangements. (I later argue that at least one plausible response to the contemporary situation of social thought does combine extreme skepticism about general social or historical explanations with equally extreme disbelief in the necessity and the desirability of contemporary social frameworks. But modest eclecticism is not this response.)

Objections to the Modest Eclectic Response

Implicit in my discussion of positivist social science and deep-structure explanation is a criticism of the modest eclectic approach to the predicament their disintegration has created. One way to make explicit this critique of modest eclecticism is to insist upon a distinction between the facts of constraint and convergence and the ways of explaining them preferred by the adepts of the ruling traditions of social analysis. It is indeed a fact that only a few major systems of governmental and economic organization have flourished in the modern world, that many campaigns against these systems have been defeated, and that many would-be alternatives have failed. But it does not follow that these triumphs and failures are best accounted for by deep-structure or positivist explanations, no matter how much these explanations may be weakened. For a thesis of my critical argument is that no weakening is ever enough. The modest eclectic avoids falling victim to further doses of the criticisms that made him modest only by surrendering more and more of the explanatory claims that drove him into his modesty in the first place. Thus, he backs himself into nihilism – the very nihilism for fear of which he both clings to the residues of the idea of the script and refuses to consider more radically antinecessitarian styles of explanation.

Consider, for example, the modernized Marxist who says that there are three or four rather than just one institutional pathway to a certain level of development of the productive forces of society. New historical learning and surprising social experiments compel him to expand from time to time his estimate of the variety of possible trajectories. With each revision the suspicion grows that his exercises in detailed analysis have lost touch with the basic Marxist story about forces and relations of production or with any story that can take its place. His approach begins to seem so elastic as to be empty. It can all too easily be adjusted, the next time around, to accommodate the most recent invention in politics or the latest discovery in scholarship. Excluding nothing, it explains nothing.

Or take the neo-Keynesian macroeconomist. He may begin by hoping to find a constant relation between aggregates such as savings and investment levels. Then he may discover that these relations vary according to factors as detailed as the nature and amount of unemployment insurance and as intangible as investor expectations about the faithfulness of governmental decisions to declared governmental policies. At the next stage he may be driven to conclude that a certain type of unemployment insurance produces a certain effect at one time but a completely different effect later, either because other attitudes and circumstances have changed or because workers, employers, and governments take into account the past effect of the arrangement. Each new source of variation can be assimilated by his methods of analysis and explanation: things are simply more complicated than they seemed at first. But as the sources of actual or potential variation in the connection among the macroeconomic constants increase, the point of searching for general relations among them becomes unclear. For what could these relations show, if they exist, other than that a certain area of social practice has not been shaken up for a certain period?

Modest eclecticism may also be criticized from the angle of its lack of clarity about the role of the framework–routine distinction. We must either accept this distinction as central or dismiss it as illusory or unimportant. If we reject it we run into the problems encountered by an unreconstructed positivist social science. But if we accept it we face unavoidable choices. We need a way to think about how such formative contexts are made and internally constituted. We must decide whether to accept the assumptions with which the framework–routine distinction has traditionally been associated: the idea that frameworks such as capitalism are indivisible wholes that stand or fall as a single piece; the appeal to the lawlike constraints or the developmental tendencies that can generate a list of possible social orders or a compulsive sequence of stages of social evolution; and the belief that contexts always keep the same relation both to the context-breaking freedom of the agents who move within them and to the constraints or tendencies that shape them. Modest eclecticism evades these choices. Better to give up the pretense of explanation altogether than to insist upon explanations as confused as the accounts that result from such equivocations.

Beyond Modest Eclecticism

The persuasive force of the case against modest eclecticism depends to a large extent upon the availability of alternatives. After all, the modest eclectic does not claim to offer a theoretical panacea, only to do the best that can currently be done with a thankless subject matter. The sole argument with a chance to convince would be the actual formulation of an alternative theoretical practice. We would have to work out the ideas that can in fact dispense with the makeshift compromises of modest eclectism and carry forward the antinaturalistic view of society. This task is taken up by the constructive work that the book in your hands introduces.

It is possible to suggest a direction for such an alternative without actually formulating the alternative. The suggestion has an appropriate role to play, even in a book primarily oriented to a critical analysis of the situation of social and historical thought. In fact, it is already implicit in the critical argument. A major theme of *Social Theory: Its Situation and Its Task* has been that the disintegration of the available traditions of social thought is no mere entropic process: the disintegrating traditions have forged many of the instruments required for their transformation. Our view of an intellectual situation, like our conception of a political circumstance, is formed in part by our ideas about how we can change it. Here, as elsewhere, no hard-and-fast distinction separates criticism and construction. A critical analysis of an intellectual situation incorporates a hypothesis about constructive opportunities. Conversely, our constructive ideas about better ways to explain social and historical events alter retrospectively our understanding of the present circumstance of social thought.

The evocation of an alternative theoretical agenda can have two roles, even in the absence of an attempt to develop the theory in detail, to put it to work, and to assess it. First, the statement of such an intellectual program can clarify precisely what it would take to break out of the intellectual predicament presented by the disintegration of these traditions of thought and by the hesitations of the modest eclectic response. If a theory like the one anticipated here were possible (judgment suspended), we could indeed do better than modest eclecticism.

Such an outline of constructive intellectual opportunities can also accomplish a second, more ambitious task. Once this alternative direction is formulated, it becomes clear that there are no reasons to reject it on its face. The alternative may turn out to be disappointing for any number of reasons. But it is at the very least not an unreasonable agenda for work, given the disarray of the current forms of social analysis and the weakness of the arguments that attribute this disarray to the infancy of a science or to the inherent nature of a subject matter. The initial plausibility of the alternative approach is strengthened by its kinship with many of the themes, categories, and conjectures that have emerged from the internal criticism and self-transformation of the dominant traditions of deep-structure social theory and positivist social science.

My presentation of an alternative to modest eclecticism passes through four stages. The first step of the argument adds one more element to my reading of the contemporary structure of controversy in social thought. The point of this addition is to show that the reach for a constructive program – indeed, for a particular type of constructive alternative – already takes place under cover of what appear to be merely destructive maneuvers. This point helps support the belief that some of the building blocks already lie at hand, forged in the course of the internal reconstruction of the available forms of social analysis. The second stage is the enumeration of some of the categories and themes of an alternative. This part of the argument very directly anticipates the theory offered by *Politics*. It is meant to perform precisely the two roles mentioned in the preceding pages. The third part of the discussion singles out a few implications of this view that have an especially direct bearing on the problems of transformative political practice. These practical implications illuminate the nature of the theoretical endeavor outlined in the preceding step of the argument. They also suggest the rudiments of a way to advance the radical project. The fourth stage of the argument indicates a way of waging the antinaturalistic campaign that differs from the route taken by *Politics* and prepared by this book. This other response ("ultra-theory") seeks to avoid rather than to revise generalizing explanations in social and historical study. Yet it does so without returning to the tacit positivist acceptance of current institutional arrangements as an uncontroversial basis on which to solve practical problems and to reconcile individual or group interests.

Before embarking on this four-step argument, remember that more is at stake than our ability to escape the twin illusions of deep-structure social theory and positivist social science. Our capacity to get critical distance on the current institutional and imaginative contexts of our societies is also on the line. Above all, the issue becomes our ability to imagine and to further the radical cause without relying on unbelievable assumptions about how things happen and what things are possible.

THE REINTERPRETATION OF CONSTRAINT

Another controversy is superimposed upon the debates discussed in my previous account of the situation of social and historical thought. This controversy reappears in all branches of contemporary social and historical studies, from the analysis of the present to the study of the past, from comprehensive social theory to specialized social science, and from empirical to normative studies. Basic, novel, and bafflingly simple, this dispute is easily missed. Its themes are regularly misdescribed by a patchwork of categories borrowed from other quarrels.

On one side of this debate stand the protagonists of the dominant traditions and methods of social thought discussed in this book. Those who take this position hold on to one of the many variants of the idea of the script distinguished in the preceding section. They see in the constraints on social invention the reality that makes possible general social and historical explanations. They attribute these constraints to relatively inflexible economic, organizational, and psychological imperatives, or to powerful developmental tendencies, or to the requirements and consequences of rational decision making and efficient resource allocation. The advocates of this view differ only in the extent to which they believe social and historical reality to be thus scripted, in the particular version of the script to which they appeal, and therefore also in the confidence with which they advance general causal explanations.

The opponents of the believers in the script do not deny the reality of constraint. But they refuse to attribute the frameworks, sequences, procedures, situations, and events emphasized by their adversaries to intractable economic, organizational, or psychological imperatives, to overpowering developmental tendencies, or to the implications of rational choice. Faced with such constraints and such alleged products of other yet deeper and more universal constraints, they often say something like: It's all politics. But what do they mean? Or, if their intentions are, as seems probable, both undeveloped and ambiguous, what should they mean?

At a minimum, they want to see the formative contexts of social life (if the critics define their ideas in a polemic with deep-structure theory) or the procedural frameworks of problem solving and interest accommodation (if they begin from a criticism of positivist social science) as nothing but frozen politics: conflicts interrupted or contained. They want to deprive these frameworks or contexts of their aura of higher necessity or authority. Above all, they want to affirm that things can be otherwise.

In this largely subterranean argument the term politics seems to have both a narrower and a broader meaning. Politics means conflict over the mastery and uses of governmental power. But it also means struggle over the resources and arrangements that set the basic terms of our practical and passionate relations. Preeminent among these arrangements is the formative institutional and imaginative context of social life. Politics in the former sense represents a special case of politics in the latter sense: governmental power is often the single most important tool for the stabilization or remaking of a formative context. Those who say that it's all politics claim that the fighting should be taken seriously, not dismissed as the mere enactment of a preestablished design.

Consider two characteristic theaters in which this controversy appears: one an explanatory discipline; the other, a field of normative controversy.

Most contemporary economists continue to hold on to stronger or weaker versions of the idea that an industrial economy changes and operates according to well-defined constraints. Politics, in either the narrower or the broader sense, can shift the distributive effects of different economic policies, assign larger or smaller areas of economic activity to market or command systems, and facilitate or obstruct efficient production and exchange. But it cannot alter the constraints, the constants, and the correlations that form the core subject of theory. There are, however, other economists, fewer in number and often disguised from others and even from themselves, who insist that *everything* depends upon power relations, upon the always surprising course of conflict over the uses of government and the nature of privilege, and upon the institutional settings within which these struggles take place.

You can claim to be a follower of Keynes, for example, and adopt either stance: interpreting the writings of the master in one case as an analysis of the economic laws of regulated market economies in democratic polities (a general type of economic organization capable of being reproduced in different countries at different times) and in the other case as a commentary on the particular consequences of particular institutional compromises. The Keynesians who prefer the latter view have a different intellectual and political agenda from the Keynesians who choose the former course. As economic analysts, they must place the interplay between detailed institutional arrangements and economic activities at the center rather than at the periphery of their studies. As citizens or policy advisers, they must insist on the revisability of these arrangements and refuse to treat them as fragments of an indivisible and repeatable type of economic organization.

The contrast between the two types of Keynesians goes a long way toward answering a superficially plausible objection to the preceding account of the controversy between the evokers of constraint and their critics. According to this objection, the contrast dissolves into a difference of degree. Economists, like all other social scientists, vary in how much of the phenomena they study they consider to be predetermined by practical imperatives that cannot be disregarded. But this objection misses the point. The economists who represent the party of politics do not merely opt for a script with more blanks;

they present a view of economic reality that dispenses with a script altogether. To develop their position into an intellectual program they must therefore show what economic analysis looks like, once the idea of general economic systems with built-in laws is abandoned.

Now, consider legal theory as a branch of social thought that, though explicitly normative in its concerns, plays host to the same dispute in other forms. Just about everyone has agreed that you cannot adequately understand the law as a system of rules that provides determinate solutions to particular problems of choice. But many believe that doubts can be settled through an appeal to impersonal policies and principles. The adherents of this rationalizing legal analysis wage a war on two fronts.

On one front they attack the methods of legal analysis that leave the body of the law as a vast heap of low-level legislative compromises and judicial analogies. Against this view of legal doctrine they demand a higher order of consistency, safeguarded by a form of legal reasoning that presents extended bodies of law as the expression of a coherent and defensible plan. They dismiss as mistaken the judicial precedents or doctrinal understandings that fail to fit the plan they see embodied in the main corpus of the law.

On a second front these rationalizing analysts fight radical theorists who insist upon seeing and treating legal doctrine as one more arena in which to carry on the struggle over the basic terms of social life. By opposition to these critics, they emphasize a sharp discontinuity between legal doctrine and all-out ideological or philosophical debate. To justify this discontinuity, it is not enough to assimilate the issue of what legal analysis should look like to the question of what judges should or should not do under a particular democratic regime. It is also necessary to claim that large areas of law can be retrospectively organized as coherent sets of principles and policies. These principles and policies supposedly articulate a plan – for efficient resource allocation, for a system of free and equal rights, or for any scheme of social order the rationalizing analyst may credit with the greatest authority.

If more than a small part of the law failed to fit this plan, the law applier would have to choose one of two solutions, either of which would be fatal to the objectives of the rationalizing analyst. On the one hand, he may give up the pretense that large parts of the law do add up to an intelligible scheme. On the other hand, he may repudiate as mistaken broad areas of existing law and doctrine. This alternative would undermine the cherished contrast between restrained legal analysis and freewheeling ideological criticism. It would also make restraints on the judicial role depend on narrowly drawn institutional or prudential considerations rather than on the very nature of legal reasoning.

The rationalizing analyst avoids these dangers by seeking to represent the law as a repository of intelligible policies and principles, somehow built into statutes and precedents that were produced by a vast array of makeshift deals and conflicting intentions. In an earlier day he could find help for this enterprise in a widely shared assumption: the idea that types of governmental and economic organization such as a constitutional democracy or a market system have a built-in legal content. In this view, people choose whether to establish such a type of social organization, though they cannot choose its content. The content is already there, as the hidden content of the package people bought when they committed themselves to a general type of social organization, and it provides the basis for intelligible policies and principles allegedly immanent in the law. But the history of modern legal thought can be written in large part as the history of the discovery of the legal indeterminacy of such vague institutional projects as a market order or a representative democracy. The result is to leave rationalizing legal analysis without a ready-made foundation.

Confronted with the ideas of the rationalizing legal analyst, the radical critic says once again: It's all politics. He sees no script that could turn the detailed stuff of the law into the expression of a coherent practical plan or moral scheme. He tells us that we may or may not want to confine certain officials – nonelected judges in the present Western democracies – to a low-level practice of analogical comparisons that leave the law as the confused and contradictory mass it really is. We may also choose to practice legal analysis outside the adjudicative setting as the explication and criticism of such compromises and contradictions or as the exhibition of small-scale institutional variations that can be used as points of departure for bolder social experiments. But the one thing we should not do is to pretend that the materials of the law add up to an intelligible and defensible order. For whatever temporary tactical advantage this pretense affords to the promotion of worthy aims seems sure to be overriden by the dangers of superstition, concealment, apology, and elitism.

Thus, the same debate between the more or less confident believers in the script and the dismissers who say that it's all politics reemerges in different forms but with similar implications in every branch of social thought. Yet, though omnipresent, the debate is also obscure. The claim of those who say that it's all politics is easy to misunderstand. It can be heard as merely the expression of a skepticism that has gone beyond modest eclectic response, evincing a more radical disbelief in the prospects for any style of social and historical explanation. When thus misunderstood, its problems merge imperceptibly into the doubts and riddles addressed by modest eclecticism. The debate then loses its independent interest.

Those who take the all-is-politics side in this dispute have often given cause for this reading of their words. They have almost always failed to grasp the consequences of their own position or to identify with clarity different ways to develop and support it. Yet the hope of working out the antinaturalistic view of society and of illuminating the path of the radical cause depends on our ability to make sense of this seemingly negativistic and paradoxical view and to carry it to a successful conclusion.

To interpret the claim that everything is politics as the disheartened, skeptical next step after modest eclecticism is to be left without a point of departure from which to undertake this effort. Nor does this interpretation do justice to the half-articulated concerns of the critics. The politicizing dissident may or may not be skeptical about general explanations and comprehensive theories. But at his most self-conscious and persistent he is radically skeptical about everything in contemporary social thought that remains attached to the idea of a script. He refuses to treat contemporary formative contexts as the expressions of unyielding practical imperatives or as flawed approximations to an ideal plan for human coexistence. Far from believing that we can explain our societies only insofar as they respond to these deeper necessities, he asserts that we can begin to explain them only after we stop looking for such illusory or misrepresented causes.

But once we have rejected the temptation to interpret the thesis that it's all politics as a move from modest eclecticism to intellectual nihilism, we must still choose between two interpretations of the thesis. Each represents a different way of carrying the outlook of the critics to its extreme conclusions without turning it into an intellectual or political abdication.

In one view, the claim that it's all politics should be taken as the announcement of an intention to formulate a theory that breaks decisively with the neonaturalistic assumptions of both positivist social science and deep-structure social theory. Such a theory would be built in part with ideas generated by the internal criticism of these traditions and in part with other ideas added to these conceptions. Unlike positivist social science this theory would affirm the overriding importance of the distinction between formative contexts and formative routine. It would show how those institutional and imaginative frameworks of social life set the terms on which problems get identified and solved and group interests are selected and reconciled. But unlike deep-structure theory this theory would reject the assumptions with which the framework–routine distinction has traditionally been associated: the belief in a list of possible social worlds or a compulsive sequence of stages of social evolution, the view that the most basic social laws specify constraints or tendencies that can produce such lists or sequences, and the conviction that the character of the relation of formative contexts to the laws that create them and to the routines they shape remains invariant – at least until a great millennial turning point in history. The theory to emerge from the substitution of these assumptions would be as comprehensive in its scope and as detailed in its conjectures as the theory it replaces. The issue is whether we can execute such an endeavor without repeating at another level the problems of deep-structure social theory.

But this route is not the only way to develop the thesis of the critics. In an alternative view, the slogan that everything is politics should be taken as the starting point for an attempt to break with general social theories. The purpose of this attempt is not just skepticism but skepticism with a point. General theories are to be replaced by a series of explanatory, critical, and constructive-utopian practices that enable us to carry forward the conception of society as artifact. The practitioner of this armed skepticism patiently discredits every historical thesis that represents a set of formative contexts or a series of context changes as the expression of irresistible necessities. He sees in the defeated alternatives of the past and in the underemphasized deviations of the present the materials with which to build alternative social orders. He believes that the way to find directions for this work of social renewal is to imagine forms of social life that extend the aspects of current experience that seem most fully to emancipate and empower us. He seeks moral learning – to the extent that it can be had – from a conversation between our unfulfilled longings and our efforts to satisfy them.

In all these ways, the armed skeptic (whom I later call the ultra-theorist) wants to free the distinction between formative contexts and formed routines from its traditional associations. But he refuses to give general answers to such questions as how frameworks are constituted or how they are made. For he believes that we cannot dispel the illusions of false necessity without putting a stop to the enterprise of general theorizing about society. The question for him is whether he can continue to get a critical distance on the past and established frameworks of social life without devoting himself to the development of such theories or whether their absence will not drive him back, against his will, to the preconceptions and equivocations of positivist social science.

Those who uphold the view that everything is politics seem rarely to have considered the implications of the choice between these two intellectual programs. Both programs might shock them: one by its extravagant theoretical ambitions; the other by its unrestrained negativism. For all their intellectual radicalism, sympathizers with the idea that everything is politics do not yet appreciate how much more radical they must be in order to carry the antinaturalistic campaign to a successful conclusion. Thus, these two accounts of their cause are less interpretations of what they mean than alternative and parallel proposals for intellectual action. *Politics* works out the extravagantly theoretical rather than the relentlessly negativistic proposal. But that is just one man's choice about what to do now. I argue here that both responses should be tried out and judged by their results.

MAKING SENSE OF THE SLOGAN "IT'S ALL POLITICS": TOWARD A RADICALLY ANTINATURALISTIC SOCIAL THEORY

Themes of a Theory

Consider now a few of the central themes of a social theory that develops the ambitious speculative version rather than the armed skeptical interpretation of the claim that it's all politics. The worth of the view that elaborates these themes cannot be assessed until the theory has been worked out in detail. The thematic outline can nevertheless show what it takes to break loose, through the means of general theory, from the contemporary predicament of social thought. It can also strengthen our sense of intellectual possibility by suggesting an alternative that we have no reason to reject out of hand.

The Theme of the Distinction Between Formative Contexts and Formed Routines. In every social and historical situation we can identify a contrast between formative contexts and formed routines. An institutional or imaginative framework of social life arises through the containment and interruption of conflict. Defeated or exhausted, people stop fighting. They accept arrangements and preconceptions that define the terms of their practical and passionate relations to one another.

These terms are then continuously recast as an intelligible and defensible scheme of human association: a set of models of sociability to be realized in different areas of social life. This reconstruction is more than an imperative of justification. It is an aspect of what it means to settle down in a social world and to make out of it a home. People then no longer need to understand the organization of society as merely the truce lines and trophies of an ongoing social warfare. They can read one another's words and deeds against a subtext of shared assumptions.

A stabilized social framework, context, or structure sets the conditions of people's material, emotional, and even cognitive access to one another. It shapes the routines of conflict over mastery and use of the tangible and intangible resources that enable the occupants of some social stations to set terms to the activities of the occupants of other social stations. These resources include governmental power, economic capital, technical expertise, and prestigious ideals or the forms of argument that claim to show implications of these ideals. Once in place, a formative institutional and imaginative context regenerates a system of social division and hierarchy, of roles and ranks. It also gives life to cycles of reform and retrenchment in governmental politics and to business cycles in the economy.

You can tell whether an institutional arrangement or a belief about the possible and desirable forms of human association deserves to be included in the definition of a society's formative context by applying two complementary criteria. First, the belief or arrangement must be taken for granted by the strategies with which people pursue their recognized individual or group interests. Second, its substitution must change the form and outcome of conflicts over the key resources of society making. (A complication in the use of this second standard is that some substitutions may be functional equivalents.)

In contemporary North Atlantic countries the institutions that satisfy these two criteria include a style of government that combines an eighteenth-century commitment to the fragmentation of governmental power with a nineteenth-century mode of partisan rivalry incongruously related to the persistent class and communal divisions of society; a form of regulated market economies that employs property rights nearly absolute in use and duration as its preferred device of economic decentralization while using regulation by professional bureaucrats and judges as its favored method of social control over decentralized economic activity; and an approach to the representation of labor and to the organization of industry that results in the differential unionization of the work force. The imaginative preconceptions that meet the two criteria are expressed clearly, though often tacitly, in the specialized discourses of party-political and legal controversy and more richly, interestingly, and contradictorily in popular expectation, argument, and sensibility. These premises include images of private community for family and friendship, of civic equality and official accountability for governmental politics, and of voluntary contract and technical hierarchy for work and exchange.

A formative context does not exist in the same sense as the atomic structure of a natural object, open to external observation. Nor does it exist as a mere set of illusions that insight can dispel. The primary sense of its existence is practical. It exists because (and in the sense that) it is hard to disturb and even to grasp in the course of ordinary activities. Its power to shape a world of routine deals and quarrels depends upon the extent to which it gains immunity – or rather immunizes itself – against the possibility of challenge and revision.

The Theme of the Relativity of the Contrast Between Context-Preserving Routine and Context-Transforming Conflict. Formative contexts must be reproduced in the banal activities of daily life such as the forms of economic exchange, the habits of party-political competition, and the discourse of moral and legal controversy. These activities generate an endless series of petty conflicts – a Brownian motion of social life. These disputes are the small wars fought to save a social world from the wars that can pull this world apart. Yet the context-preserving disputes can always escalate into context-transforming struggles. For no ultimate difference divides them other than their relative scope and intensity. Some circumstances encourage escalation while others discourage it. But neither the actual occurrence of this escalation nor its outcome is governed by higher-order laws.

As practical or imaginative conflict widens and intensifies, different parts of the formative context are shaken. As a result, established assumptions about group interests, collective identities, and social possibilities also begin to come unstuck. For these assumptions are never more secure than the arrangements and preconceptions that supply the armature of a stabilized social world.

In a theory like Marxism, escalating conflict acts out the directional forces that lead from one preordained mode of production to another. It therefore also clarifies the logic of class interests embodied in each mode of production, or each transition between modes. But in a theory such as this one, the effect of escalation is just the opposite: to obscure and ultimately to dissolve the logic of class and communal interests. Nor is there any substitute system of interests waiting to take the place of the system that has been dissolved.

The more radically a formative context is disrupted, the more people find themselves thrown into a twofold circumstance of insecurity and openness. On the one hand, they descend into a Hobbesian war in which individuals and groups try to grab whatever apparent benefits they can seize and social life is consumed by a search for preemptive security. On the other hand, people divide into parties of opinion whose recruitment fails to map the preexisting lines of communal or class division and whose orientation fails to echo the interests and ideals that their members recognized at the earlier moment of stability. Instead of making the script fully explicit, escalation shows that there is no script.

Such a view recognizes that people will fight to retain the gross benefits and privileges of their acquired positions or to grab the privileges and benefits that, in the climate of expanded conflict, they no longer believe to be irretrievably beyond their reach. To account for this self-defensive or grasping activity, you need make no large assumptions about alternative systems of class interest: you need only acknowledge the impulse to seize the nearest and most tangible advantages in the midst of danger. Even this crude worldliness will be disturbed by the anxieties, animosities, and uncertainties of the moment.

The fierce struggle over material preferment will be accompanied by another series of events that the adherent to a theory like hard-core Marxism must try to dismiss as a temporary and self-correcting aberration. People whose class positions and material circumstances were similar when the fighting accelerated will find themselves disagreeing more often and more deeply than before. They will be divided by conflicting opinions and assumptions about what is good for them – or for the rest of society – and what they can reasonably expect or fear from the troubled situation. This fragmentation and regrouping will be all the more acute because the views of collective opportunity and of the social ideal on which they depend are incurably controversial. No simple historical sequence or list of alternative social orders exists to show each group its next best chance.

Thus, this view predicts that the experience of aggravated group struggle will regularly be a strange mixture of straightforward individual or collective self-aggrandizement and high conflicts of vision. Both the selfish and the ideal aspects of ordinary struggle will be exaggerated and, in their exaggerated form, they will taint each other ever more pervasively, until people can no longer tell them apart. Classes, rather than becoming more and more themselves, will, at least for the duration of the intensified conflict, become indistinguishable from parties of opinion. Indeed, in a very real way, parties of opinion will replace classes. Such predictions supply ways of testing the superiority of this view over its rivals. They will also be seen to have important practical implications.

The Theme of the Variability of Entrenchment. Formative contexts differ in the extent to which they are entrenched, that is to say, protected against being challenged and revised in the midst of ordinary conflicts and deals. The more entrenched a formative context, the greater the number of intermediate steps that must be traversed before context-preserving routines become context-transforming struggles. For example, before some of the society's formative institutional arrangements are seriously jeopardized, the habits of conflict over the mastery and uses of government that characterize a relatively more entrenched framework will have to undergo a longer and more easily interruptible process of escalation than the corresponding practices in a relatively less entrenched context. Similarly, the style of legal argument in a relatively more entrenched context will have to expose more concealed disharmonies among recognized principles or between pretense and practice before it turns into an attack on the dominant imaginative scheme of possible and desirable forms of human association.

Relative entrenchment and disentrenchment are not just things that happen to a formative context. They are consequences of particular ways of organizing and understanding social life. An advance toward disentrenchment should therefore not be mistaken for a move toward anarchy. A relatively more denaturalized or disentrenched context is at least as distinctive and detailed in its content as its relatively more disentrenched counterpart. In fact, if anything, it is richer in worked-out detail because the people who establish and reproduce it are more keenly aware of its artifactlike character. Compare, for example, the relatively more disentrenched frameworks of the contemporary North Atlantic countries to the relatively more entrenched contexts of the prerevolutionary monarchies. The former are no less richly defined than were the latter. Nor is there any reason to suppose that other, even more revisable orders would have any less detailed and distinctive substance.

The arrangements and preconceptions that compose a formative context shape social roles and hierarchies. The more entrenched are the preconceptions and arrangements, the more stable and rigidly defined become the hierarchies and roles that they support. For the privileged holds upon resources, or the discriminations of propriety and allegiance, implied by social division and ranking survive intact only so long as they remain hard to challenge and even hard to recognize. In fact, the relation between the revisability of a formative context and the force with which it imposes a system of division and hierarchy is so constant that the relative rigidity of roles or hierarchies may be considered part of the definition of entrenchment.

Thus, we can relate the spectrum of entrenchment to very distinct styles of social ranking. Hereditary castes or corporately organized estates, for example, occur in societies whose formative contexts are relatively entrenched. At the opposite extreme of disentrenchment, society would be divided only by freely formed parties of opinion whose membership bore no relation to any antecedent structure of social divisions or hierarchies. Somewhere toward the middle of this spectrum stand contemporary class societies, familiar with political parties that both speak and do not speak for particular classes and communities. The interplay between the weakened and fragmentary hierarchies of class and a practice of party politics that both reflects and transcends these hierarchies is a mark of societies partly, but only partly, emancipated from the constraints of false necessity.

Disentrenchment holds great practical interest for us because it can serve as the basis for a broad range of varieties of individual and collective empowerment. By opening social relations more fully to recombination and experiment it can contribute to the development of productive capabilities. By weakening roles and hierarchies it can help reconcile the enabling conditions of self-assertion: the need for engagement in group life and the countervailing need to avoid the dangers of dependence and depersonalization that attend all such engagement. By giving us a more conscious mastery over the settings of our practical and passionate relations it can turn us more truly into the architects and critics, rather than the puppets, of the social worlds in which we live. Call the sum of these varieties of empowerment that result from disentrenchment negative capability.

Disentrenchment also matters for another, related reason. We have grown accustomed to thinking that our lives in society are overshadowed by a series of unyielding tensions between, for example, the attractions of the social control of economic activity and the benefits of decentralized markets or, at a still more primitive level, between autonomy and community. But principles like social accountability and economic decentralization or ideals like autonomy and community have little meaning apart from the practical arrangements that are made to represent them in fact. Just as the content of these tensions varies, so does the extent to which they are indeed recalcitrant rather than open to partial resolution. Cumulative disentrenchment, if it can be achieved, may increase the part of these disharmonies that can be reconciled. Thus, for example, a market system based on rotating capital funds rather than absolute property rights may extend the opportunities for *both* the social control of accumulation and the decentralization of economic decisions.

The Theme of Possible Movement Toward Disentrenchment: Cumulative Change Without Evolutionary Compulsion. A thoroughly antinaturalistic social theory takes the final step in the development of the historical point of view. It affirms that we can change not only the content but also the force of our formative contexts: their relative immunity to challenge and their active encouragement to a structure of social division and hierarchy.

Because more disentrenched frameworks make possible a range of forms of empowerment, a cumulative move toward greater revisability is possible. Such a move may occur as a result of intentional action: more disentrenched arrangements may be inaugurated by groups and ruling groups who want to secure the benefits of negative capability for themselves or their countries. Alternatively, the move may result from a social counterpart to natural selection: the more disentrenched contexts outdo the less entrenched in the worldwide rivalry of practical capabilities and ideological seduction. Cumulative emancipation from false necessity may even result from efforts that override the contrast between intentional and unintentional agency. For example, more disentrenched practices and organizations may initially emerge as the unexpected by-products of other endeavors and without benefit of any understanding of the relation between disentrenchment and empowerment. Yet these organizations and practices may seem worth preserving for the sake of the advantages they produce. Moreover, the people who control them may have to develop a conception – of, say, enterprise management or legal doctrine – that requires an implicit, fragmentary understanding of negative capability and its conditions.

The advance toward greater disentrenchment is never more than possible. It can be reversed or overridden by other factors. Above all, it does not preset its own practical forms and implications. We can say that a particular formative context is more disentrenched than another. But we cannot generate prospectively a list of the institutional arrangements or imaginative preconceptions that correspond to different degrees of disentrenchment. In our efforts to build more revisable and hierarchy-subverting frameworks we work with the materials of the institutional and imaginative contexts that we are in or of past or remote sequences of context making that we study and remember. Even our boldest and most original inventions represent penumbral extensions of these legacies.

Each formative context influences its own sequel without determining it. For some parts of such an institutional and imaginative framework are usually less open to change than others: harder to replace without also replacing other arrangements or preconceptions. The biases that a formative context imparts to its own transformation can reinforce one another over time and thereby open up another source of cumulative context change.

In an evolutionary deep-structure theory such as Marxism the sequence of social frameworks can never be more than an outward product of the directing forces in history. But in a theory organized around these themes the pull of negative capability and the push of the sequential effects of formative contexts are independent influences that disturb and reshape each other. On the one hand, an advance in negative capability limits the force of sequential effects: when formative contexts become more disentrenched, their influence over their own sequels also diminishes. On the other hand, when we set out to change the character as well as the content of our frameworks, we have nothing to work with but the outcomes of many loosely connected histories of context change.

The Theme of the Piece-by-Piece Replaceability of Formative Contexts. While positivist social science disregards the distinction between formative contexts and formed routines, deep-structure social theory sees every social framework as an indivisible package. Once we define a formative context with enough detail to show how it shapes routines of social conflict, we see that its components do not in fact develop simultaneously nor come together in a single moment of closure. The major institutional or imaginative components of a formative context are often changed piecemeal. Their replacement reshapes some of the deals and conflicts that reenact a scheme of social division and hierarchy and that determine the uses to which economic capital, governmental power, and scientific knowledge are put. Such revisions typically destabilize some parts of the established framework while strengthening others.

Like the style of social theory it exemplifies, the illusion of the indivisibility of formative contexts has dangerous practical consequences. It suggests that all changes short of total revolution must amount to mere conservative tinkering. It thereby induces in its adepts a fatal oscillation between unjustified confidence and equally unjustified prostration.

A view of the internal constitution of formative contexts is always just the reverse side of an account of context making. Thus, the approach to context change outlined earlier suggests an approach to the composition of social frameworks. This approach allows for a piece-by-piece reconstruction of social frameworks. Yet it also identifies constraints upon the replacement and recombination of the elements that make up such an ordering of social life.

These elements may not be able to coexist for long if they represent widely disparate degrees of emancipation from false necessity. Consider in this light the relation between two major parts of a formative context: the method of capital allocation and the organization of government. The property-based regulated market system of the contemporary North Atlantic countries can coexist with many different styles of democratic or authoritarian polities. But it is hard to see how this property regime can survive side by side with arrangements that closely link caste or class privileges in government and privileged degrees of group control over land and labor. Such arrangements are found in formative contexts more resistant to challenge and more supportive of rigid roles and hierarchies than the democratic or authoritarian regimes that ordinarily accompany economic decentralization based on absolute property rights. Neither is that property regime likely to coexist with polities even less entrenched than the polities that now accompany property-based market systems. Such systems include a mobilizational democracy committed to open up every feature of the social order to collective challenge and revision and to liquefy all rigid roles and hierarchies or a mobilizational dictatorship determined to shift people around according to an artificial plan for economic and military strengthening. For different reasons and with different consequences, these political orders would not tolerate the exercise of private privilege and the restraint on social control that nearly absolute and eternal property rights imply.

Institutional solutions at such different levels of negative capability give irreconcilable messages about the extent to which we can or should remake and reimagine society. More important, they permit and require very different degrees of collective engagement from the bottom up or of reformist initiative from the top down.

Practical Implications

The antinaturalistic social theory whose themes I have just outlined has many implications for transformative practice. The evocation of these practical lessons may help elucidate the character of the theory that inspires them.

A Mission for Programmatic Thought. Programmatic thinking gains a secure place in our ideas only when we believe both that the formative contexts of social life can be remade and reimagined and that the outcome of this reconstructive activity is not foreordained. Positivist social science denies the first of these two conditions by disregarding or downplaying the difficulty of explaining the frameworks of our deals and conflicts in the relatively noncontroversial way in which we justify choices within these frameworks. Deep-structure social theories fail to meet the second condition by imposing predetermined limits on the results of context revision. In a view like Marxism such limits are especially severe. We are told little about the next stage of social evolution (socialism), yet are discouraged from usurping the prerogatives of the dialectic. If a detailed description of the next stage were to fill this gap, we would still be left with no more room for invention than the protagonists of past modes of production enjoyed. Our role would be merely to suit a necessary structure to local variations.

But in an antinaturalistic social theory like the one anticipated here, programmatic thought has its work cut out for it. The formative institutional and imaginative contexts of social life can be remade and reimagined – though rarely all at once. Moreover, the results of this transformative work are not preestablished. For the directional forces invoked by this view do not even select a list of possible frameworks, much less a compulsive sequence of frameworks.

A social theory with the central themes outlined in the preceding subsection does not merely give programmatic thought a mission. It also provides our programmatic efforts with a measure of guidance. It offers us the beginnings of a credible account of context change. It thereby allows us to escape a striking consequence of current views of social reality, which is to equate the realism of a proposal for reconstruction with its proximity to current arrangements. By giving content to a conception of the meaning and conditions of human empowerment, the theory also helps identify a goal for social reconstruction. In particular, it frees the definition of the radical project from unnecessarily restrictive assumptions about the possible forms of social organization and personal experience.

The Search for Alternative Institutional Forms of Market Economies and Representative Democracies. Even those who hold no conscious allegiance to the assumptions of deep-structure social theory and positivist social science habitually treat abstract types of governmental and economic organization such as command and market economies or representative democracies as if they had a detailed, built-in institutional content. Thus, people speak as if they had to choose among different blends of market and planning but not among radically different ways to centralize or decentralize and to combine centralism and decentralization in the economy. They take for granted an identity between the abstract idea of a market – as an order in which many economic agents bargain on their own initiative and for their own account – and a particular system of contract and property rights. They equate the social control of economic activity with familiar methods of nationalization or regulation. They make the idea of representative democracy equal the peculiar combination of eighteenth-century liberal constitutionalism and nineteenth-century party politics that history has bequeathed them.

Liberals and radicals share these prejudices with conservatives. Liberals fail to confront the constraints that inherited institutional forms impose on the realization of their ideals. Radicals take liberals at their word. They seek alternatives to current market economies in an unnecessary rejection of market principle. They often attack bourgeois democracy in a futile quest for direct democracy and permanent civic engagement.

The antinaturalistic view sketched previously liberates us from these prejudices. It turns our attention to the work of imagining alternative forms of market economies and representative democracies. Economic regimes – it suggests – differ in the success with which they resolve the tension between the social control and the decentralization of economic activity; we can achieve more of both. Democratic regimes differ in the seriousness of the explicit or implicit obstacles they set in the way of bold institutional experiments and of attacks on privilege. Systems of legal rights differ in the facility with which the devices established to safeguard the individual against governmental or private oppression lend themselves to the exercise of subjugation over other people and restrict the plasticity of social life. The interest lies in the practical details of these variations. The liberal and the radical do not awaken from their slumber until they seize the opportunities such variations create and set themselves to the work of imagining and establishing less entrenched frameworks of social life.

The Provisional Force of Group Interests. A theory like the view outlined in this section presents an approach to transformative political practice that recognizes the force of established group interests yet treats these interests as no more secure than the institutional arrangements and the imaginative preconceptions that help sustain them. The transformative movement that begins its work in a relatively stable social situation (and no situation can be more than relatively stable) knows that the ranks and communities into which society is divided have recognized interests. The movement must take care to relate its cause to these interests. However, it also needs to think and act with the awareness that these definitions of interest are not for keeps. They rest on assumptions about collective identities and social possibilities. These assumptions in turn depend on the serenity of established institutional arrangements and enacted models of sociability that shape a world of routine deals and quarrels.

Escalating conflict over such arrangements and models shakes assumptions about group membership and transformative possibility, and it reshapes conceptions of group interest. The direction taken by the new views of group interests depends on the precise ways in which formative contexts have been changed. Because there is no closed list of possible frameworks, and no preestablished sequence of formative contexts, there is also no secure limit on the changes that a current system of group interests can undergo. Thus, the transformative movement must take established conceptions of group interest seriously while anticipating how these conceptions may shift as new institutional or imaginative elements enter into the framework of routine conflict and exchange.

This approach has an important corollary. In a stabilized social world some class or communal alliances are easier or harder to establish than others. Some classes or communities are more likely to welcome or to oppose a given transformative program. But there is no permanent logic of group collaboration or hostility and no class or community anointed to serve as the indispensable agent or vanguard of a particular change of the social order.

The Means of Stabilization Generate Opportunities for Destabilization. In the theory whose themes I have sketched, the fighting that goes on within a stabilized social framework is only a more truncated version of broader and more intense struggles about the framework. Formative contexts differ in the extent to which they effect and enforce this truncation. All practical or imaginative conflicts can get out of hand. None need await the cue to play an assigned part in the script. Through the give-and-take of alliance and animosity, of compromise and contradiction, each petty quarrel hints at opportunities of human connection beyond the possibilities countenanced by the established order.

An antinaturalistic social theory formulated on these lines enables us to understand how a formative context gains a semblance of deep necessity after practical and imaginative conflict has been contained or interrupted. But the theory also shows how each of these methods of stabilization creates opportunities for destabilization.

Thus, for example, a pacified formative context is both presupposed and reinforced by a set of explicit or implicit deals among groups and of accommodations between groups and parts of the governmental apparatus So, too, such a context serves as a template for assumptions about collective identities and social possibilities, which in turn help shape conceptions of group interest. Once the deals, the accommodations, and the conceptions of group interest are all in place, the institutional and imaginative order begins to seem almost immutable.

Look closer, though, and you find hidden disharmonies, ready to be seized on and developed. For example, even the most narrowly conceived group interest can always be defended through two different strategies. One strategy clings to the group's present station and prerogatives and defines the closest or the immediately inferior groups as rivals and enemies. The other strategy makes common cause with these groups against higher-ups. These two methods have radically different implications. While the former reaffirms the established order, the latter sooner or later challenges it. For what begins as a transitory tactical partnership often leads to a new collective identity, encourages new views of group interest, and contributes new preconceptions and arrangements.

Thus, too, a stabilized institutional and imaginative order of social life serves as a foundation for the development of a distinctive technological and organizational style. Everything from the way enterprises are managed to the way machines are designed begins to take the basic institutional and imaginative settlements of the society for granted. The overturning of these settlements poses a real threat to a dominant managerial and technological style. The dimension of the threat increases as this style spreads through a system of nation-states at unequal levels of economic and military power. The reforming elites of the more backward countries discover only slowly that they can reach the most advanced levels of productive or destructive capability on the basis of novel social arrangements. Even after they have made this discovery, it takes time to develop an alternative managerial and technological approach.

Nevertheless, practical pressures and rivalries also provide opportunities for destabilization. The development of practical productive or destructive capabilities may require that people and resources be moved around not just once but repeatedly. The arrangements capable of ensuring this greater plasticity can be either coercive or consensual in their temper, and they can either minimize or maximize the break with the preexisting pattern of group interests. A perennial stream of middle-level crises supplies occasions to begin fighting over the future order of society.

If the transformative movement can find opportunities for destabilization in the very methods of stability, it can discover inspiration in the failure of a formative context fully to inform people's practical and passionate dealings or to supersede the residues of past and distant versions of social life. The vestiges, the anomalies, the deviations, the transgressions represent countless small-scale experiments in the making of alternative social orders. Yesterday's defeated alternative, recast in new institutional terms, becomes tomorrow's triumphant solution.

No decisive crisis ever ensures that any particular reconstruction of an institutional and imaginative order will succeed. But with such opportunities and inspirations, no stability is tranquil enough to give the would-be subversive an excuse for prostration.

The Primacy of Revolutionary Reform. A political imagination formed by positivist social science is predisposed to prefer incremental social reform. For this mode of social analysis encourages us to bring the established procedures for problem solving and interest accommodation closer to a supposedly noncontroversial ideal of neutrality and efficiency. It prompts us, for example, to ask how a given market economy can be rid of oligopoly without jeopardizing the ability to take advantage of economies of scale, how the harms that an entrepreneur imposes on other people may be incorporated into his cost of doing business, or how social needs may be protected by administrative regulation that restricts and supplements market allocation. Those who press such questions ordinarily take for granted particular institutional forms of economic decentralization and social control. By contrast, the deep-structure social theorist treats the formative institutional and imaginative frameworks of social life as indivisible units, each of which stands or falls as a piece. As a result he believes that political action always faces a choice between a revolutionary substitution of the entire formative context of social life and a reformist tinkering that merely wards off serious change.

But for a theory built on the themes sketched earlier the normal mode of transformative action is revolutionary reform, defined as the substitution of any one of the loosely and unevenly connected arrangements and beliefs that go into the making of a formative context. The criterion for the occurrence of revolutionary reform is a corollary of the standard for the inclusion of a practice or belief in the definition of a society's formative context. A revolutionary reform changes the institutional and imaginative presuppositions taken for granted in the everyday struggles over the uses and mastery of the resources – of capital, governmental power, technical expertise, or legal and moral justification – that enable the occupants of some social stations to set terms to what the occupants of other social stations do. As a result, such a reform changes the plan of social division and hierarchy in content and even in character. The existing cycles of governmental policy and economic prosperity or decline acquire a new structure and new consequences. And a different set of biases is imparted to the effects that forces exogenous to the formative structure – such as demographic or technological change – will exercise on social life.

Thus, in the circumstances of the contemporary Western democracies it would be a revolutionary reform to impose a version of public control over the basic flows of investment decisions in the economy or, on the contrary, to prevent elected governments from influencing investment decisions through differential fiscal policies; to set up a special branch of government with the mission of reconstructing large-scale organizations and major areas of social practice in conformity with unfulfilled ideals of the legal order such as nondiscrimination among classes, races, and genders or, on the contrary, to prevent current administrative or judicial officials from pursuing any more modest variant of this reconstructive activity; to require the unionization of all labor (e.g., putting a corporatist labor-law regime in place of a contractualist regime), to prohibit unions altogether, or to replace unions as an instrument of labor representation by a system of joint public and workers' control of enterprises.

Revolution becomes the limiting case of transformative action rather than the sole alternative to the statecraft of stability through tinkering. The vulgar idea of revolution includes two elements. The first part is a process: a violent seizure of the central government, with the participation of large masses of ordinary people and the paralysis or active collaboration of the repressive machinery of the state. The second part is an outcome: the comprehensive reconstruction of an entire form of social life, of its distinctive arrangements and its established hierarchies and divisions. But the process often occurs without the outcome, if indeed this outcome ever takes place at all. Moreover, a revolution in the sense defined by violent upheaval is an event so uncertain in its course and so dependent for its occurrence upon government-shattering events like war and occupation that we are fortunate not to depend on it in order to remake our contexts.

TWO WAYS TO DEVELOP THE IDEA THAT EVERYTHING IS POLITICS: SUPER-THEORY AND ULTRA-THEORY

The claim that everything is politics can be developed in two radically different directions. These twin agendas offer alternative responses to the predicament of social thought, alternative ways to go beyond both deep-structure analysis and positivist social science. Let me label them here, ironically, super-theory and ultra-theory.

The response of super-theory is to develop a comprehensive view, rich in explanatory claims about social facts and historical events. Such is the intellectual direction whose major themes and practical implications are outlined in the preceding section and developed by *Politics*. Super-theory rivals deep-logic practice in the scope, generality, and concreteness of its hypotheses and arguments. It preserves the first move of deep-structure analysis – the distinction between formative context and formed routines. But it also replaces the second and third moves – the subsumption of each framework under an indivisible and repeatable type of social organization and the recourse to the lawlike constraints and tendencies that can generate a list or sequence of such types. The view offered shows how general explanations in social and historical study can dispense with the conception of indivisible and repeatable types of social organization while nevertheless specifying constraints on what can be combined with what within a single framework. It offers an account of context making, indeed even of the possibility of cumulative change in the character as well as the content of our frameworks. Yet this anti-naturalistic social theory does not rely on the ideas of a world-historical evolutionary logic or of a set of criteria that any possible social world must satisfy. Nor does it imply any qualitative contrast between the social knowledge available to historical agents and the insight of a theorist who describes and explains their actions.

The resulting method of social analysis vindicates the principal intention of deep-structure theory – the understanding of social order as made and imagined rather than as given – against the scientistic baggage that has compromised the realization of this intellectual project. It therefore pushes to the limit the internal criticism of deep-logic work, recognizing the fragments of a constructive view in what may otherwise seem merely a long series of disappointments. Such a response to the problems of social thought shifts the sense we give to our practices of social and historical explanation and to our modal categories of contingency and necessity. But the reformed explanatory style continues to be recognizable as general theory. In some ways it may be even more ambitious in its self-conception than the theory it replaces. It therefore also remains vulnerable to the objection that it merely carries deep-logic analysis to another plane, perpetuating its deficiencies in novel or disguised form.

Politics takes the direction of super-theory. The argument of this book anticipates by diagnosis and criticism the broad outline of the super-theoretical view presented more fully in the constructive work that follows. The merit of the proposed view depends in part on its success at escaping the objections leveled against deep-structure analysis and in part on the comparison of its achievements with the results of alternative ways of dealing with the problems of social thought.

For super-theory is not the sole possible response to these problems. There is at least one other intellectual agenda open to whoever comes to share the critical perspective on the situation of social thought described in the earlier parts of this book. Call this alternative ultra-theory. Let me add immediately that ultra-theory, like super-theory, is a project, not an accomplishment. Nobody has actually developed its program or codified its practice though many fragments of both its practice and its program have long been available.

The key difference between super-theory and ultra-theory is that ultra-theory rejects the attempt to develop a theoretical system. The ultra-theorist believes that the quest for comprehensive and systematic explanations betrays the principle that everything is politics (man as maker, society as artifact, conflict as tool) and leads to another version of the problems of deep-structure thought. He sees the deep-logic endeavor as an example of the quest for foundational ideas: for the big picture, the underlying reasons, the ultimate causes, and the hidden truths. He believes, on the basis of his reading of intellectual history, that, whatever its proclaimed intentions, a systematic and comprehensive theory will compromise with foundationalism. And foundationalism in social thought, he adds, means the appeal to controlling structures or to the laws that govern them. It means hedging on the insight that everything is politics. From this standpoint, the ultra-theorist suspects the super-theorist of falling into a new version of the errors of deep-logic analysis. Even the super-theorist can agree with him that the weak point of super-theory is precisely that it might fail in the end to solve the problems from which deep-structure theory came to grief.

Like super-theory, ultra-theory rejects positivist social science and naive historiography. It therefore makes at least one exception to its habitual theoretical negativism: the exception necessary to affirm the central importance of the difference between formative contexts and formed routines. It therefore also insists on the discontinuity and originality of particular contexts. But it does not seek to develop these insights through more defensible counterparts to the second and third moves of deep-structure analysis.

More generally, the ultra-theorist denies that his negativity produces intellectual paralysis or that it undermines a critical perspective on existing society. On the contrary, he insists that only by following his path can we avoid replacing necessitarian superstitions by ideas that resemble them. Ultra-theory defines itself by its recurrent use of a set of intellectual practices rather than by its adherence to a theoretical system. The ultra-theorist believes not only that these practices require no comprehensive system of explanations but that they cannot be reconciled with any such system. Consider three characteristic practices of the ultra-theorist.

The first activity is a negativistic explanatory therapeutic. Each time the ultra-theorist encounters a deep-logic explanation of a social transformation he shows how the same events can be fully explained without deep-structure arguments. He presents them as the outcomes of a particular history of practical and imaginative conflicts. Each time he finds a conventional social-science treatment of a topic he shows how the explanation has been skewed or trivialized by the failure to understand the controlling influence of a framework. But he rejects the attempt to develop a general theory of frameworks, of their making and their internal constitution. He is much less interested in making abstract points than in puncturing the illusory accounts offered by the deep-structure theoretician and the positivist social scientist. What others may deride as intellectual emptiness he defends as a refusal to be drawn to his adversaries' level of discussion.

A second distinctive practice of ultra-theory is the vindication of repressed solutions, of yesterday's missed opportunities, today's forgotten anomalies, and tomorrow's unsuspected possibilities. The ultra-theorist (and in this, as in so much else, he resembles the super-theorist) sees a connection between insight into social reality and sympathetic interest in the losers. The vindication of defeated or deviant solutions follows directly from the criticism of deep-structure or conventional social-science accounts of what actually happened. To the extent that dominant institutions or ideas cannot be adequately explained as the result of an evolutionary logic or of entrenched economic, organizational, and psychological constraints, to that extent they must be ascribed to particular causes and conflicts. No deep change in human nature or social reality would have been required for the result to have been different. If the triumph of certain institutions and ideas was relatively accidental, their replacement can also more easily be imagined as realistic.

The ultra-theorist denies that he needs any general theory of frameworks and of their making in order to develop these themes of contingency and replaceability. He wants, instead, to nurture an imagination of the particular that does not depend on the pretense of a comprehensive knowledge or of a privileged vantage point. He remembers, he anticipates, and he defies, but he does not claim to disclose secret and fundamental knowledge.

A third practice of ultra-theory is constructive and prescriptive. The ultra-theorist may go beyond criticism and explanation to develop anticipatory visions of more ideal forms of social life. But here too the ultra-theorist avoids first principles or elaborate theories. Rather than relying on a general view of realistic trajectories of transformation, he seeks analogies to the successful changes of the past. Rather than working out the implications of fundamental ideals, he seizes on the deviant elements in our present experience that suggest ways to realize more fully our received ideals and to reevaluate them in the light of these new realizations. If he is pressed to state the standards by which he chooses one such deviant solution as more worthy of extension than another, he denies he has such preestablished standards. He appeals instead to a pretheoretical experience of repressed or disappointed aspirations, and he frankly acknowledges that we have to choose between these aspirations by acts of commitment, choices that are also gambles, gambles that are also experiments.

The weak point of ultra-theory is the difficulty it has in resisting the standpoint of conventional social science without the help of a countervailing theory of formative contexts, of their genesis and internal composition. Though the ultra-theorist claims to acknowledge the influence of institutional and imaginative frameworks and the distinctiveness of the ways of life they shape, he can affirm this acknowledgment only by implication or through narrowly focused acts of criticism, explanation, or utopian vision. Except for a long memory and a vigilant intention, he has no prescription against the danger of taking a particular context for granted. He has no way, at least no general and discursive way, to justify any particular approach to frameworks and their history. He must even deny that he is committed to a particular approach. Nor can he easily explore a theme like the idea that the formative contexts differ, among other things, in their relation to the context-revising freedom of the people who live within them. There is only a tenuous distinction between not having a theory of formative contexts and not having a way to talk about them. When this distinction crumbles, ultra-theory lapses back into positivist social science, like a once militant leftist party that repeats the rhetoric of structure-defying activism while surrendering completely to the politics of structure-respecting redistribution.

When ultra-theory escapes the slide into conventional social science it stands exposed to another peril. It risks expressing a precommitment to a particularly perverse and misleading version of modernism. This version is the existentialist idea that true freedom consists in the perpetual defiance of all settled structure, in the endless flight from one context to another. This existentialist reading of the modernist message fails to take into account both the bad news that we must live and think most of the time in a context and the good news that we can create contexts that more fully respect and encourage our context-revising freedom. Having asserted that all our structures are historical, the existentialist does not see that the relative force with which they imprison us and turn us into the victims of unseen compulsions is itself up for grabs in history.

The project of ultra-theory has a more than superficial affinity with this form of modernism. Both the rejection of explanatory or prescriptive theories about our formative contexts and the commitment to trash every argument for the necessity or authority of a given context suit a view that sees in the "endless labor of negation" the sole true source of authentic humanity. At the same time the absence of a theory of frameworks suggests by default that, as constraints on freedom, frameworks will be frameworks. No wonder many of the most cogent foreshadowings of the program of ultra-theory are found among the defenders of this modernist heresy.

Ultra-theory may seem at least easier to carry out than super-theory. It does not require a big book, only an open collection of particular exercises. It may not make such sudden and comprehensive claims on knowledge and research nor demand so arduous a translation into small-scale explanatory and programmatic discourse. It may therefore also more easily inspire and be inspired by our ordinary experience of social understanding and social criticism. But the impression of relative facility begins to dissipate once you remember how much must be done to keep ultra-theory from degenerating into positivist social science and to either prevent or to justify its alliance with the negativistic, existentialist version of modernism.

There are nevertheless no persuasive a priori reasons to prefer either super-theory or ultra-theory as responses to the contemporary situation of social thought. Each represents a research agenda, and research agendas have to be judged ultimately by what people do with them. Prospectively, each student makes a gamble, informed by guesses about the relative fruitfulness of a line of work and by his assessment of his own strengths and weakness. Retrospectively, we compare results.

Politics pursues the super-theory route unequivocally and unabashedly. The super-theory perspective already overshadows the ideas of this critical introduction. But I hope the ultra-theorists are out there working away.

7

The Philosophical and Scientific Setting of an Antinaturalistic Social Theory

TURNING THE SCIENTISTIC PREJUDICE UPSIDE DOWN

SOCIAL theory has traditionally defined itself by its uncertain relation to the prestigious explanatory methods of natural science. Throughout the history of modern social thought the natural sciences have embodied the most successful and aggressive forms of causal explanation. It is therefore not surprising to find that programs of social theory have repeatedly taken as their model whatever explanatory methods seem to hold the day in natural science. Thus, both deep-structure social analysis and positivist social science presented and present themselves as extensions of a canonical scientific method to social phenomena, although they interpret the implications of this method in very different ways. Others have reacted to such scientistic claims by seeking to merge social theory into the humanities. But the result has often been to abandon the causal explanation of social and historical events to positivist social science while staking out a special terrain on which considerations of value and intention become paramount.

An antinecessitarian social theory like the one this book works toward may seem to increase the tension between natural science and social understanding, to take sides with the humanistic party, and with this party, to relinquish rather than to transform the practice of causal explanation. The aim of this section is to dispel these impressions. A politicized social theory can coexist with natural science without either imitating its methods or claiming an unjustified exemption from the responsibilities of causal analysis.

The point might not be worth arguing if the aim of the exercise were merely defensive. But in the course of illuminating the relation of natural science to social theory, we can discover in modern science itself and in its wider philosophical setting the means with which to refine some of the central arguments of this book. The purpose is not merely to overcome a dangerous obsession, but to turn the obsession into insight. The discussion proceeds by addressing two connected sets of issues: problems raised by the relative contingency of social facts, and difficulties presented by the historical particularity of these facts.

The social theory foreshadowed in this book can easily be misinterpreted as making a claim for the unexplained and explanation-subverting contingency of social situations and historical events. Thus misinterpreted, the argument is likely to elicit a commonsense objection. Of course, the objection goes, social phenomena are not as closely determined, nor even as subject to chance, as natural phenomena, if only because of the influence of intentional action. But social facts are not uncaused. It is because they are constrained or conditioned that we can explain them; even intentional analysis presupposes a view of the relative effectiveness of alternative ways to achieve chosen goals.

The objection largely misses the point of the style of social theorizing for which this work argues. True, this politicized social theory emphasizes a distinctive form of human freedom: our freedom not only to resist the influences of the institutional and imaginative frameworks of routine activity but also to increase the extent to which we can revise these frameworks in the course of normal social life. Some circumstances favor this resistance to context; others discourage it. However, neither our institutional and imaginative contexts themselves nor any system of social laws supposedly underlying them can determine the history of these acts of submission or defiance. The intention of the social theory advocated here is less to emphasize historical contingency over historical necessity than to give a different content to our notions of necessity or contingency and to change our view of the relation between them.

Conceptions of necessity and contingency can never be more than abbreviated statements of particular explanations. We know this through a series of discoveries made by modern philosophy and natural science. These discoveries have a twofold relevance to the project of a politicized social theory. On the one hand, they help undermine the idea that natural science provides a well-defined model of necessity and determination that can be extricated from its detailed explanatory setting for use in social analysis. On the other hand, these contemporary findings suggest a distinctive view of the relation of our thoughts to our presuppositions. This view illuminates, extends, and supports the conception of our relation to our contexts that informs all the critical and constructive arguments of *Politics*. Thus, what seemed to be a mere admonition (Do not be taken in by the flaunting of science to justify a narrow view of explanation!) turns into a source of encouragement and guidance.

The other, related issue addressed in this discussion is the difficulty of causal explanation when applied to unique situations that serve as causes and effects in many loosely connected historical sequences.

The idea that social theory can but embody with greater or lesser stringency a version of necessity anchored in the prevailing natural sciences goes hand in hand with a prejudice about generalization: that a direct relation exists between the importance of historical particularity and the impossibility of general explanations. Thus, we must either downplay the historical quality of social life (in the fashion of deep-structure analysis) or relinquish the effort to generalize (in the manner of antinomian historiography).

The following criticism of this prejudice begins with the implications of historicity for generalization within natural history itself. Discussion of these implications serves as a point of departure for the development and defense of a thesis: the subversive effects of historical particularity on certain forms of generalizing explanation run parallel to other traits of natural and social reality that open up compensatory explanatory opportunities. Social explanations – at least explanations suited to the style of social theory suggested here – are not just more qualified versions of unhistorical explanation. They are special.

This thesis relies on a metaphysical picture of different orders of reality and of the styles of explanation suited to each of them. The picture cannot be directly verified or falsified. But it does lay itself open to two tests. We can ask whether it is compatible with our scientific knowledge. We can also treat it as the ideology of a series of research agendas and assess it by judging the value of the work conducted under its aegis. It is a fable designed, as so much in the ensuing discussion, to serve as an antidote to the enlistment of natural science in the service of the received forms of social analysis.

NECESSITY AND CONTINGENCY

The Thesis Stated

This book works toward a social theory that pushes to extremes the idea that everything in society is frozen or fluid politics. Such a theory seems to make very general and controversial assumptions about the contingency of social worlds. It therefore also seems to require a preliminary definition of the conception of contingency and of the related conceptions of necessity and possibility. To attempt such a definition, however, would be a mistake. To see why is to take the first step toward dissipating the philosophical prejudices that help prevent the development of a social theory free from the superstitions of false necessity. In particular, these prejudices lay the social theory anticipated in this book open to the misinterpretation that it must be merely claiming that all historical events and social situations are contingent, thereby both denying the reality of constraint and abandoning the task of general explanation.

Here is the key thesis presented in the following pages. No ideas about contingency, necessity, or possibility (so-called modal categories), and no conception of the correct relations among these conceptions, can be defended or even understood outside the setting of a particular view of how things happen in a particular time and place. The intuitive core of the idea of contingency is the notion that all things or some things might be otherwise than they are. But aside from the extreme necessitarianism I later discuss and reject, every theory recognizes that states of affairs can be other than what they are. A conception of contingency, necessity, or possibility always amounts to a shorthand allusion to a particular explanatory theory or family of theories. It summarizes the way a theory relates events. Because such a conception is shorthand it is also characteristically ambiguous. In order to resolve its ambiguities you need to make more and more of the implicit theoretical context explicit. You resolve the ambiguities completely only when you have fully retranslated the conception into the detailed explanatory account for which it stands.

You can certainly stipulate in advance a set of abstract definitions of contingency, necessity, and possibility and then show how a particular explanatory theory exemplifies these definitions. But this procedure can easily mislead. There is no fixed list of types of contingency, necessity, and possibility that is anything more than the incomplete summary of an explanation. Between any two stated conceptions of contingency, a third conception may be found to be required by a change in our explanatory ideas. Even the metaphor of the continuum is too restrictive: no invariant scale exists along which conceptions of contingency can vary. Each substantive theory, if it is general or novel enough, changes the relations among the meanings and senses of necessity, contingency, and possibility.

The thesis that the categories of necessity, contingency, and possibility have no explanation-independent meaning has an important corollary. The claim that a theory asserts the radical contingency of certain states of affairs, whether in natural science or social study, should be met with suspicion. The would-be claim of contingency is much more likely to represent both a refusal to believe in the kind of necessity a reigning theory presupposes and an attempt to describe and explain relations in a different way. The direction of social theory for which this book argues does indeed give a larger role to a context-revising freedom than does deep-structure analysis. It severs the link between the denial of this freedom and the strategies of general social or historical explanation. It resists the idea that we can understand ourselves only to the extent that we see ourselves as puppets of our social contexts or of the laws that supposedly govern their emergence and persistence. But the point is less to tilt the scales in favor of freedom and against constraint than to change the detailed ways in which we think about the relation between constraint and freedom.

My discussion begins by considering under what conditions the idea of a context-free sense of necessity, contingency, or possibility holds up. It turns out that this metaphysical thesis becomes secure only within a certain picture of the world labeled here extreme necessitarianism. This picture is a hypothetical construct. No celebrated philosopher has ever subscribed to extreme necessitarianism though some have come close. The purpose of the construct is to show what would have to be true for contingency, possibility, and necessity to have a meaning and a sense independent of particular explanations. Once you abandon extreme necessitarianism you are driven to the thesis that the categories of contingency, necessity, and possibility gain their sense and meaning from the particular explanatory theories to which they implicitly refer. The ideas about mind and nature that support this argument have special interest because they also supply many of the insights that enable us to relate a politicized social theory to the contemporary forms of natural science.

The Limiting Case of Extreme Necessitarianism

Extreme necessitarianism is the belief in the existence of relations among states of affairs that cannot be otherwise, represented by ideas or categories of thought that are themselves unchanging. For extreme necessitarianism to be true, the lawlike regularities that science takes as its topic must be untransformable except by rules of transformation that are themselves stable. If these rules can change they must change according to a higher-order set of laws that either remains invariant or governs its own variations.

As aggressive in its claims as this objective aspect of extreme necessitarianism may be, it does not suffice to define the extreme necessitarian position. The more surprising requirement is subjective. Our appreciation of these strongest necessities must be so deeply rooted in features of knowledge and perception that it remains immune to revision. Of course, we can say that all our beliefs about nature are completely revisable and nevertheless attribute a quality of absolute necessity to the relations that serve as the subject matter of these beliefs. Our ideas about the relations would always be in flux. Earlier beliefs would constantly be shown up by later beliefs as too partial or even as utterly mistaken. But through all these shifts of conviction we would always claim that certain relations cannot possibly be other than what they are. The relations themselves are absolutely necessary. Unfortunately, our capacity to tell what these relations really are would, in this view, remain ineradicably fallible. According to such a conception, the laws of celestial mechanics may or may not be true but there would be nothing contingent about the relations in nature that they portray.

Such a fallibilist solution, however, would be wholly unsatisfactory to the extreme necessitarian. It would be just as unsatisfactory as the idea of a constraint on perception, language, or thought that lacked an objective basis in external reality and that could not be either amended or tested. For the idea of the absolute necessity of states of affairs would then become a postulate without practical explanatory force: it would have no impact on content or method. Moreover, the extreme necessitarian would be disturbed to find that the revision of his substantive ideas would end up forcing him to revise his abstract conception of necessity. Despite his determination to hang on to an uncompromising view of necessity, the actual content of his discoveries would push him in the opposite direction.

What ideas then can satisfy the extreme necessitarian? They must be features of thought, language, or perception that we unavoidably deploy in every extended picture of reality but features that remain immune to revision as we revise the pictures. Extreme necessitarians may differ in the relative prominence they assign to this invariant element. If, however, the invariant element is allowed too large a place, it begins to preclude the revisability, and therefore the objectivity, of thought. If its role is too severely restricted, it fades into truth by stipulation.

Again, extreme necessitarians may give different philosophical interpretations to this invariant element in thought. But, for the reasons I have mentioned, the extremists will not be satisfied with the idea that this unrevisable, or less revisable, element simply reflects something about the way we are (in the manner of the later Wittgenstein's treatment of logical compulsion). They will not treat the unrevisable element as a mere condition of practical success (in the fashion of a pragmatist who also happens to be an extreme necessitarian). They will not even resign themselves to the notion that the unrevisable element describes the conditions of possible experience (in the manner of Kant's theoretical philosophy). They will want to assert that these permanent structures also reveal something objective about the world. The intentions of the most extreme necessitarians must thus be realist as well as necessitarian. (By realism here I mean the belief that an indispensable part of the justification for any extended set of beliefs about the world must be grounded in features of the world external to the mind and to our practical interests.)

Plausible candidates for this strongest degree of necessity of thought are our ideas of space and time and the propositions of logic and mathematics, which are put to use in extended pictures of the world. Though capable of cumulative revisions they seem to reflect something fundamental about the workings of the imagination. Yet they may also be taken, by the extreme necessitarian, as a revelation of the way things are and have to be in the world. He may find a justification for assigning such objectivity to these ideas in the combination of three facts: that they are not just strings of tautologies, that they remain invariant, and that we have independent criteria of objectivity and success in science. As science advances, according to such independent criteria, it makes ever more extensive use of these invariant structures of the imagination. Though science uses them as more than just a language, it never has occasion to revise them. This is how the extreme necessitarian would argue. But he would be wrong.

My discussion of extreme necessitarianism advances in two steps. First, I argue that no part of our ideas about the world is privileged, in the sense of being immune to the implications of change in our empirical beliefs. Nothing in our ideas can be lifted above the flux of our empirical beliefs. The thesis is pressed through a discussion of the ways in which our conception of the necessity of even the most necessary relations is affected by shifts in a particular class of beliefs, namely, our ideas about the origin and history of the universe. The second step of the argument considers a range of discoveries in modern philosophy, natural science, and psychology. By connecting these seemingly disparate discoveries and by working out their implications for our view of discourse and inquiry, we can generalize the thesis that there are no privileged methods or representations.

This thesis matters to the argument of the book because it frees us from the prejudice that there is a single, uncontroversial conception of necessity and contingency most fully expressed in natural science and applicable to all branches of knowledge. So long as we adhere to this prejudice we remain tempted to cast social and historical understanding in a number of false roles. On the one hand, we may see social and historical study as seeking to approximate the one true method of scientific explanation and the one true model of necessary relations. The more strict and more ambitious versions of deep-structure social theory or positivist social science try to come close to that model and that method. The more subtle and skeptical forms (e.g., the Marxists who play up the relative autonomy of class conflict and the diversity of pathways from one mode of production to another and the economists who recognize the importance of unique and variable sets of institutional arrangements) emphasize the diverse and historical quality of their subject matter (too many causal sequences too loosely connected). From this quality they infer that social and historical explanation must remain content with less of the very same type of necessity and more of the very same type of contingency exhibited by natural science. On the other hand, we may give up on causal explanation and seek in a humanistic concern with the explication of values and intentions and the description of subjective experience an exemption from the frustrating responsibilities of causal understanding. The imitation of natural science and the abandonment of causality are equally fatal to the theoretical endeavor set out in this book. For this endeavor represents an attempt to redefine and redirect rather than merely to retrench the explanatory ambitions of deep-structure analysis and positivist social science.

The effort to generalize the thesis that everything in thought is empirical or sensitive to changes in our empirical beliefs has a broader and more surprising purpose. The philosophical, psychological, and scientific discoveries that support the generalization of the thesis also help to elucidate and to confirm the view of our relation to our contexts that animates the project of antinaturalistic social theory. For those discoveries contribute to an account of the imagination that is itself only a special case of this view of the self in context.

The Empirical Revision of Conceptions of Necessity: A Cosmological Example

Among our beliefs about the world some have a special role in determining the sense attributed to the necessity of necessary relations. These beliefs are the general truths of cosmology. Different accounts of the origin and history of the universe have different implications for our beliefs about the character of contingency. When we probe these differences we discover that there are numerous ways in which these laws can be necessary. In fact, there are as many ways as there are cosmological views. Even a minor adjustment in cosmological ideas may change the sense in which something cannot be otherwise than what it is.

Consider two of the most widely held sets of cosmological ideas at the present time: the steady state and the big bang (the "standard model"). It makes no difference to my argument whether either of them is actually true; presumably, both will be superseded by other, yet unheard-of cosmologies. But the contrast between them illustrates the relation between the content of beliefs about the universe and the sense of necessity.

The heart of the steady state theory is the idea that the average properties of the universe never change with time. As the universe expands, if it does expand, new matter is continuously created and keeps the density of the world constant. The steady state theory dispenses with the notions of a beginning and an end of the universe.

From the standpoint of the conception of necessity, the most interesting characteristic of this cosmology is its requirement that all features of the universe be self-propagating. The requirement of self-propagation implies that the laws of nature determine the actual contents of the universe. If there were no such requirement, the laws might be limited to showing how one state of affairs changed into another or what the initial properties of the universe would have had to have been in order to have produced the present universe. But those initial properties might still have been entirely different from what, in such a view, they in fact are. Thus, the steady state theory supports a stringent conception of necessity. At any time, the universe can have only those properties that make constant density possible.

But even this version of necessity is far from the idea of a world that could not have been otherwise than what it is. The picture that emerges from this cosmology cannot live up to the requirements of extreme necessitarianism. It cannot therefore provide the conception of necessity with an uncontroversial basis. In the terms of the steady state theory, two fundamental qualifications apply to any such unconditional necessity.

First, there is a metaphysical qualification. You may still ask why the universe must be so designed as to possess the quality of self-propagation. This question cannot be answered within the steady state theory itself. You can certainly develop alternative coherent views that dispense with the constancy of matter; the proof that you can is the existence of rival cosmologies. Whatever mysteries these alternative accounts may leave unexplained are no greater than the mystery of why the universe has turned out the way it has.

The other qualification to an absolute sense of necessity is the counterpart to this metaphysical query within the steady state theory itself. In order to squeeze out all but ultimate metaphysical contingency the steady state theorists would have to show that only matter with certain specified properties can have the quality of self-propagation. But even if the implications of constancy can be shown to possess this degree of determinacy, a related difficulty bars the way to absolute necessity. You cannot understand matter and its properties without actually dealing with matter. An earlier argument against extreme necessitarianism showed that no particular understanding of the physical world can be derived from pure schemes of the imagination, if only because there is no fixed limit to the schemes that may be invented. You have to study matter in order to find out how it behaves. Your ideas about what self-propagation requires already presuppose an acquaintance with a certain variety of matter.

The impossibility of an a priori deduction of the qualities of matter is of more than epistemological interest; it restricts the explanatory force of steady state cosmology or any other physical theory. You cannot ensure yourself by deduction (or by any other theoretical operation) against the possibility that an entirely different universal stuff might also be self-propagating. To ask, independently of appeals to particular experience, what kinds of matter can display the quality of self-propagation is to pose an unanswerable question. Thus, the element of arbitrariness in the initial properties of the universe, which the steady state theorists claimed to avoid, reappears, more modestly and surreptitiously, within the steady state theory. It resurfaces in the residual arbitrariness of the observed behavior of matter.

When someone who accepts this cosmology says that the laws of nature are necessary, his use of "necessity" incorporates, by reference, these several qualifications. The physical relations that, for him, appear most necessary are nevertheless necessary only in this variously qualified and contextually defined way. Everything else is less necessary. The sense in which things cannot be different from what they are remains relative to the truth of these particular cosmological ideas. Within this particular theory, necessity includes an ineradicable trace of contingency, of brute givenness, in the constitution of matter.

Now consider the major alternative to the steady state theory, the theory of an initial explosion (big bang). In one of its versions it had become successful enough to be called the standard model. Take the following speculative variation on this model. The universe began in an initial state of enormous density and pressure. It may continue to expand indefinitely into infinite rarefaction if its total mass falls below a certain critical density. But if its mass happens to exceed this point, the universe will eventually collapse back into a state like the one in which it had began. Thus, there might be a cycle of expanding and collapsing universes. The transformation of particles at each initial moment would have been so rapid that events prior to each moment of maximum collapse would have no effect on events in the ensuing world. The properties of each exploding universe would be determined solely by the events that occurred at the time of its formation.

If this variant of the standard model were true, the laws of nature would be contingent in a more far-reaching sense than is implied by the steady state theory. But again the precise sense depends on the detailed content of the cosmological ideas. You can trace the properties of the present universe back to properties it must have had at its beginning. But you cannot show that these are the only properties that any universe might have had. The moment of maximum temperature exhibits, directly, symmetries that can only be discovered scientifically and represented mathematically now that the universe has cooled down. They are the symmetries of this universe alone. Earlier or later universes may have had entirely different laws. Any view of possible universes is inconclusive because based on inferences from the actual universe. There is no way to confine the force of the element of randomness at the initial moment.

Within this cyclical extension of the standard model, the universe has a history. To state the laws of nature is not to describe or to explain all possible histories of all possible universes. Only a relative distinction exists between lawlike explanation and the narration of a one-time historical sequence. The conception of a law of nature is no more stable or self-defining than the idea of necessity itself. By laws of nature we mean nothing more than the most general invariant relations. Our view not only of what these relations are but of the kinds of relations they are varies with the substance of our beliefs about the world.

Any modification of these beliefs immediately affects the sense in which these relations cannot be otherwise than what they are. If, for example, the universe were not homogeneous and isotropic (the cosmological principle) or if there were a continuity of determination between the moment of maximum collapse and the events that preceded it, the sense of necessity would shift once again.

This summary comparison of cosmological ideas illustrates the following point. If you are asked what you mean by the necessity of the laws of nature (that is to say, by the necessity of the most necessary relations), you can legitimately respond only by laying out the substance of your cosmological and other scientific ideas. People who appeal to fixed conceptions of necessity, contingency, and possibility are simply confused.

The Thesis Generalized

The thesis that everything in our ideas about the world, including our conceptions of contingency, necessity, and possibility, is sensitive to changes in our empirical beliefs can be made clearer and more persuasive if we first recall, interpret, and relate certain seemingly unconnected discoveries in contemporary science, philosophy, and psychology. In the course of establishing the principle that there are no privileged methods or representations, these discoveries also help develop a view of the imagination. This view exemplifies and supports a conception of our relation to our contexts that inspires both this book and the constructive social theory into which it leads.

Consider first the discovery of the empirical character of space and time. Whether Riemannian geometry, for example, turns out to be true, Euclidean geometry can no longer be viewed as self-evidently correct. We should not dismiss this change in scientific belief as a mere alteration in the meaning of certain words, as if, say, the new geometry simply meant by curved line what the older one, or the layman, meant by straight line. The old meaning, or the layman's meaning, was claimed to be, if not wrong, at least merely a special case of the later view. According to the new theories the received conception of straight line fails to hold up, no matter how you interpret it. No major element in our inherited views of space and time remains untouched by similar controversies; all are drawn into the contest among rival scientific theories. Far from being refinements of ordinary perception, some of the new conceptions of space and time violate our commonsense assumptions and our perceptual biases. Though inconceivable (by which I mean untranslatable into the language of everyday perception), they may nevertheless be true.

A second discovery was that many relations previously thought to be true by definition receive an empirical interpretation in new physical theories. Consider this example taken from Hilary Putnam. For Einstein, the traditional definition of kinetic energy enshrined a conjecture about the world. In his hands that conjecture became a crude approximation to a better view of what things are actually like. Again, such a shift amounts to more than an arbitrary change in the definition of terms. What at one time seems an uncontroversial definition appears at a later time to be an empirical hypothesis incompatible with a new body of scientific ideas (in this instance, the requirement of Lorentz invariance). Any relationships that figure, or that might figure, in the statement of general laws, can meet a similar fate, even if they seem to be true by definition. For what is a matter of stipulation in one theory becomes a subject for empirical revision in another theory or at a later moment in the history of the same theory.

A third discovery was the collapse of any significant distinction between analytic and synthetic judgments. Since Kant, analytic judgments have been defined as judgments that are true by definition or judgments in which the subject "contains" the predicate. In more modern language, analytic statements are statements true by virtue of meanings, independent of fact. The concept of the analytic judgment may be saved for certain trivial statements that are truly *only* matters of definition. But if these supposedly analytic statements refer to relationships that may be subject to general laws, then they can also be revised in just the way indicated by the earlier physical example. In any sustained explanation of reality the difference between statements true as a matter of meaning (or by definition or stipulation) and statements true as a matter of fact is no more than relative. A proposition treated at one moment as a matter of linguistic convention may be reinterpreted at the next moment as a revisable statement about the world.

Even the statements less immediately connected with experience draw their justification from their membership in whole bodies of thought that are themselves vulnerable to whatever tests of success and failure apply to science in general. Each of these extended theories stands or falls as a whole rather than statement by statement. A move to rescue the theory in the face of threatening observations may lead deep into the territory of the theory and cause statements to be revised, statements that had previously been regarded as "analytic" and therefore unrevisable.

The idea of analytic truth may, indeed, be rescued by being narrowed down to statements that are true by linguistic stipulation *and* that do not employ as subjects or predicates terms that became elements in scientific controversy. But even this more trivial version of analytic truth is controversial. Whether this conception of analytic truth holds up depends, for example, on our success at finding a definition of synonymy that does not presuppose the very conception of analyticity that it is needed to elucidate.

The criticism of the distinction between the analytic and the synthetic nevertheless bears in an indirect way on the claims of an extreme necessitarianism. If there is any truly nonrevisable element in an extended explanation, then it can be nonrevisable for only one of two reasons. It may describe invariant features of reality by schemes of imagination that are themselves invariant though not analytic (e.g., Kant's synthetic a priori). But all the plausible candidates for this role, like the conceptions of space and time, have been shown to be revisable in the same way that the most general principles of any scientific theory are. Alternatively, the allegedly nonrevisable idea may be true as a matter of stipulated meanings. But then this idea is also corrigible, as a part of the body of thought to which it belongs, unless it is entirely trivial because it cannot figure within any developed theory. Triviality is the sole guarantee of immunity. Within a theory, the difference between statements entrenched against any surprising discovery and statements susceptible to disconfirmation and amendment is always a difference of degree, and an unstable one at that.

A fourth set of discoveries took place in mathematics. Many branches of mathematics cannot be fully axiomatized. Gödel showed that the consistency of a formal system adequate for number theory cannot be proved within the system and that any such system contains a formula that is not decidable and whose negation is not decidable. Church proved that there exists no decision procedure for determining whether a formula of the pure predicate calculus of the first order is decidable. Tarski generalized these discoveries into a theory of undecidability. At the same time, the antinomies of set theory became unmistakable. These antinomies have to do, in one way or another, with the impossibility of giving a precise mathematical sense to the concept of a set of all sets. No particular mathematical structure can serve as a model for the conception of a totality of all sets. More sets can always be added to any such structure.

The arguments about undecidability and the antinomies of set theory have often been invoked in defense of broad philosophical claims – such as an intuitionist view of mathematics – that they in fact fail to support. But there is one implication of these arguments that can hardly be disputed, for it merely generalizes what they actually state and prove. At any moment you can discover mathematical truths not derivable from any preexisting system of axioms and decision procedures or indeed from any system that can be completely and conclusively stated. Any formalization is incomplete in the sense that it fails to limit what people may discover to be true. No mathematical or logical system can turn out to be the context of all contexts for mathematical reasoning and invention. The powers of mathematical and logical reason cannot be circumscribed once and for all. In what sense is this state of affairs a situation that cannot be otherwise?

There is no self-evident link between this fourth set of discoveries and the three series of insights listed earlier. But their connection to one another, within the setting of the larger argument against extreme necessitarianism, may be brought out by a fifth group of findings, superficially unrelated to any of these other lines of thought. Consider the approach to cognitive development pioneered by Vygotsky and Piaget. Their central conception was the idea of the steps by which the fundamental organizing schemes of the imagination develop. They held that the most basic schemes of relations among ideas do not spring complete from the mind and do not emerge, continuously, as the gradual refinement of a single set of organizing principles. Instead, there is a series of breaks between different schemes of relationship. The child develops these schemes – ideas of chance and causality, or of entailment and contradiction, for example – together with his substantive knowledge about the world. The schemes are only relatively more invariant than the child's substantive ideas about the world. Moreover, these conceptual structures, no matter how general and how basic, do not limit, once and for all, what the child can discover about the world. The emergence of new and more successful structures of thought is preceded by activities and insights that are anomalous or unjustifiable in relation to the existing structures.

At each stage of development the formal schemes are not purely formal at all: they serve as organizing principles for some pictures of reality, and they are incompatible with other pictures. Thus, they cannot properly be regarded as a transparent medium – like a natural language – capable, with the right adjustments, of giving expression to any truth. They themselves have truth values if any complex group of beliefs does. Yet this characteristic simply serves to highlight an irreducible practical element in claims about the truth or falsehood of extended beliefs. The superseded schemes of thought are not simply flat mistakes about the world; they are less successful than the schemes that replace them in the organization of cognitive and practical activities. If you are a philosophical realist, you believe that the greater success of the later schemes reveals better insight into external reality.

This line of thinking in cognitive psychology suggests the relation between discoveries about the incompleteness of mathematical generalization and the failure of all attempts to isolate an element of thought that, whether "analytic" or "synthetic," remains true, come what may. Every significant scheme of conceptual relationships, no matter how formal it may appear, is, to an important extent, empirical. It is a more or less successful framework for hypotheses about the world and therefore, at one remove, a hypothesis itself. But no explicable set of schemes, no matter how infinitely transparent or adjustable or self-evident it may appear, draws a permanent limit around what people can discover about the world. Precisely because all formal schemes of thought are only relatively less empirical than the beliefs they help organize, every formalization of insight remains incomplete.

These views find independent support in other features of mathematics, logic, and science. Undecidability means the inability both to prove and disprove a proposition in relation to a consistent system of axioms. But the occurrence of undecidable propositions in any formal system does not mean that the system as a whole, or even the undecidable propositions it generates, is without any truth value. On the contrary, the argument can be turned on its head. The undecidable propositions may be true; their truth may be borne out by another system of axioms and another set of conceptual and practical activities into which they enter. It is just because insight can outreach consistency in this way that realism has a case: we can be assured of not being simply the unwitting prisoners of mutually reinforcing presuppositions. The discovery of undecidable propositions within a formal system can be understood as simply the first stage in a two-stage process whose second stage is the extension or reconstruction of the system itself. The reasons that justify this second step do not ultimately differ from the grounds for revising any empirical beliefs.

Thus, two related ideas unite the five sets of discoveries recalled in the preceding pages. One idea is that no significant element with any role at all to play in our developed beliefs about the world is immune to empirical disconfirmation and revision. All distinctions between invariant and revisable truths are only relative. The other unifying theme is that our power to discover what is in fact the case exceeds the limits of any list of possible forms of inquiry, inference, or discourse we can state prospectively. We can always discover more to be true than we can yet prove, verify, or even make sense of. We can always formulate retrospectively the systems, practices, or assumptions that enable us to prove, verify, or make sense of what we have discovered.

These two themes are the reverse sides of each other. They doom extreme necessitarianism. They therefore also discredit the attempt to give to our ideas about necessity, contingency, and possibility a meaning that can be specified apart from our other empirical beliefs.

These twin themes also imply a view of the imagination that exemplifies and, by exemplifying, supports the thesis about our relation to our contexts that an antinaturalistic social theory seeks to develop. Our forms of inquiry, inference, or discourse supply the contexts within which our routinized perception and thinking take place. The power to see and to think beyond what any given system of methods, rules, and premises can countenance illustrates our context-breaking capability.

HISTORICAL PARTICULARITY AND GENERAL EXPLANATIONS

The Problem Introduced

The preceding discussion has been designed to remove the obstacle that a spuriously self-evident conception of necessity, headquartered in the contemporary natural sciences, places in the way of an attempt to develop a thoroughly antinaturalistic social theory. Once we overcome this barrier, we can relate social theory to natural science without either casting it as a weak imitation of the one true scientific method or exempting it from the responsibilities of causal explanation. But no sooner do we dispose of this difficulty than we confront another very much like it: the constraint that historical particularity imposes on general explanation. The particularizing aspect of the subject matter is the existence of infinitely diverse phenomena that concern us more for what distinguishes them than for what they share. The historical aspect is the multiplication of countless causal sequences, only loosely connected and mired in unique circumstances.

The problem of historical particularity seems to impose on us the same disastrous option as the belief in an exemplary model of necessary relations. On the one hand, we may insist on that inverse relation between the prospects for generalizing explanation and the prominence of historical particularity we profess to see in natural science. The more self-confident and the less self-confident versions of deep-structure social theory and positivist social science simply strike different balances. Thus, the more self-confident variants (e.g., hard-core Marxism and game-theoretic approaches) make use of deterministic or probabilistic generalizations purporting to show that social facts are not as particularistic as they seem. The less self-confident variants (e.g., the styles of Marxism that play up the differences between national or regional histories of class struggle and the modes of positivist social science that emphasize the historically given and particularistic quality of the assumptions from which problem solving and interest accommodation must depart) trim their efforts at generalization, the better to expand their recognition of historical particularism. Still other styles of social thought try to opt out of the dilemma by professing agnosticism about causal relations and by replacing causal accounts with the description of subjective experience and the explication of values and intentions. But this escape is neither correct in its assumptions nor capable of being reconciled with the theoretical project espoused here.

The antinaturalistic view to which this book points allows for general explanations as ambitious in their scope as the deep-structure and positivist explanations they displace. Yet this view rejects the basis on which generalization rests in positivist social science. Particular practices of interest accommodation and problem solving in particular societies cannot be treated as better or worse approximations to a universal standard of rational choice. For the terms on which problem solving and interest accommodation must be practiced are decisively shaped by unique institutional and imaginative contexts that cannot be explained as the mere residues of past exercises in problem solving and interest accommodation. Nor can the basis for generalization in a politicized social theory be laws that determine the realization or the succession of social frameworks, as in deep-structure social theory. By insisting on the real though limited influence of contexts that are not themselves subject to higher-order laws and that do not even fully govern the beliefs and conduct of the people who take them for granted, the social theory foreshadowed here seems to deny itself the traditional tools for managing the tension between the commitment to general explanations and the claims of historical particularity.

The discussion follows the pattern of my earlier treatment of the problem of necessity and contingency. It begins with examples drawn from natural history that present the issue of general explanation and historical particularity as it arises outside the area of social studies. It then goes on to develop the central point made by the use of these examples: the idea that as historical particularity undercuts certain styles of general explanation it opens opportunities for other styles.

Once we grasp these opportunities, we free ourselves from the hold of a single, exclusive model of explanation and from belief in a simple inverse relation between the prominence of historical particulars and the capability for explanatory generalization. The earlier analysis of contingency and necessity helped vindicate the view of our relation to our contexts that an antinaturalistic social theory seeks to develop. The following discussion of generalization and historicity specifies the explanatory opportunities on which such a social theory must rely as it sets out on what may at first appear to be a self-destructive course.

Historical Particularity as a Challenge to General Explanation: Examples from Natural History

Imagine, reader, that you were a neophyte student of mineralogy at some time in the twentieth century. (The mineralogical example suits my purpose especially well because it is drawn from the realm of inanimate nature and skirts the special problems that the emergence of life introduces.) You would be struck by the fact that the genesis and properties of the different kinds of rocks you studied were not equally amenable to explanation by reference to laws couched in general physical and chemical terms. (By laws in this setting I mean not the regularities themselves but the propositions that state them.)

The igneous rocks, which crystallize from a molten liquid, could be explained directly by reference to the composition, temperature, and cooling rate of the parent magma. On the basis of these factors, you could formulate a well-defined classification: there was no confusing the phaneritic and the aphanitic varieties, either with respect to origin or to properties.

The metamorphic rocks, which result from the effects of temperature and cooling on preexisting rocks, presented greater difficulties. Composition, temperature, and cooling determine the results, only much more imperfectly. Many other factors may be at work, and they may combine in different historical sequences. Thus the broad classification of these rocks into foliated and unfoliated is much looser than the classification of the igneous rocks. The categories of classification define only the grossest properties of the individual rock: no piece of gneiss is very much like any other piece. There are multiple pathways to the same final piece of gneiss. The metamorphic rocks are sunk in historical particularities. These historical particularities made successful reduction of the mineralogical facts to physical and chemical laws – or indeed to any laws at all – much less successful. They also weakened the force of any typology and added to the individuality of members of a type.

You found these difficulties further aggravated in the study of the third major type of rock. Sedimentary rocks are produced by the settling of particles through aqueous media, by organic secretion, or by direct precipitation out of water or brines. Each of these processes works through particular combinations and sequences. These sequences cannot be shown to have simple or close connections to general physical and chemical laws, nor can their rich detail be explained by a small number of laws of any other sort. The classification of sedimentary rocks is complex and tentative; there is even a special branch of geology – stratigraphy – devoted to the topic. Each rock body is an entity with a multifarious individuality of its own.

Thus, within a single field of study, you could witness large disparities in the role performed by generalizing laws in the explanation of particulars. With the move from the igneous to the metamorphic and from the metamorphic to the sedimentary came a steady decrease in the power of known physical and chemical laws to determine, closely and immediately, the details of the phenomena. The difficulty in reducing mineralogical explanations to physical or chemical laws amounted to a difficulty in reducing them to lawlike statements of any brand; there were no laws of any other kind.

The chief obstacle to reduction and generalization was the idea that historical particularities played a much larger role in the formation of some rocks than of others. Three elements in this idea of historicity should be distinguished. Consider them one by one, and notice how each has manifestations far beyond mineralogy.

The first and most important element in the idea of historicity is an increase in the scope of what has to be taken as given in comparison to what can be explained as a regularity. In the standard scientific explanations certain elements are just unexplained facts: the initial conditions or the values of the variables. These facts may or may not be elucidated by other lawlike explanations. To the extent that they are, you can hope eventually to draw the several explanations together into a unified theory.

To say that a natural science becomes increasingly historical is, in this sense, simply to say that more and more of the facts have to be taken as given or as subject to fragmentary explanations whose ultimate connection remains unclear. The determining power of the regularities – or of the lawlike statements that enunciate them – becomes correspondingly weaker. All the explanations together fail to add up to anything like a sufficient condition for the results.

In a more historically oriented branch of natural science, lawlike explanations do not suddenly cease to be applicable, nor are they replaced by explanations of a clearly distinct type. Darwinian selection theory, for example, even when combined with microbiology seemed to leave a great deal unexplained. (For example, why did ancestral species continue to coexist alongside their evolutionary descendants? Why did diverse species flourish in an absolutely homogeneous environment? Why, apart from constraints of physical design or from an independent genetic directionality, did animal populations develop so many traits that seemed to serve no reproductive or competitive good?) In order to make Darwinism's rather weak, though certainly not trivial or tautologous, explanations work, you had to resort to a host of givens that were themselves unexplained or that became the subjects of other explanatory accounts with a similarly compromised force. Other elements in the idea of natural history help define more precisely the sense in which natural history is historical and committed, for that reason, to special styles of explanation.

One of these additional elements is the existence of a large number of causal processes that develop on their own terms, with only loose or ultimate ties to one another. Consider, for example, the relation of continental drifts, as studied by plate tectonics, to competitive natural selection in determining the characteristics of the higher mammals. Suppose that the animals in one isolated continent had been subject to intense noncompetitive extinctions as a result of severe climatic conditions and that the survivors had benefited from a development of cranial capacity and other related advantages. Suppose that for reasons also associated with the unique relations between the shape of the land masses and the diffusion of animal populations, the mammals favored by the noncompetitive extinctions happened to be placentals. Suppose that a marsupial mammal population had long since arrived in another continent. There, unthreatened by extinction it had failed to develop the capacities of its placental counterparts. Later, the two continents were reconnected. The more capable or versatile placentals had gone on to liquidate their marsupial rivals. At the start, there had been no inherent structural or functional link between the distinctive traits of marsupial or placental mammals and the capacities that ultimately tipped the scales in favor of the invading placentals.

That placentals came to hold the main line of mammalian evolution and that marsupials had eventually been relegated to minor status resulted in part from the ways in which the floating of the continents on the surface of the planet happened to interact with other factors more closely linked to animal evolution itself. Compared with these other factors the particular effect of continental drift was simply a fluke. The fluke might nevertheless be significant if the resulting placental option turned out to impose distinctive constraints or to create distinctive opportunities in future animal evolution. In some ultimate sense, the laws – if there were any – that governed these heterogeneous strands in animal history might be reducible to a single set of more basic regularities. Even if this reduction could someday be effected, it would be compromised by many mediating links of explanation. For practical purposes, the movements of the continents would continue to be regarded as an independent factor in explaining particular incidents in the history of animal populations.

The example is both simplified and hypothetical. The theoretical assumptions it relies on may be superseded. The situation it imagines may never have been realized (though it may well describe an aspect of the actual history of South American marsupials). But the complication it illustrates – the development of independent causal processes, often in great number – is familiar to every naturalist. It is part of what made the study of stratified rocks difficult. It helps define the counterpart to history in nature, or the idea of a natural history.

Another defining element in this idea of natural history is the importance of sequence. This element has two aspects: one has to do with properties of the sequences themselves; the other, with a feature of our knowledge of them.

Many processes in natural history share an attribute that may be called the property of divergent sequence. Consider the strongest case. The same events, run in a different order, prove to have different effects. This, too, is a naturalist's commonplace. In late twentieth-century biology, for example, the average genetic structure of any biological population depends on the historical sequence of environments, not just on their static probability distribution. Identical selection pressures, in reverse order, produce different histories and different average behavior. In an average probabilistic system, information grows and uncertainties about characteristic properties decline as the number of observations (like the number of throws of the dice) increases. This fact is the gist of the law of large numbers. But this property of perfectible information fails to characterize the relation of a genetic pool to environmental constraints: gene frequency may, for instance, respond more vigorously to recent environments than to remote ones.

This feature of natural sequence would not by itself add anything to the idea of a natural history if the naturalist's knowledge were independent of the sequences that had actually occurred: if he could confidently formulate the theory of all possible sequences and fully account for the occurrence and qualities of any actual sequence within the larger realm. He is prevented from doing this, however, by a basic characteristic of the historical science he practices. The naturalist's knowledge of events does not depend solely on a general physical, chemical, or biological theory of possible states of affairs. It depends as well on inferences drawn from the surprising world he actually encounters. To this extent he understands phenomena less by locating them within a well-defined system of possible natural worlds than by observing and imagining marginal variations in the world that actually exists and in the unique and irreversible history that has actually happened.

The coexistence of this feature of knowledge with the property of divergent sequence described in the preceding page has an important consequence. It is always hard for the naturalist to tell which aspects of the developed natural world are due to the particular divergent sequences that have occurred and which aspects hold, no matter what the sequence. The problem recurs at many different levels of generality and scope. All the available explanations put together could not have predicted the distinctive form or even the overall direction of natural history. Scientific insight makes merely retrospective sense of the glittering diversity and the implausible inventions of nature.

The qualities of historicity are more prominent in some natural sciences than in others. All these qualities, however, are drastically accentuated when you pass from natural science to social theory. And many factors other than the independence of causal processes and the importance of divergent sequence also enter into the historicity of social worlds. What was true of the study of sedimentary rocks by comparison to the analysis of igneous rocks holds, in spades, for social thought by contrast to natural history.

So long as the deep-structure theories of social transformation retained a semblance of plausibility, the implications of historicity remained in check. There was hope of finding laws which, although not cast in physical terms, might achieve a generality and determining power comparable to those of natural science. The disintegration of these theories seems to undermine all defenses against extreme historical particularity. To take sides with the party in each area of social thought that claims that everything is politics seems to carry historicity to the extreme. But the further you move in this direction, the more you seem to abandon the task of offering general causal explanations or, indeed, any explanation at all.

It is not enough to invoke the idea of a mode of narrative explanation that accounts for events merely by placing them in a rich context of sequence and by appealing to vague criteria of plausible connection. If there is anything to narrative explanation other than a still weaker and more fragmented version of the kind of context-dependent analysis used in stratigraphy, you need to know what it is. In the study of history and society as in every branch of thought, you can understand what things are only by resorting to a view of transformative possibility. But how can such a view be found and justified if the particulars of history devour all insight?

Again, it does not suffice to say that the space left vacant by generalizing explanation can be occupied by an intentional analysis: the comparison of social events and their consequences to the ideas and intentions of historical agents. You cannot move from the ideas and intentions of individuals to the large-scale structures of society and the long-run transformations of history unless you can find guidance in a more general conception of social reality and social opportunity. You cannot derive such a conception, in any simple or direct way, from the ideas and intentions of particular individuals and groups. Every approach to history has to account for a sense of constraints that hardly seem reducible to the intentions and ideas of particular individuals or (if you knew how to sum them up) of everyone's intentions put together. Every approach must allow for the possibility that the relation of actions to results over time may be shaped by forces the agents neither intend nor understand.

The Explanatory Advantages of Weakened Constraint

The geological example shows that the problem of historical particularism is not unique to social study. In fact, the example even suggests the possibility of styles of general explanation that can turn what appears to be an explanatory embarrassment into an explanatory advantage. To develop this suggestion, the following analysis distinguishes three orders of reality. These orders, which only imperfectly parallel the familiar distinction among inanimate, living, and social phenomena, are marked by distinctive types of relations, requiring and justifying distinctive styles of explanation. The main point is to show how what may at first appear to be weaker orders, resulting in weaker explanations, are in fact different orders, permitting different types of explanation.

My earlier treatment of contingency and necessity concluded with an account of modern discoveries that had the incidental advantage of exemplifying, elucidating, and supporting the thesis about our relation to our contexts worked out in this antinaturalistic social theory. Similarly, the following remarks strengthen this thesis by showing how it may be reconciled with the science of our day. Thus, the distinction among types of order is a quasi-empirical myth, a story about the reconciliation of historically specific and transitory forms of knowledge and discourse. This story is no more uncontroversial than the ideas it brings together. Nor is it the sole possible way to represent a peaceful coexistence between natural science and politicized social theory within a larger view of imagination and reality.

The three kinds of order I have in mind may be roughly described as an order of deterministic and probabilistic processes, an order of self-regulating and self-referring structures that interact with probabilistic and deterministic influences, and an order of imaginative and institutional frameworks. Such frameworks differ from the self-regulating and self-referring structures that distinguish the second type of order because they neither control their own transformation nor follow a pattern set by higher-order laws. Whenever one of these three types of order dissipates, another seems to be superimposed upon it. Each supervening order brings with it an explanatory advantage that compensates for the explanatory crisis induced by the loosening of more rigid or determining varieties of order. These discontinuities in the modes of order and explanation do not coincide in any simple fashion with the boundaries between inanimate and living matter, or between living matter and society. Nor do the supervening forms of order and explanation fully displace the forms on which they supervene.

In the course of this overlaying of forms of order and explanation, the distinction between what must be accepted as given (by way of initial conditions or the value of the variables) and what can be rationally explained begins to wane. The contrast between order and disorder loses its clarity, together with the contrast between the nature of formative structure in theory and in the phenomena that theory explains. The conceptions of reason and order become increasingly subtle and capacious.

A scientific theory abstracts from phenomena to focus on particular facts. Within these limits it distinguishes what can be determined by explanation from what has to be accepted as merely given. It simplifies in order to bring out the structural and functional aspects of a complex, underlying reality. A parallel process is at work in nature itself. This process generates a first type of order.

This first-level order relies on a constraining scheme that simplifies an aspect of matter and, through this simplification, allows structures to be specified and functions to be coordinated. Such a scheme thereby creates opportunities for further transformation. Constraint, coordination, and the creation of developmental opportunities are linked. The chemical bond, for example, may be understood as a simplified structure of this sort with respect to the microscopic, quantum description of matter. Whatever the ultimate dynamic reason for the emergence of such constraints, their effect on the organization and history of nature is unmistakable.

In order to perform a coordinating role at "higher levels," a simplifying structure may require an optimum level of detail. It cannot specify too many details (like a crystal) or too few (like a gas). As you move toward the realm of living matter, you find that the simplifying and liberating traits acquire characteristics of which they earlier showed only faint traces. One of these traits is the arbitrary connection between the uses to which the coordinating structures put certain pieces of matter and the physical structure of these pieces (e.g., the amino acid assignments in the genetic mechanism). Another feature is the capacity of the constraining structure to refer to itself:

to contain messages about its own order. This capacity is indispensable to the self-replication and the developmental regulation of living matter.

The simplifying structures with these twin characteristics of self-regulation and self-replication share so many features and give rise to so many common problems that such structures deserve to be considered a second type of order. The emergence of this second mode of order runs parallel to the aggravation of the conditions that imply ever more severe degrees of the historical particularism familiar to the natural historian. The parallelism is only rough: the causes of the dissipation of one type of order relate only indirectly and obscurely to the causes of the rise of another. Thus, historicity may in some cases go very far with a relatively modest development of structures that possess the qualities of self-regulation and self-reference. The most history-dependent geological phenomena prove the point.

Whenever such self-referring and self-regulating structures do emerge, they compensate for the disadvantages caused by the march of historicity. Deterministic or probabilistic processes operate on these simplifying structures (e.g., the influence of natural selection on genetic endowments). What appears at first as pure randomness and particularity in the phenomena results in part from the imposition of an intermediate level of order between the general forces of the physical world and the organism and its life. The operations of this intermediate order – the coordinating structures or "programs" – can be understood by suitably adjusted and reinterpreted analogies of purpose and programming drawn from a human setting. This understanding softens the contrast between what is arbitrarily given, as initial conditions, and what is rationally explained, by lawlike statements. It brings design and accident closer together. It makes the occasions and devices of limiting structure and developmental opportunity intersect.

It is tempting to imagine that our social and intellectual lives exemplify the same self-referring and self-regulating type of order that occupies a central place in biology and natural history. The social counterparts to the second type of order are the practical arrangements and the preconceptions about the possible and desirable forms of sociability that, together, shape a complex world of routine deals and conflicts. The cognitive parallels to the second type of order are the substantive and methodological presuppositions that shape our ordinary explanatory and discursive practice. But there is a basic objection to the analogy between these cognitive schemes or social frameworks and the self-regulating and self-referring structures of which the biologist speaks. Different as they may be from each other, our theoretical presupposition and our social contexts share a way of fitting in our lives that announces the presence of a third, distinct type of order. People act both as if their thoughts and actions were governed by institutional and imaginative contexts with these same self-referring and self-regulating properties (as well as by a brute residuum of material influences unassimilated or untamed by these structures) and as if they could think and act, at a higher level, where they are ruled by no such frameworks or schemes. Sometimes one and sometimes the other aspect of their situation seems preeminent, but neither is ever entirely absent. This pattern of simultaneous structure dependence and structure transcendence is so basic that it applies to the most diverse and seemingly unrelated aspects of human experience.

Thus, we can always discover more than our established modes of discourse allow us to validate, verify, or make sense of. No part of thought is invariant; every part can be reinvented. The capacity to replace even the ideas or the methods that seem most uncontroversial already presupposes an ability to think beyond them to a point where the presuppositions become unclear. Revised presuppositions emerge retrospectively from the insights that have been gained. No one conceptual practice, nor any prospective list of conceptual practices, exhausts the inventive and revelatory powers of reason.

The same features that characterize systems of thought and the ideas by which they are revised also mark social orders and the practical or imaginative activities by which they are made and remade. Each social world conditions insight and action. But no social world, however closed and self-sustaining it may appear, can defend itself against actions and thoughts that cross its boundaries and that undermine its core practices and beliefs. The low-level practical and imaginative conflicts indispensable to the maintenance of these societies are only contained versions of the more intense struggles that can destroy these same societies. The direct, passionate relations among individuals already contain, in undefined, undeveloped, and unreflective form, materials for forms of sociability excluded by the dominant institutional and imaginative order of society. As conflict becomes more intense and as its scope widens, the signs of this ability to think and act beyond the boundaries become more visible.

Relations among people have, to an even greater degree, the same properties of self-reference and self-regulation that characterize the structures in the biological realm. Two forces qualify the influence of these social counterparts to biological structures.

The first such force is the existence of causal effects not fully integrated into the collective structures of belief and practice. These influences begin in the biological endowment of humanity and the facts of material scarcity. But they also include the totality of events that mankind has been through, together or in separate nations and classes. This half-forgotten history shapes people's dispositions and hopes even when their overt forms of belief and practice fail openly to reflect it. Such qualifications to the primacy of the coordinating structures have counterparts in the earlier, biological style of order: the deterministic and probabilistic processes that act on the organizing constraints. But even the nature of this qualification is subtly changed by the appearance of another qualification lacking any parallel in the earlier realm of order: the capacity to think and act beyond the limits imposed by any extant or nameable structures. The interplay between the influence of these cognitive schemes or these institutional and imaginative frameworks of social life and our power to defy these frameworks and schemes defines a third type of order.

Thus, there appear to be two basic sources of explanatory embarrassment in social theory. All the defining features of historical particularism appear with aggravated force. At the same time, the surrogate order that might have compensated for this weakening and provided a basis for generalizing explanation becomes less determinate. The institutional and imaginative frameworks that represent the imperfect analogy to the self-regulating and self-referring structures of the biologist do not fully govern either their own transformation or the routine activities they help shape. Nor are they themselves ruled by probabilistic or deterministic laws.

In these embarrassments, however, you can find a compensating explanatory advantage. This whole book represents an effort to describe the advantage. To draw out the implications of the fact that people can make and imagine more than what any enumerable set of structures can account for is to take sides with the extremists who claim that everything is politics. Everything is politics not in the sense that the will and the imagination work without resistance but in the sense that there is no predefined limit and no metalogic to their destructive and creative work. To find and to exploit the explanatory advantage is to begin developing an antinaturalistic theory of society.

By way of anticipation this advantage may be described in three equivalent ways. Only the entire theory can show the precise sense of each formulation and the basis for their equivalence. But the main idea can be grasped, tentatively, even before the theory has been laid out. Each aspect of the compensating advantage has a forerunner in the part of nature and natural science that deals with the other types of order: the type marked by deterministic and probabilistic processes and the type distinguished by the interplay between such processes and self-regulating and self-referring structures on which and through which they act.

A first statement of the advantage draws out the consequences of the relative convergence, in the realm of society and its history, between the nature of theory and the character of the reality that theory describes and explains. I have already pointed out that any simplifying order in nature can be interpreted as a counterpart to the simplifying and explanatory order of a scientific theory. The analogy becomes more precise when we reach the self-referring and self-regulating structures that characterize living matter. There, the constraints display most of the features of human symbolism, including the traits of self-reference and of arbitrary connection between signifier and signified. But there is one characteristic of explanatory systems that the coordinating structures in the biological and proto-biological realm possess only marginally or obliquely if at all. This missing element is precisely the capacity to think and act beyond the limits of determinate structure without ever being able to reach unconditional insight and satisfaction.

No mind and no society can ever make the structure that would never again need to be broken for the sake of further satisfaction and insight. This inability to reach the definitive context coexists with the power to shatter all particular contexts. Thus, the similarity between the nature of structure in the mind and in society increases, and increases all the more as society emancipates itself from false constraints and realizes in its everyday life a condition of experimental freedom.

Social theory is not imposed on a reality arranged according to principles different from the principle that generates its own intellectual order. Everything people say and think about themselves and their life in common becomes the sketch of a picture that social theory can at best correct and complete. (This is the element of truth in the methodological programs that look to an "interpretive understanding" beyond mere "explanation.") All history, finished and future, represents a testing ground for the conjectures of social theory. And social theory itself becomes a weapon and a guide in the imaginative and practical conflicts that make and undo social worlds.

Together with this unique intimacy of social thought with its subject matter goes a special variety of perfection: the perfection of a mode of discourse that is itself an example (or a close counterpart) of the same mode of order it tries to disclose in the phenomena it studies. A corollary of this affinity and this perfection is the evasion of any rigid contrast between order and accident, the rationally explained and the gratuitously given. A theory capable of imagining a being whose thoughts and actions no enumerable set of imaginative or institutional orders can contain is a theory that refuses to contrast brute facticity and rigid schematism. It progresses by the refinement of its operative notion of what order can be like and what reason represents. Each step in this advance allows it to take possession of more of its subject matter.

A second statement of the explanatory advantage focuses on the way in which the repeated destruction or enlargement of determinate imaginative or institutional order, when carried to an extreme of uncertainty and iconoclasm, provides social theory with a theme. The constraints that distinguish the first two types of order already show how simplifying structures can multiply the developmental options available to an organic or inorganic system. In the macrophenomena of evolution we can see how the power not to depend on any particular environment may override the advantage of perfect suitability to a particular environment. Nothing succeeds like plasticity.

Pushed further, much further, in history than in the living, non-human world, this enormous negative capability, this endless work of denial, becomes a force in the organization of practical or imaginative activities that counts more than any particular causal influence or affirmative commitment. For the social theory into which this book leads, the institutional and imaginative frameworks of social life differ in the force with which they control us as well as in their distinctive content. Some frameworks go further than others in effacing the contrast between context-respecting routine and context-transforming struggle and in diminishing the constraints that rigid roles and hierarchies impose on practical collaboration and passionate attachment. From the more revisable, hierarchy-subverting structures we may gain a host of advantages: some related to the practical benefits of openness to experimentation, others to the fuller reconciliation between our need for engagement in group life and our fear of the dependence and depersonalization such engagement may bring, and still others to an emancipation from a superstitious identification of particular social forms with the permanent requirements of human association. A relentlessly antinaturalistic social theory takes modern historicism to the final step: understanding that the relation between freedom and structure is itself up for grabs in history. Such a theory explores the interplay between the attractions of empowerment through the invention of less imprisoning social contexts and the countervailing forces that prod us into the prison.

Consider a third equivalent formulation of the explanatory advantage that accompanies the explanatory embarrassments of social and historical thought. The double failure of the formative institutional and imaginative contexts of social life fully to determine us or to be themselves fully determined ensures that society and history lack a script. The central place that such an automatism might have occupied is filled up instead by the living, suffering, aspiring individual and by the open-ended experiences of practical collaboration or passionate attachment. These experiences constantly outreach, defy, and subvert the institutional and imaginative frameworks that partly shape them. Forever hesitating between the desire to credit a partial and provisional structure with absolute reality and value and the iconoclastic rejection of each context-bound insight and satisfaction, the person becomes the ultimate subject matter and the real protagonist. In studying society or personality we always get a second chance. Every truth about people can be seen twice: as a truth about societies and their history and as a truth about the individual and his passions.

8

Conclusion

The Radical Project and the Criticism of False Necessity

THIS book develops a polemic with a constructive point. The central thesis of the book combines an intellectual and a political hope. Modern social thought, I have argued, has begun to forge the instruments with which to carry to extremes the idea that originally inspired it – the view of society as artifact. Modern students of society and history have done the most for the execution of this constructive task precisely when they seemed to be at their most negativistic. For it is then that they have been most relentless in destroying the neonaturalistic assumptions on which comprehensive social and historical explanations have so often relied. If only we push yet further the criticism of these assumptions and bring together its many strands, we may be able to imagine ourselves more fully as the context-bound yet context-resistant and context-revising agents we really are. We may learn how to use the distinction between formative contexts and formed routines without having to rely on the ideas traditionally bound up with this distinction. Among such ideas are the conception that the institutional and imaginative frameworks of social life are indivisible and uncombinable units, the appeal to determinate constraints or developmental tendencies that generate a short list of possible types of social organization or necessary stages of social evolution, and the belief that we can change the content but not the character of formative contexts – their relation to the context-revising freedom of the agents who inhabit them.

The development of an antinecessitarian social theory contributes to the advancement of the radical project – the cause that liberals, leftists, and modernists (those radicals of personal relations) confusedly share. Such a social theory promotes the radical cause because it helps form a social understanding freer from the taints of institutional and structure fetishism.

Institutional fetishism is the imagined identification of highly detailed and largely accidental institutional arrangements with comprehensive and vague ideals like freedom and equality. The institutional fetishist may be the classical liberal who identifies representative democracy and the market economy with a makeshift set of governmental and economic arrangements that happen to have triumphed in the course of modern European history. He may also be the hard-core Marxist who treats these same arrangements as an indispensable stage toward a future, regenerate order whose content he sees as both preestablished and resistant to credible description. He may even be the positivist social scientist or the hard-nosed political or economic manager who accepts current practices as an uncontroversial framework for interest accommodation and problem solving. Institutional fetishism draws its inspiration from styles of social thought that either downplay the importance of the framework–routine distinction or tie this distinction to the characteristic ambitions and assumptions of deep-logic social theory.

Structure fetishism is a related mistake cast at a higher order of generality. The structure fetishist denies that we can change the quality as well as the content of formative contexts – the extent to which they impose on our practical, passionate, and cognitive relations a script we cannot easily rewrite. He may be the historicizing skeptic turned apologist who tells us that, denied transcendent standards of value and insight, all we can do is to choose a social or mental world and to play by its rules. Alternatively, he may be the defiant and despairing negativist who asserts that we can find freedom only in the perennial rebellion against all fixed conventions and institutions. Each of these two variants of structural fetishism is just the reverse side of the other. Each fails to take modern historicism to the final step: understanding that the relation between our contexts and our freedom is itself up for grabs in history. The implications of structure fetishism are more familiar in debates about knowledge and morals than in controversies about social reorganization. But its political importance becomes clear once you begin to appreciate how much the varieties of human empowerment depend upon the development of practices, institutions, and beliefs that soften the contrast between framework-preserving routine and framework-transforming conflict.

Institutional fetishism and structure fetishism keep the radical endeavor fragmented and disoriented, divided into rival camps. For lack of apparent alternatives, each camp holds fast to assumptions about personal and collective possibility that have become literally incredible. We cannot rid ourselves of these assumptions simply by announcing that we no longer believe in them. For we cannot think about social frameworks and their remaking without having something to put in place of the deep-structure or positivist ideas that give life to institutional and structure fetishism. The replacement may look like another comprehensive theory (i.e., super-theory), or like a range of critical and constructive practices that do not add up to a theory (i.e., ultra-theory). But, whatever its distinctive character, the alternative approach has to be fought for.

To be sure, people can come up with programmatic proposals for the reform of social institutions or personal relations by just refusing to take seriously the preconceptions of deep-structure social theory or positivist social science. But the more far-reaching and the further removed from the pressures of a particular circumstance their reconstructive ideas are, the harder the proponent of alternative social arrangements will find it to dispense with a way of thinking about the institutional and imaginative contexts of social life, about their composition and reconstruction.

In the absence of the ideas that enable us to gain critical distance on the established settings of social life, the transformative imagination can easily be disarmed. For lack of a credible view of how social worlds get remade we come to measure the realism of a proposal by its closeness to whatever exists. The utopian plans we then devise turn out on closer inspection to be merely the announcement of a longing. We erect whatever we feel to be missing in our current experience of social life into the generative principle of an alternative social order. The utopianism that merely inverts what it cannot believably reimagine or effectively reconstruct presents as great a danger to our transformative hopes as the institutional and structure fetishism with which it so often coexists. Like the fetishistic habit, the utopian inversion has to be corrected the hard way – by an exercise of understanding that develops hand in hand with a collective practice of transformation.

The social theory anticipated in this book confronts a central riddle of social and historical explanation. We act according to two different and seemingly incommensurable logics. On the one hand, we behave as if we were the passive objects of the formative institutional and imaginative contexts of our societies and the victims or beneficiaries of the tendencies and constraints that shape these frameworks of social life. On the other hand, however, we sometimes think and act as if our pious devotion to the practical or argumentative routines imposed by these structures had been just a ploy, to be continued until the propitious occasion for more open defiance. When our defiance of the context goes far enough, it seems also to disregard any system of lawlike tendencies and constraints we can prospectively describe. The first logic – the logic of routinization – may appear to prevail most of the time. The second logic – the logic of transgression – may often seem confined to exceptional moments of runaway social conflict and radical social invention. We may therefore be tempted to disregard the second logic for most purposes of social description and explanation. For it is troublesome as well as anomalous; it seems to impose a limit upon our explanatory capabilities.

But the history of the most ambitious efforts of modern social thought is the history of our failure to dispose of the problem of routinization and transgression by disregarding it. The logic of context breaking persists as an inconvenient residue in even the most routinized social situations. The ease with which people pass from one logic to another depends on the content and character of the society's formative arrangements and preconceptions. We cannot explain the occurrence and outcome of context breaking by closed historical or social laws. Our inability to explain the remaking of our contexts in this way changes the sense in which we can be said to obey our social contexts, when we do obey them. This capacity-producing incapacity discredits the attempt to present the routines of a social world as the work of practical and imaginative structures shaped by constraints or tendencies precise and irresistible enough to predetermine possible types of social organization and unstoppable sequences of social evolution.

Contemporary students of society and history often cling to the residues of deep-structure and positivist assumptions, fearing that to recognize the unstable relation between these two logics of social life would be to give up on all but the most causally agnostic forms of social study. People with transformative commitments have an additional reason for concern. Explanatory skepticism threatens to deprive them of the intellectual tools with which to affirm a larger conception of the possible against the delusive self-evidence of current arrangements.

But this book has argued that the fear is misplaced. To recognize our context-breaking capabilities is the beginning of insight, not the abandonment of explanatory ambitions. We do not need the idea that society and history follow a script. We can dispense with the thesis of the script and still develop a social theory that recognizes the institutional and imaginative contexts of social life and illuminates the ways in which we can change these contexts in content and character.

The sole persuasive demonstration of our ability to get rid of the notion of the script is actually to do it and to show how the result makes a difference for the way we understand the content, the claims, and the prospects of such commitments as the radical cause. *Politics* sets out to execute just this plan. In this introductory book I have argued that many of the conjectures, categories, and methods required for the execution of this task already lie at hand. They are the by-products of the very processes of intellectual disappointment and self-criticism that seem to have brought us ever closer to an unqualified skepticism.

If we succeed at this effort we can turn what looked like intellectual disintegration into a more powerful vindication of the original, inspiring ideas of modern social thought. To succeed we must learn to get intellectual nourishment wherever we can find it, even in a seeming desert of theoretical disillusionment. We must refuse to give up on the causal explanation of social facts and historical events but must nevertheless insist on enlarging our repertory of explanatory practices. We must distinguish the styles of social explanation that we want to establish and those we want to reject, without taking a stand on the broader and vaguer conundrums of free will and determinism. And we must acknowledge the existence of different routes to the same intellectual goal, differences exemplified by the contrast between super-theory and ultra-theory.

We can find encouragement not only in the constructive work that modern social thought has silently begun to accomplish but also in the emergence in many areas of thought of an image of man that emphasizes both his context-bound predicament and his context-smashing capabilities. Thus, the redirection of social thought along the lines foreshadowed in this book represents an attempt to bring our practices of social explanation and social criticism more fully into accord with our experience and our conception of ourselves. It takes a theory that dissociates the distinction between formative contexts and formed routines from the project of deep-structure social theory to imagine the activities of a free being. It takes such a theory to imagine agents who themselves possess imagination. For the imagination is less a separate faculty, as the old school psychology described it, than a quality of all our mental faculties: the quality of seeing more things and making more numerous and varied connections among ideas about things than any prospective list of theories and discourses can countenance.

The imagination works by a principle of sympathy with the suppressed and subversive elements in experience. It sees the residues, memories, and reports of past or faraway social worlds and neglected or obscure perceptions as the main stuff with which we remake our contexts. It explains the operation of a social order by representing what the remaking of this order would require. It generalizes our ideas by tracing a penumbra of remembered or intimated possibility around present or past settlements, and it then subjects this enlarged sense of possibility to the tests of further comparison and practice. By all these means it undermines the identification of the actual with the possible.

Close to the heart of the social theory anticipated in this book lies an idea that long predates modern times and that reappears in many branches of contemporary social thought. According to this view, society moves forever between hot and cold, fluid and rigid, moments.

There is the moment of widening conflict over the basic terms of people's access to one another and to the resources of society. At such times people catch a glimpse of the indefinite range of social possibilities. As long as the fighting goes on and no one gives up, who knows what might come? But this openness is just the reverse side of indefinition and violence. Wills remain in contest and imaginations sealed off from one another. Then comes the moment in the life of society when one faction achieves a victory great enough to impose an order. The open-ended fighting turns into a set of accepted roles and hierarchies, and the relations among people become enmeshed in a thick tangle of accepted dependencies. The ideological free-for-all gives way to authoritative beliefs about the proper form of social relations in different domains of social existence. A detailed though always ambiguous and contested image of civilized life comes to stand in place of the open-ended idea of society. Self-deception, self-concern, and sheer exhaustion combine to encourage the substitution. Bewitch us, bewitch us, men and women cry, bewitch us and enslave us, that we may live!

Thus, civilization, for all its practical and spiritual accomplishments, appears as the child of an illusion and a surrender: the illusion that there is something natural and permanent about a particular plan of social coexistence, the surrender that stopped the fighting. The trance disappears into struggle, and is then restored.

These two moments, of trance and struggle, mingle in the real life of society: an undercurrent of conflict and disbelief always counteracts the routines of dependence and deference. Society, no matter how impregnable it seems to its inhabitants, always stands at the edge of the cliff. The petty practical quarrels and normative disputes, endlessly refought to reproduce a social world in the face of divergent interests and changing circumstance, can escalate at any moment into broader and more intense conflicts that put this world at risk.

The most ambitious modern social theories – theories that combine deep-structure assumptions and functionalist methods – have subjected this ancient view to three transformations. Nowhere can these revisions be more clearly seen than in Marx's social theory, the most powerful example of the synthesis of deep-structure approaches and functional explanations.

The first change was to give greater precision to the description of the social orders that undergo periodic upheaval. The idea of a system of formative arrangements and beliefs, identified by its effect on certain activities, came to describe the thing that undergoes periodic breakdown and reconsolidation. Thus, in Marx's theory it is modes of production that are occasionally disrupted and replaced.

The second revision was to put a conception of progressive evolution in place of a picture of random or cyclical change. The history of breakdown and reconstruction follows a preestablished sequence. This sequence has a developmental logic that theory can make explicit.

The third shift was to represent this perennial smashing of social worlds as the occasion for the development of human faculties. In particular the progression of social orders promises both to develop our practical productive capabilities and to cleanse social life of its taint of enslavement: the enslavement of the occupants of some social stations to the occupants of other stations and the enslavement of the oppressed and the oppressors alike to the requirements of stereotyped stations. Thus, the repeated disintegration of societies represents an ordeal of collective empowerment rather than the reenactment of a fruitless disaster.

The social theory to which this book points imposes on the old theme of the trance and the struggle, of the rigid and the fluid moments of social life, a further series of transformations. These additional revisions root out the necessitarian assumptions of deepstructure theory. But as the earlier discussion of necessity and contingency suggests, antinecessitarianism is no more than a convenient polemical label for a connected series of critical and constructive arguments on behalf of a change in explanatory style. The alternative explanatory moves are indeed less restrictive. They do not generate groups of necessary and sufficient conditions for the remaking of formative contexts. They do not predict a one-to-one relation between particular sets of formative institutions and beliefs and particular levels of success in the development of our practical capabilities or in the diminishment of subjugation and depersonalization. They do not treat the institutional and imaginative frameworks as indivisible units. They do not give us a list of possible types or necessary stages of social organization.

But the most important fact about the alternative explanatory moves is not that they are less restrictive but just that they are different. They account for constraints on the recombination and replacement of the elements that compose every social framework without treating such frameworks as examples of indivisible types in a predetermined list or sequence of such types. They enable us to explain and to anticipate the possibility of cumulative change in the character and content of our contexts without appealing to developmental tendencies that imply a particular succession of social orders. They allow us to see how the different aspects of human empowerment may be served by the development of social frameworks that impart to the rigid moments of social life some of the qualities that define the interludes of heightened fluidity.

The arrangements and beliefs of these more disentrenched contexts are no less detailed and definite than the beliefs and the arrangements they replace. But they make themselves more fully available to challenge and revision in the course of ordinary social activity; they present themselves more fully as the mutable artifacts they really are. The more disentrenched a context becomes, the looser and lighter is the grid of social division and hierarchy with which it frames our practical or passionate dealings and the weaker the bias it imposes on its own revision. In both these ways the disentrenchment of formative contexts strikes at the facts that delude us into thinking that society and history have a script. We do not make the antinaturalistic view of society fully persuasive until we have grasped its constructive practical implications and then have acted them out.

A theory that carries to extremes the conception of society as artifact makes a vital contribution to the radical project – the commitment that liberals, leftists, and modernists can share ever more fully and consciously as they free themselves from unnecessarily restrictive assumptions about personal and social possibility. The effort to associate an approach to the understanding of society with a line of social reconstruction may seem an open invitation to wishful thinking and theoretical prejudice. The constructive work that builds on this book argues for an intimate and frankly controversial relation between an explanatory view of society and a programmatic orientation toward the remaking of our formative contexts. A looser, tentative association between the radical cause and the antinaturalistic understanding of society can rest on two loose and relatively uncontroversial ideas.

The early pages of this book presented one justification for the link between the understanding and the cause: the special cognitive interest of the radical perspective. The radical wants to break down the fixed internal divisions within mankind and to disrupt the ongoing compulsions within history; radicals differ among themselves according to the compulsions and divisions they mark for destruction. The radical, in his efforts to imagine how far, by what means, and with what results he can hope to advance his enterprise, puts to the test the necessity of the arrangements and of the forces he opposes. To view society and history through his eyes (even though not with his heart) is to subject to a passionate and practical skepticism the restrictions on social and personal possibility we ordinarily take for granted. You may disagree with the radical's aims and nevertheless find your understanding of your goals changed by the results of this cognitive exercise.

An additional reason to connect an antinecessitarian understanding of social life with a radical perspective on society has to do with the combination of a characteristic of our ruling social ideals and an attribute of the relation between any social ideal and the assumptions about social possibility this ideal presupposes. There is a real sense in which almost every contemporary political movement has joined the radical cause. Increasingly, the modern conservative is not the old-European-style reactionary who upholds the sanctity of a particular scheme of social division and hierarchy and defends the personal habits that accompany this scheme. Instead, he is the reformed classical liberal. He identifies a purified version of current contractual, proprietary, and governmental arrangements as the best possible approximation to the system that channels resources to those who can use them to the greatest social advantage and that enables individuals and groups to pursue their freely chosen goals with the fewest possible restraints. The conservative radicals differ from the radical radicals less by a distinct conception of the social good – for all preach the modern gospel of the illegitimacy of a preassigned system of social stations – than by different views of what the alternatives are and how they work.

One aspect of this opposition deserves to be singled out even in this preliminary discussion. This aspect suggests how an antinaturalistic social theory bears on the debate between the contemporary right and the contemporary left. More generally, it also illuminates the relation of social ideals to assumptions about the possible.

No one can adequately understand social ideals by considering solely the vague and contradictory rhetoric that ordinarily expresses them. To grasp what people mean by an ideal like democracy we must read our professions of democratic faith against a richly detailed but largely implicit background of institutional assumptions and traditions. If someone then proposes a very different set of institutional means with which to realize our democratic commitments, we may dismiss the proposal as unrealistic. But if we can be persuaded to take it seriously, we are likely to be jarred. Faced with the alternative, we soon discover ambiguities in our preexistent conception of the meaning and the requirements of democracy. The seeming transparency of our democratic ideal depends in fact on the unchallenged meshing of an indistinct image of human association, the practices that stand for this image, and the area of social existence in which these practices apply. Once this fit of the image, the practical form, and the domain of application are upset, we may find ourselves forced to choose among competing trajectories of institutional change. These trajectories represent alternative views of what really matters most to us about a received ideal like democracy.

A developed understanding of society can inform choice among such views. At the very least it can enlarge and refine the appreciation of practical alternatives. At its most ambitious it can help us decide which of several pathways to the reform of our practices for the sake of our ideals, and to the criticism of our ideals for the sake of our unfulfilled and inexplicit aspirations, we ought to choose. For our conception of society and of its transformative possibilities helps shape our sense of the content and implications of our many-sided efforts at individual and collective self-assertion. These dim, confused, and tenacious strivings form the raw material that social ideals try to express and to order. Our thoughts penetrate and reshape this material.

A radically antinaturalistic social theory like the view anticipated in this book contributes to the radical project in several ways. It criticizes and, by criticizing, unifies the major strands in the radical tradition – strands that until now have seemed only obscurely related and even overtly antagonistic. It connects this enlarged conception of the radical cause to a more defensible account of the conditions and content of human empowerment. Most important, it detaches our conception of the radical commitment from the utopian, millenarian claims that have so often undermined the credibility of the radical project.

A thoroughly politicized social theory revises and regroups the liberal, leftist, and modernist contributions to the radical cause. An antinaturalistic social theory encourages this unification by developing a social theory that frees liberal and leftist ideas from their institutional fetishism – their take-it-or-leave-it attitude toward the contemporary institutional and imaginative contexts of social life – and that frees modernist ideas from their structure fetishism – their take-it-or-leave-it attitude toward the context-bound character of our activities. From this double correction emerge both a more inclusive view of what the radical project is for and a livelier appreciation of the variety of practical and institutional forms the radical idea can assume. The broader definition of aims develops together with a less restrictive conception of their practical forms and means.

In the more comprehensive view that results from this argument, the radical endeavor shifts its meanings. It ceases to be primarily about protected spheres of individual action (as the classical liberal believes), or the destruction of class society through the radical substitution of those same arrangements (as the traditional orthodox Marxist thinks), or even the need to choose between the relativistic acceptance of whatever contexts there are and the negativistic rebellion against all contexts (as a certain type of modernist would have it). The radical cause concerns the creation of formative institutional and imaginative orderings of social life that have two connected qualities. Such contexts diminish the extent to which a preestablished, unchallengeable scheme of social roles and ranks shapes our practical or passionate dealings. At the same time these valued contexts lay themselves more fully open to identification, challenge, and revision in the midst of our ordinary practical and argumentative activities.

This redefinition of the radical project redirects our attention to the task of finding the connected institutions and beliefs that enjoy such qualities to a greater degree than past or present societies have possessed them. This task we can now accomplish unburdened by the untenably narrow assumptions of current styles of social analysis – free from the alleged need to choose between reformist tinkering with current frameworks and total framework change, free from the alternatives that are presented to us as a ready-made sequence or list, and free to imagine practical forms of representative democracy and economic decentralization that can more effectively further the radical cause.

Once we recast the radical project in this way, we can connect it more tightly and persuasively with a view of the content and conditions of human empowerment. As a result, we can strengthen and broaden the appeal of the radical commitment. The key to this connection is the idea that the conditions for two major aspects of human empowerment can overlap. One of these aspects is the development of practical productive capabilities. The other aspect is the diminution of dependence and depersonalization. It is just as vital to recognize that the overlap between the conditions for these two types of empowerment is not inevitable as it is to affirm that nothing in the general facts about personality, society, and history prevents it from occurring.

At certain levels of relative poverty, savings over consumption may be a more powerful constraint on the development of productive capabilities than are the rate and nature of innovation. The advantages of the coercive extraction of resources and manpower through the nearly automatic operation of social hierarchies, and of the arrangements and beliefs that sustain these hierarchies, may prove decisive. They may then override the countervailing benefits of greater freedom to recombine and replace both factors of production and the organizational settings of production and exchange.

But as society overcomes poverty the paramount condition of material progress becomes the plasticity of social life: the relative ease with which people can subject their forms of production and exchange, of machine design and work organization, to the logic of problem solving. The keynote of this logic is the interplay between the redefinition of practical tasks and the reorganization of the technical and organizational means to their execution. There is much in recent historical learning to suggest that plasticity becomes more important than surplus extraction even in societies that remain poor by our contemporary standards. Thus, the relative level of savings over consumption seems to have been at least as great in some of the great agrarian-bureaucratic empires of the past as it was in the Western nations that pioneered the industrial revolution.

Even when recombination becomes paramount it can be achieved in ways that are either coercive or consensual, either dictatorial or democratic. Plasticity may be imposed on the resistant body of society by a ruthless central authority that rearranges people and capital at will. Or plasticity may be built into decentralized and participatory institutions that minimize the stranglehold individuals or groups may impose on the tangible or intangible resources of society.

These two pathways to plasticity have vastly different consequences for the character of social life. But viewed from the narrow standpoint of the interests of practical progress, each has pitfalls. The coercive solution may subordinate the development of productive opportunities to the power interests of the planners. The consensual solution may subject the organization of production to private goals that fail to coincide with productive advantages for society.

The collective interest in the growth of our productive capabilities may therefore be satisfied in ways that conflict with the other aspects of human empowerment. Marxism seems to recognize this truth. Yet Marxist social theory both misrepresents the point – by overemphasizing the importance of coercive surplus extraction as the practical justification for mankind's long and painful detour through class society – and undermines its force – by putting its faith in an irresistible evolutionary dynamic that can be counted on to resolve the conflict between the development of the productive forces of society and the overthrow of social oppression.

A thoroughly antinecessitarian social theory does not ensure a present or future coincidence between the conditions for the development of productive capabilities and the emancipation of social life from rigid roles and hierarchies. But it encourages the search for the arrangements that may satisfy more fully both these sets of conditions. The coercive and hypercentralist forms of the approach toward greater plasticity loosen the constraints of preestablished roles and ranks on our practical and passionate relations. However, they also create new varieties of oppression by central imposition and new versions of hierarchies founded on the relative access of individuals and groups to governmental power. The democratic alternatives seek to break society open to politics through organized conflict and through the denial of factional strangleholds over the means and resources of society making. These alternatives allow us to reconcile the conditions for collective practical success with a different brand of human empowerment.

This other empowerment directly concerns the quality of our relations to one another. Its mark is the easing of conflict between two basic imperatives of self-assertion: the need for engagement in shared forms of practical, emotional, and cognitive activity and the ability to avoid or contain the threats of oppression and depersonalization posed by every form of group engagement. Each version of group life threatens to enmesh us in relations of dependence and domination. Each threatens to cast us as placeholders in a system of social stations that determine our experience and life chances. To the extent that these threats are carried out, we suffer disappointment in our varied efforts at self-assertion. For we can then avoid the cost of engagement only by paying the price of isolation.

By developing formative contexts that loosen the structure of social division and hierarchy and that diminish the gap between context-revising conflict and context-preserving routine, we can weaken the force of rigid roles and ranks. We can thereby moderate the conflict between the enabling conditions of self-assertion. Moreover, we can do so in a way that also provides a more favorable basis for the development of practical capabilities. As a result, we can combine more easily two major aspects of human empowerment. We can diminish the likelihood that the effort to purify the quality of human association will be sacrificed to the seduction of worldly success and to the economic and military rivalries of nation-states.

The path of social reconstruction that gives us a chance to reconcile our worldly ambitions with the ennoblement of human solidarity also allows us to become more fully the masters of the social worlds in which we live. It undermines the contrast between pursuing interests on the basis of institutional and imaginative assumptions we take for granted and arguing or fighting about these assumptions. By allowing us to diminish the sense in which our contexts are arbitrary and recalcitrant givens, such a program of social reform enables us to cut through a dilemma that also disempowers us.

This dilemma, embodied in structure fetishism, increasingly dominates our ideas and our sensibility as we lose faith in the existence of standards that transcend particular social frameworks and cultural traditions. One horn of the dilemma is to accept our contexts just because they are there and because they are ours. Knowing that one context is ultimately as groundless as another, we seek to quiet disbelief through active involvement in the practical and imaginative transactions of a particular society and culture. The other horn of the dilemma is to remain at permanent war with all established institutions and conventions, seeking in the practice of defiance more than in its outcome the sole way to assert our transcendence over our context.

By changing the character of our contexts we partly resolve this dilemma. By partly resolving it we make it possible to achieve a wholehearted engagement in our societies that does not rest on illusion and bad faith. The availability of such engagement is itself a form of empowerment. Indeed, it is the form most directly connected to the practices, the institutions, and the beliefs that enable us to reconcile more successfully the other major aspects of human self-assertion.

An antinaturalistic social theory contributes to the radical project not only by freeing it from arbitrarily restrictive institutional assumptions and by connecting with a more inclusive and defensible view of human empowerment but also by rescuing it from the perfectionist or utopian illusion. Radicals have often escaped belief in a sudden, definitive regeneration of society only by ceasing to be radical – that is, by seeking economic redistribution within an institutional and imaginative structure they no longer challenge. But escape the utopian tone the radical must, for it is a confession of weakness, a declaration of failure to relate radical goals to a credible view of social change.

The advance of the radical project is never more than possible. Nothing ever guarantees that we will succeed in establishing or even in identifying reforms that reconcile the conditions for the development of practical capabilities with the requirements for the improvement of our relations to one another. Nothing deep or permanent about the character of social life rules out such a reconciliation, and much in the record of broken constraint suggests its possibility. Local and temporary obstacles, however, may defeat us just as surely as obstacles built on permanent economic, organizational, or psychological imperatives.

The radical project is interminable and reversible. There are no unique or predetermined practical forms it must assume in the course of its advance. We do not select institutions, practices, and beliefs from a well-defined list or a preestablished sequence. Our exercises in social invention begin with the relatively makeshift, accidental arrangements we have inherited. We go from there. Every claim that a particular set of revolutionary reforms is best suited to advance the radical cause in a particular historical circumstance remains controversial. The controversy over such claims is always mired in a contest of perceived group interests and half-developed beliefs.

Moreover, each advance toward greater plasticity and disentrenchment creates new dangers of reversion to less revisable and more oppressive orderings of social life. Every additional opportunity to deliberate, to mobilize, and to experiment can be turned, under the pressure of privatistic self-concern, into an opportunity for the more ingenious, the more resolute, and the more persuasive to change temporary advantages into permanent privileges. The quest for preemptive security and the indulgence in apprehensive fantasy can make people into the perpetrators – not just the spectators – of such regression. An enlarged freedom from determination by our contexts increases rather than lessens the sense in which history is a gamble, and "a throw of dice does not abolish chance."

The radical project is morally perilous. It does its work by using and accelerating the succession of the hot and the cold, the fluid and the rigid, moments of social life. At worst, the practical and imaginative strife it unleashes overshadows the attempt to promote and to reconcile the different facets of human empowerment. At best, many loyalties embedded in established contexts of social life must be betrayed, and many passionately held views about the requirements of happiness must be overturned.

The radical project is not enough. Imagine the radical cause carried forward to its extreme triumph. People would still reach out beyond the transparent, created social world – this joy, this dazzling game, this work of art – to the dark world they had not created. They would still crave kinship with nature and desire to become a deathless, self-sustaining part of a realm in which union has no need of will and imagination. They would still reach toward a transcendent reality, absolute and unconditional, beyond this life of transience and illusion. And they would feel the conflict between the longings for kinship with nature and for transcendence over nature all the more fiercely as the material problems and collective divisions of society waned.

Despite its contingency, its reversibility, its moral ambiguity, and its partiality, the radical cause can speak to us with authority. An antinaturalistic social theory helps show why. All our major forms of empowerment depend on the success of that cause. Moreover, we can hardly avoid the continued breakdown of constraints upon practical recombination and social invention. The readiness to innovate is bound up with the conditions for the development of practical capabilities; no society can resist the imperative of plasticity without risking failure in the race for economic advantage and military security. The real issue is whether we shall overcome obstacles to a heightened social experimentalism in ways that serve our desire to be both free and connected, both self-conscious and engaged.

In their better and saner moments men and women have always wanted to live as the originals they all feel themselves to be, and they have sought practical and passionate attachments that express this truth. As soon as they have understood their social arrangements to be made up and pasted together they have wanted to become the coauthors of these arrangements. Some modern doctrines tell us that we already live in societies in which we can fully satisfy these desires; others urge us to give them up as unrealistic. But the first teaching is hard to believe; the second is hard to practice.

The constraints of society, echoed, reinforced, and amplified by the illusions of social thought, have often led people to bear the stigma of longing under the mask of worldliness and resignation. An antinecessitarian social theory does not strike down the constraints but it dispels the illusions that prevent us from attacking them. Theoretical insight and prophetic vision have joined ravenous self-interest and heartless conflict to set the fire that is burning in the world, and melting apart the amalgam of faith and superstition, and consuming the power of false necessity.

Bibliographical Notes

AIMS AND NATURE OF THESE NOTES

HERE you have a bibliographical commentary on a book that anticipates a work in speculative social theory. *Social Theory: Its Situation and Its Task* is not a fragmentary or schematic history of modern social thought nor an exegesis of particular writings and authors. It represents an effort to discern what serves, and what impedes, the advancement of a certain intellectual endeavor.

The reader who looks in this book for something like an intellectual history will be disappointed to find that it rarely mentions particular thinkers or texts. The focus is different because the concerns are different. I assume that opposing ideas regularly coexist in the writings of the same thinkers and that some of these ideas serve the endeavor to which I want to contribute while others frustrate its progress. When dealing with the distinctively intellectual aspects of the condition of social and historical studies I am much more interested in identifying the ideas and in assessing their relation to my constructive purpose than in understanding the particular way in which they work together in a certain writer or book. My discussion confirms the commonplace that, in theory as in politics, insight and fecundity count for more than consistency. Every thinker betrays his most subversive intentions in the process of carrying them out. It is better to betray them less than to betray them more. But it is also better to let vision outreach theory building than to see and to say only what you can already formulate coherently and persuasively.

Much of this book represents a polemic against what the text labels deep-structure social analysis. The writings of Marx and his followers provide the most powerful and detailed illustrations of the deep-structure moves. Yet Marx's own writings contain many elements that assist the effort to free ambitious theorizing from deep-structure assumptions. People working in the Marxist tradition have developed the deep-structure approach. Yet they have also forged some of the most powerful tools with which to build a view of social life more faithful to the antinaturalistic intentions of Marx and other classic social theorists than Marx's original science of history. Herbert Spencer was a more consistently deep-structure theorist than Karl Marx. But that does not make him a more rewarding exponent even of the deep-structure approach itself.

The criticism of intellectual currents need not be vague simply because it is detached from the in-depth study of particular writings. Forms of intellectual practice like deep-structure social analysis can be defined very precisely and shown to be more or less present in a particular text. But the emphasis in this book falls on the character of the obstacles and the encouragements to a particular intellectual project wherever they may be found. The advantage of this procedure from the standpoint of an intellectual campaign (as distinct from intellectual history) is to connect criticism, directly and transparently, with a reconstructive purpose. The disadvantage is that it is easy to miss – because the net is too gross – ideas that might assist the affirmative endeavor. So, let's try it this way, and then let's try it all the other ways we can imagine, including the way of close textual analysis.

These aims shape the character of this bibliographical commentary. The following notes are designed to elucidate more than to prove or support, and their scope is minimal rather than exhaustive. They include two main groups of references. The first group consists in direct debts for ideas, arguments, and observations. The second, larger group consists in the names of authors and the titles of books that exemplify to a greater or lesser extent the tendencies of thought discussed in the text. This second series is meant to diminish some of the difficulties of understanding that inevitably result from the lack of textual focus in the book. But these citations are not intended to bridge the gap that separates my argument from detailed intellectual history and criticism.

Some sections, especially those dealing with the practical political context of theoretical reconstruction, are very sparsely annotated. Others, which address the inherited traditions of social thought, are dealt with at greater length. Titles appear in English whenever English translations are readily available. Authors are sometimes named without reference to particular works. A list of references departs from chronological order whenever another sequence seems preferable. The text page numbers to which the commentary refers appear at the outside margin. Themes that key in with the text are in italics.

GENERAL BACKGROUND

The diagnosis and criticism presented in this volume lead into a constructive social theory. The inspirations of the criticism also represent sources of the diagnosis. It may therefore help to transcribe here the same list of nine major influences on the constructive view present at the beginning of the bibliographical commentary to *False Necessity*. The ideas and arguments of this introductory book and of its constructive sequel do not represent a synthesis of the conceptions contained in the following sources. But neither are the components of the list a random assortment of ideas, linked only by the accidents of one individual's intellectual trajectory. They rank among the materials available today to whoever wants to combine, as *Politics* does, the reconstruction of social thought along antinecessitarian lines with the anticipation of practical forms of social life that can more fully realize the radical project. Each of the nine sets of ideas, themes, or forms of intellectual practice contained in this list can be, and has been, used in ways that conflict with the intellectual program advocated in this book. Yet all nine together can be enlisted in the execution of this program. Their availability lends support to the claim that we already have at hand the building blocks of an antinaturalistic social theory able to give new life and new meaning to the cause that leftists, liberals, and modernists share.

    1. The theme of the rigid and the fluid, the hot and the cold, moments of social life. This theme has been present, in one form or another, in virtually every period and tradition of social thought. Its most famous formulation in classic European social theory can be found in Durkheim's discussion of the moments of collective ecstasy (*The Elementary Forms of Religious Life*, trans. J. W. Swain, Free Press, New York, 1969, pp. 240–242), and in Max Weber's treatment of charisma and routinization (*Economy and Society*, ed. Guenther Roth and Claus Wittich, Bedminster, New York, 1968, vol. 3, chap. 14, pp. 1111–1155). It reappears as a central idea in Sartre's late work; see *Criticism of Dialectical Reason*, trans. Alan Sheridan-Smith, New Left Books, London, 1976, pp. 256–404. It plays a prominent role in the writings of Victor Turner; see *The Ritual Process: Structure and Anti-Structure*, Cornell, Ithaca, 1977. Francesco Alberoni has given this idea its most elaborate and rewarding contemporary formulations; see, particularly, *Movimento e Istituzione*, Il Mulino, Bologna, 1981.

    2. Karl Marx's criticism of English political economy, particularly as evidenced in the *Poverty of Philosophy*, the *Grundrisse*, and the early sections of *Capital*. This criticism represents an example of how the portrayal of an extended area of social practice as an expression of eternal laws of social organization may be attacked with the purpose of changing the content and character of social and historical explanations. The task is to find an affirmative explanatory voice more responsive to the spirit of this critique than Marx's affirmative explanations, with their search for the "laws of motion" of capital and their story about the succession of modes of production.

    3. The writings of Marxists, or of writers sympathetic to Marxism, who emphasize and explore the autonomy of politics, in both

the narrow and inclusive sense distinguished in the text: the conflict over the mastery and uses of governmental power and the strife over any of the formative terms of social life. Some have been thinkers and activists who attempted to theorize transformative political practice. See Antonio Gramsci, "The Modern Prince" and the "Critical Notes" on Bukharin in *Selections from the Prison Notebooks of Antonio Gramsci*, trans. Quintin Hoare and Geoffrey Nowell Smith, International Publishers, New York, 1971, pp. 123–205, especially pp. 136–145 and 419–473. Others are contemporary historians who have studied traditions of collective organization and class consciousness. See, for example, E. P. Thompson, *The Making of the English Working Class*, Vintage, New York, 1963; Robert Brenner, "Agrarian Class Structure and Economic Development in Pre-Industrial Europe," *Past and Present*, no. 70 (1976), pp. 30–75, and "The Agrarian Roots of European Capitalism," *Past and Present*, no. 97 (1982), pp. 16–113; Gareth Steadman Jones, *Languages of Class: Essays in English Working-Class History, 1832–1982*, Cambridge, Cambridge, 1983. Still others are sociologists who have probed comparatively the relations among class structure, state conflict, and governmental politics. See, for example, Barrington Moore, Jr., *Social Origins of Dictatorship and Democracy*, Beacon, Boston, 1966; Theda Skocpol, *States and Social Revolutions: A Comparative Analysis of France, Russia, and China*, Cambridge, Cambridge, 1979.

These varieties of political Marxism should be distinguished from the related tendency to put in place of the privileged causal connections emphasized by Marx a notion of generalized reciprocal causation. See the classic expositions in Georg Lukács, "Reification and the Consciousness of the Proletariat," in *History and Class Consciousness: Studies in Marxist Dialectics*, trans. Rodney Livingstone, MIT, Cambridge, 1968, pp. 83–222; Karl Korsch, "Marxism and Philosophy" (1923), in *Marxism and Philosophy*, trans. Fred Halliday, Monthly Review, New York, 1978, pp. 29–97.

At times the political Marxists have sacrificed the development of their insights to the desire to retain a connection with the central theses of historical materialism. To them these tenets have seemed the only available basis for theoretical generalization and for critical distance from the arrangements and circumstances of the societies they lived in. At other times, the political Marxists have simply given up on theory. See, for example, E.P. Thompson, "The Poverty of Theory or an Onnery of Errors," in *The Poverty of Theory and Other Essays*, Monthly Review, New York, 1978, pp. 1–210. They have then paid the price in the loss of ability to convey a sense of sharp institutional alternatives for past, present, and future societies. The constructive theory of *Politics* just keeps going from where the political Marxists leave off. It does so, however, without either renouncing theoretical ambitions or accepting any of the distinctive doctrines of Marx's social theory.

4. A loose and apparently unrelated set of forms of twentieth-

century social analysis that have emphasized the institutional indeterminacy of abstract types of social organization such as a pluralistic democracy or a market economy and that have demonstrated the dependence of supposed economic or social laws on unique, transitory institutional arrangements. I have found the most interesting discussions of the interplay between institutional arrangements and social or economic regularities in the writings of interwar economists. One group of writings concerns the strategies of economic recovery in the West (Keynes, Kalečki, Hayek). Another body of literature grows out of the Soviet industrialization debate, so intimately connected to the formative events of the late 1920s (Preobrazhensky, Bukharin). On the other hand, the idea that there can be markets or democracies radically different from the democratic or market systems we normally take for granted or imagine possible has been most extensively explored by the critical legal studies movement in the United States. See the discussion in Roberto Mangabeira Unger, *The Critical Legal Studies Movement*, Harvard University Press, Cambridge, 1986, pp. 5–8, 22–40, 97–99. Once you get the point of institutional indeterminacy, the old-fashioned literature of German, French, and English institutional history becomes a priceless storehouse, providing countless illustrations of the unique character of different institutional arrangements, of their made-up and pasted-together quality, and of their decisive effects.

Political thinkers and practical politicians alike have always understood "that what are called necessary institutions are only institutions to which one is accustomed and that in matters of social constitution the field of possibilities is much wider than people living within each society imagine" (Alexis de Tocqueville, *Recollections*, trans. George Lawrence, Doubleday, Garden City, 1970, chap. 2, p. 76). The point is to turn this ironic proviso into a principle of insight.

5. The ideal aspirations of nineteenth-century liberal thinkers, like Benjamin Constant, Alexander Herzen, Wilhelm von Humboldt, Alexis de Tocqueville, John Stuart Mill, and T. H. Greene, reinterpreted from the standpoint of a continuing though submerged strand in Western social thought. This strand relates political pluralism, in the narrow sense, to the prosperity, the empowerment, and the collective self-organization of the "little people." Three stages in the evolution of this tradition of thought can be found in James Harrington, *The Oceana*, in *The Oceana and Other Works*, Scientia Verlag, Aalen, 1980 (reprint of the London 1771 edition), especially the second part of the preliminaries, pp. 57–72; Henry Sumner Maine, *Village Communities in East and West*, Murray, London, 1871, which should be read together with his *Lectures on the Early History of Institutions*, Murray, London, 1875; and Barrington Moore, Jr., *Social Origins of Dictatorship and Democracy*. The classical liberal creed supplies a motivating impulse. But the other mode of thinking, with its focus on the practical bases of pluralism, helps save the impulse from unwarranted identifica-

tion with the institutional commitments of nineteenth-century liberals. The help doubles in force when the resulting insights combine with the ideas about institutional arrangements — their trumped-up character and their crucial influence — suggested by the sources mentioned in item 4 of this list.

In this connection there is much to learn from the study of the recurrent problems of social reform in the great agrarian-bureaucratic empires that shaped so much of world history. The boldest reforming statesmen in these empires repeatedly tried and failed to preserve the independence of a class of smallholders who might provide central governments with a direct fiscal and military base and counterbalance the influence of landowning magnates. Such efforts were undoubtedly inspired by a policy of state security and social stability rather than by a devotion to pluralism and equality. But few things can better strengthen a sense of the relations between the vitality of social pluralism at the grassroots level and the particular institutional design of a society than a study of the attempts of, say, the Toba regime during the period of disunity between the Han and T'ang dynasties in China or the Macedonian dynasty in Byzantine history to make an intensely hierarchical society safe for a class of state-serving smallholders.

6. The tradition of petty bourgeois radicalism. The importance of this tradition has been borne out by a renewed appreciation of the continuing role played in modern Western history by predominantly petty bourgeois movements and publicists in challenging the dominant form of Western industrialism. Publicists like Proudhon, Blanc, and Lassalle tried to combine practical proposals and speculative conceptions in ways that resisted the archaizing impulse.

An encouraging development in contemporary historical writing has been the appearance of studies that emphasize, against the shibboleths of orthodox liberalism and orthodox Marxism alike, the significance, the tenacity, and the suppressed potential of challenges to what eventually became the system of mass production and of property-based markets. Some of these writings have a plangent tone, underlining the ties that bound the radicals to social aspirations and forms of rights consciousness current in preindustrial and prerevolutionary Europe. See, for example, Fernand Braudel, *Afterthoughts on Material Civilization and Capitalism*, trans. Patricia M. Ranum, Johns Hopkins, Baltimore, 1977; William H. Sewall, Jr., *Work and Revolution in France*, Cambridge, Cambridge, 1980; Craig J. Calhoun, *The Question of Class Struggle: The Social Foundation of Popular Radicalism During the Industrial Revolution*, Chicago, Chicago, 1982. But other studies have demonstrated the continuity of the alternative that has been pejoratively labeled petty or simple commodity production, its reemergence under new guise in the most advanced sector of modern manufacturing, and its value as a model for more far-reaching industrial reconstruction. See Charles Sabel and Jonathan Zeitlin, "Historical Alternatives to Mass Production," *Past and Present*, no. 108 (1985), pp. 133–176. Whether despondent or hopeful, this literature supplies an alternative to the traditions of conservative or radical necessitarianism that have dominated thinking about the history of the institutional forms of production and exchange. But it does so without embracing the simple and sentimentalized story of big bad people eating up good little people that has too often appeared to be the sole available alternative. See, as an example of the earlier challenge to the conservative or radical mainstreams, R. H. Tawney, *The Agrarian Problem in the Sixteenth Century*, Harper, New York, 1967 (reprint of the 1912 edition).

7. Ultra-leftist ideas about collective mobilization and grassroots organization, current today throughout the third world. These ideas are relevant to the effort undertaken in this book not only as points of departure for programmatic thinking about social reconstruction but also as examples of attempts to think about social contexts and context change in a way that is free from the confining assumptions of deep-structure social analysis. Though often clothed in Marxist language, their distinctive concern is better described as the attempt to perpetuate in ongoing routine activity what the sources mentioned in item 1 of this list would call the fluid or hot moment of social life and to do so for the sake of a vision of the individual and collective empowerment that may result. There is no handy doctrinal source in which to study these ideas. Yet they are everywhere. Sympathy for them may appear irreconcilable with an interest in the revival and reconstruction of the petty bourgeois alternative mentioned in item 6. But the impression of irreconcilability begins to dissipate with the help of two intellectual transformations encouraged by the approaches evoked in items 2 through 6 of this list.

The first such change results from the conclusion that the program of petty bourgeois radicalism cannot succeed until and unless it abandons the stubborn dream of privatistic withdrawal into a protected domain of family property and local concerns. In the place of this dream it must put forms of decentralized economic and governmental organization that can prevent concentrations of power and wealth more effectively than current representative democracies and regulated market economies are able to do.

The second indispensable transformation is to disabuse ultra-leftism of its prejudice against detailed programmatic proposals and institutional commitments. If the vague ideals of contemporary ultra-leftists have a chance of being partly realized in the world, the reason is that formative institutional and imaginative contexts differ in the extent to which they impart to routine social existence the qualities of the fluid, context-revising moments of social life.

8. The portrayal of human nature in modernist writers like Proust, Joyce, and Beckett and the discursive counterpart to this image of man in the writings of such philosophers as Heidegger and Sartre. That such a modernist image of man in fact exists, that it can be understood as a recognizable transformation of the Chris-

tian-romantic tradition of thinking about personality, and that it can be weaned away from its habitual indifference or hostility to political concerns and from its disbelief in the possibility of changing the relation between freedom and structure are theses argued in my book *Passion: An Essay on Personality*, Free Press, New York, 1984. The view of personality and personal relations developed in that book and the account of society and society making presented in *Politics* are meant as parallel explorations, different in focus and level of detail but mutually reinforcing.

9. The philosophical attack on the belief in privileged methods and representations — that is to say, in representations and methods whose privilege consists in their insensitivity to changes in our empirical beliefs. This attack has been carried out by the second generation of analytic philosophers, led by such thinkers as Quine and Putnam. Their work helps free social and historical thought from the prejudice that received views about necessity and contingency, causality and explanation, enshrined in the natural sciences, must be dealt with on a take-it-or-leave-it basis. Moreover, as polemically interpreted and extended, this attack on the unavowed remnants of the synthetic a priori becomes easy to connect with the assault on comprehensive, necessitarian historical narratives that has been mounted from a very different philosophical tradition. See Richard Rorty, *Philosophy and The Mirror of Nature*, Princeton, Princeton, 1979. The combined criticism of privileged beliefs and metanarratives serves as a source of encouragement in the attempt to free radical social criticism from deep-structure assumptions.

Politics is also the product of two very different experiences. One experience is exposure to the rich, polished, critical and self-critical but also downbeat and Alexandrian culture of social and historical thought that now flourishes in the North Atlantic democracies. This social-thought culture suffers from the influence of a climate of opinion in which the most generous citizens hope at best to avert military disasters and to achieve marginal redistributive goals while resigning themselves to established institutional arrangements. The other shaping experience is practical and imaginative engagement in the murky but hopeful politics of Brazil, a country at the forward edge of the third world. There, at the time of writing, at least some people took seriously the idea that basic institutions, practices, and preconceptions might be reconstructed in ways that did not conform to any established model of social organization.

Much in this work can be understood as the consequence of an attempt to enlist the intellectual resources of the North Atlantic world in the service of concerns and commitments more keenly felt elsewhere. In this way I hope to contribute toward the development of an alternative to the vague, unconvinced, and unconvincing Marxism that now serves the advocates of the radical project as their lingua franca. If, however, the arguments of this book stand up, the transformative focus of this theoretical effort has intellectual uses that transcend its immediate origins and motives.

Aside from the intellectual and practical influences enumerated earlier, the approach this introductory book takes to the circumstance of social thought has also found inspiration in other sources more directly related to the criticism of received theories. The most important of these sources is the work of the theorists who have reevaluated and transformed from within the traditions of deep-structure social analysis and positivist social science that this book criticizes. Later parts of this commentary give examples.

I am indebted to an old tradition of writing about historicism and classical European social theory for insights into the modern history of ideas about the artifactual quality of social orders. See, for example, Friedrich Meinecke, *Die Entstehung des Historismus*, ed. Carl Hinrichs, *Werke*, Oldenbourg, Munich, 1959; Carlo Antoni, *Dallo Storicismo alla Sociologia*, Sansoni, Florence, 1940; Pietro Rossi, *Lo Storicismo Tedesco Contemporaneo*, Einaudi, Turin, 1956; Carlo Antoni, *Lo Storicismo* (Radio Italiana, Rome, 1957). Other aspects of the vicissitudes of attempts to connect general social explanation with a vindication of the constructed character of social life are explored in Louis Althusser, *Montesquieu, Rousseau, Marx: Politics and History*, trans. Ben Brewster, New Left Books, London, 1982. A recent, close study of political ideas in nineteenth-century Britain shows how explicitly connected to controversies about social reconstruction the debate over the willed and nonwilled elements in social life once was. See Stefan Collini et al., *That Noble Science of Politics: A Study in Nineteenth Century Intellectual History*, Cambridge, Cambridge, 1984.

My view of the relation of this critical introduction to the constructive work that follows it conforms to a traditional Aristotelian formula of philosophical and legal works. This formula presents constructive views as responses to a set of historically defined questions and controversies. Quentin Skinner has recently enlarged the sense of the reference to context by emphasizing the parts of the situation of thought that cannot be found in books. See *The Foundations of Modern Political Thought*, 2 vols., Cambridge, Cambridge, 1978. *Social Theory: Its Situation and Its Task* follows something of the same approach, only applied to the present rather than to the past and subordinated, in the antique mode mentioned earlier, to the interests of a particular constructive endeavor.

INTRODUCTION: SOCIETY AS ARTIFACT

1–9 The idea of the special opportunities and difficulties presented by *the artifactual and makeshift character of social orders* long antedates nineteenth- and twentieth-century European social theory. It takes one form in Hobbes (*Leviathan*, Clarendon, Oxford, 1967, Chap. XVII, pp. 128–132), another form in Vico (*The New Science of*

Giambattista *Vico*, trans. Thomas Bergin and Max Frisch, Cornell, Ithaca, pp. 96–97 para. 331). The idea is rendered in psychological terms and confined to a transitory role in Hegel's discussion of the terror in *The Phenomenology of Mind*. For a study of the artifactual theme affirmed in a non-Western setting but under the pressure of similar experiences, see Masao Maruyama, *Studies in the Intellectual History of Tokugawa Japan*, trans. Mikiso Hane, Univ. of Tokyo, 1974, pp. 189–319.

A turning point occurs when the conception of society as artifact becomes part of a detailed explanation of social situations or historical processes. A preeminent example of this transformation is Marx's criticism of economic laws. See, for example, the *Grundrisse* (*Foundations of the Critique of Political Economy*), trans. Martin Nicolaus, Vintage, New York, 1973, Introduction (Notebook M), section 3; "The Method of Political Economy," pp. 100–108, and *Capital*, International Publishers, New York, 1967, vol. 1, chap. 1, section 4: "The Fetishism of Commodities and the Secret Thereof," pp. 71–83. Another example is Max Weber's view of the rationalization and bureaucratization of social life as a social experience that also provides social theory with its standpoint. See especially *Economy and Society*, ed. Guenther Ross and Claus Wittich, Bedminster, New York, 1968, vol. 3, chap. 11, section 8, pp. 983–990.

Each of these versions of the idea of society as artifact remains, however, tainted by its combination with other ideas that qualify the artifactual thesis. Thus, Marx's criticism of political economy coexists with the attempt to discover the "laws of motion of capital." Though Marx ascribed these laws to a transitory type of social organization rather than to the inherent nature of economic life, he also held the succession of types to be governed by lawlike evolutionary tendencies. Similarly, Weber's argument about rationalization leads up to the thesis that rationalizing tendencies relentlessly impose well-defined organizational imperatives that override partisan divisions and frustrate ideological aspirations. See *Economy and Society*, vol. 1., chap. 2, section 14, pp. 109–113.

THE CONDITIONAL AND THE UNCONDITIONAL

The view of our relation to the practical and discursive contexts of 18–25 our activities presented here is more fully discussed in my book *Passion: An Essay on Personality*, Free Press, New York, 1984, pp. 5–20.

This conception of contexts and context breaking can be placed in two different controversial settings. On the one hand, it can be contrasted to the views, from psychological reductionism and behaviorism to deep-structure social theory, that deny the reality, or eviscerate the significance, of our context-breaking capabilities. In a sense, this whole book represents an argument against such views.

The argument identifies the more considerable adversary as the deep-logic theorist rather than the reductionist or the behaviorist. On the other hand, and more intimately, this view of contexts stands opposed to two pervasive themes in modernist thought. Both these variants of the modernist outlook share with the doctrine about contexts espoused in the text the rejection of belief in the existence of a natural cognitive or social context. According to one of these doctrines we have nothing to go on but the particular traditions of shared discourse and shared life that exist in the world. The message is: Accept one of these shared social worlds on its own terms, or give up. The sharpest and most inclusive formulation of this view can be found in the later writings of Wittgenstein. See *Philosophical Investigations*, trans. G. E. M. Anscombe, Macmillan, New York, 1958, and Saul A. Kripke, *Wittgenstein on Rules and Private Language*, Harvard, Cambridge, 1982. The other doctrine holds that we are free and truly alive only so long as we rebel against all established institutions, conventions, and roles. But we rebel for the sake of the experiences that rebellion makes possible. We can expect no diminution of the arbitrary and oppressive character of instituted forms of social life. This view is most often associated with existentialism. Sartre's middle philosophy provides telling examples. See *Being and Nothingness*, trans. Hazel E. Barnes, Philosophical Library, New York, pp. 481–509, the discussion of "freedom and facticity." Notice that neither of these variants of modernism recognizes the third thesis of the view of our relation to our contexts accepted in *Politics*: our ability to modify the extent to which our contexts respect and nourish our context-revising capabilities. The rejection of the third thesis changes the sense given to the other two theses. Consider also that the problem of our relation to our contexts is far more familiar in moral or epistemological reflection than in social thought. But this book argues that the problem is no less important to our ideas about society.

THE IDEA OF THE TRANSFORMATIVE VOCATION

26–35 For the presence of the idea of *the honorable calling*, see E. P. Thompson, *The Making of the English Working Class*, Vintage, New York, 1963, p. 263; Charles Sabel, *Work and Politics: The Division of Labor in Industry*, Cambridge, Cambridge, 1983, pp. 82–89. See also the discussion of the related themes of personal discretion and group solidarity in Alan Fox, *Beyond Contract: Work, Power and Trust Relations*, Faber, London, 1974, pp. 30–39. The idea of *the transformative vocation* has usually been applied only to the specialized, notorious figure of the political agitator. For a hostile view, see Alexis de Tocqueville, *The Old Regime and the French Revolution*, trans. Stuart Gilbert, Doubleday, 1955, part 3, chap. 2, pp. 156–157. For a better deal, see Edmund Wilson, *To the Finland Station: A Study in the Writing and Acting of History*, Doubleday, Garden

City, 1947. For treatments that reach beyond the role of the agitator and that achieve greater psychological subtlety, look to novels. See, for example, George Eliot's *Middlemarch*. For the generalized conception of the transformative vocation, I am indebted to a discussion of this novel in Alan Mintz, *George Eliot and the Novel of Vocation*, Harvard, Cambridge, 1978, pp. 53–72.

CREDIBLE IDEALS AND TRANSFORMATIVE INSIGHT

The disintegration of what the text labels the naturalistic ideas of 36–47 community and objectivity is a favorite trope of modern thought. Literary examples include Georg Lukács, trans. Anna Bostock, *The Theory of the Novel*, MIT, Cambridge, 1971, pp. 29–39; and Northrop Frye, *The Anatomy of Criticism*, Princeton, Princeton, 1973, pp. 33–67. An example of the application of this trope to the history of moral ideas is Alasdair MacIntyre, *After Virtue: A Study in Moral Theory*, Notre Dame, Notre Dame, 1981. The counterparts to this disintegrative image in the history of political ideas are discussed from different perspectives in Leo Strauss, *Natural Right and History*, Chicago, Chicago, 1957; J.G.A. Pocock, *The Machiavellian Moment: Florentine Political Thought and the Atlantic Republican Tradition*, Princeton, Princeton, 1975.

The treatment of the theme in this section of the book differs from these approaches in two ways. First, its emphasis is transformation rather than dissolution: it looks toward a revised view of the ideas of community and objectivity, refusing to see nihilism as the direction toward which modernism is naturally headed or to accept antimodernist reaction as the condition for evaluative confidence. Second, the discussion relates this change in the content of basic social ideals to certain efforts at human empowerment. In both respects, the argument comes closer to Hans Blumenberg, *The Legitimacy of the Modern Age*, trans. Robert M. Wallace, MIT, Cambridge, 1983. For a modernist reassessment of both the conception of human solidarity and the practice of ascribing normative force to views of personality or society, see again *Passion*.

THE CONSTRAINTS ON TRANSFORMATIVE ACTION

The argument of this section presupposes no special knowledge 48–67 other than what an active civic life and a reading of the newspapers in the contemporary West (rich or poor) would normally provide. The discussion of partial emancipation from false necessity may easily be misunderstood as the expression of an evolutionary faith. But it alludes to a view — developed in the succeeding, constructive volume — that is evolutionary only in a highly qualified sense.

The discussion of the Brazilian experience reflects the author's 67–79 experiences as a sometime participant in the late 1970s and early

1980s. The ideas here summarize the views I have developed in a series of articles — "O País àsTontas" — published as a supplement to the *Folha de São Paulo* of January 14, 1979. For a discussion of the economic background, see Peter Evans, *Dependent Development: The Alliance of Multinational, State, and Local Capital in Brazil,* Princeton, Princeton, 1979.

THE CIRCUMSTANCE OF SOCIAL THEORY
SOCIETY AS MADE AND IMAGINED

80–83 For the fortunes of the idea of *an absolute frame of reference*, or of a context of all contexts, in early modern European philosophy, see Bernard Williams, *Descartes: The Project of Pure Enquiry*, Penguin, New York, 1978, pp. 244–252. For the contemporary mopping-up operation in the criticism of the idea of an absolute frame of reference, see Richard Rorty, *Philosophy and the Mirror of Nature*, Princeton, Princeton, 1979.

84–87   For the *naturalistic idea of society* in its modified, modern version, see the classic statement in John Stuart Mill, *A System of Logic Ratiocinative and Inductive*, Toronto, Toronto, 1973, book 6, chap. 9, pp. 907–910, and chap. 10, pp. 911–930. See also the analysis of this program for a naturalistic science of society in R. C. Collingwood, *The Idea of History*, Oxford, New York, 1956, pp. 81-85; Robert Denoon Cummings, *Human Nature and History*, Chicago, Chicago, 1969, pp. 36–83.

The perspective from which the present book criticizes the remnants of the naturalistic thesis can be usefully contrasted to a different, influential approach to the legacy of classical social theory. This alternative is the view developed by Talcott Parsons, *The Structure of Social Action*, (1937), 2 vols., Free Press, New York, 1968; and recently revised by Jeffrey Alexander, *Theoretical Logic in Sociology*, 4 vols., Univ. of California, Berkeley, 1982. Parsons and Alexander treat classical social theory as the gradual, yet unfinished development of an understanding of social life that combines material–instrumentalist and ideal–normative components within an integrated account of the interplay between individual action and collective order. A difficulty in comparing the approach taken here to the account offered by Parsons and Alexander is that they want to present an analysis of what really happened in the history of social thought, in the hope that such an analysis can inform the practice of social science. This book, on the contrary, merely introduces a detailed constructive project. It surveys the situation of social and historical studies with an eye to the obstacles this endeavor must surmount and to the resources on which it can draw. It is a marshaling of forces that makes no claim to be intellectual history. Two main points of contrast nevertheless stand out.

1. Parsons's view is meant to stabilize social analysis as a method more complex but recognizably similar to the dominant, Hempel-type conception of scientific method. (See Carl G. Hempel, *Aspects*

of Scientific Explanation, Free Press, New York, 1970.) The possibility of explanation depends on the reality of constraint. Progress lies chiefly in respecting the integrity of different causal factors and levels of analysis and in correctly balancing technical or ideological constraints against opportunities of voluntary action. By contrast, my argument is concerned with identifying ideas that can help us both sever and historicize the connection between the constraints of context and the opportunities of explanation. The result is to move social and historical analysis much further away from received ideas of what explanations can and should look like.

2. By presenting every social world as the product of complex individual and collective, material and ideal factors, the Parsonian view lends itself easily to the belief that each such world is what it is. Though not inevitably conservative, the approach inspires respect for the actual. (This tendency becomes, of course, more evident in Parsons's constructive theoretical work). By contrast, the view foreshadowed in this book suggests disrespect for what happens to exist or what happens to have taken place. It throws our cognitive interest in explanation on the side of our transformative interest in recognizing the trumped-up, revisable character of our social contexts. It follows up by connecting our prospects for individual and collective empowerment with our ability to change in particular ways both the content of the institutional and imaginative frameworks of social life and their relation to our framework-revising capabilities.

DEEP-STRUCTURE SOCIAL THEORY: GENERAL NOTION

Remember the earlier remarks in these notes about the motives that 87–96 prompt me to focus on tendencies rather than on particular thinkers and texts. In line with those observations, bear in mind that the most interesting places in which to look for examples of the deep-structure moves are also the best sources in which to search for the beginnings of an antidote. Marx and the Marxist tradition provide the preeminent instance, discussed later in the main text and in this commentary. Similar contrasts appear in the work of other leading social theorists. Consider two other members of the classical canon, Durkheim and Weber.

Durkheim's *Division of Labor in Society* accepts all the key deep-structure tenets. It even embraces the particular combination of deep-structure and functionalist ideas described in the text. Yet *The Division of Labor* also shows, in its discussion of the demographic pressure on the move from mechanical to organic solidarity, traces of an uncomplicated model of causal explanation that dispenses with deep-structure assumptions. See *The Division of Labor in Society*, trans. George Simpson, Free Press, New York, 1969, book 2, chap. 2, pp. 263–266. Durkheim's later work, most notably *The Elemen-*

tary Forms of Religious Life, develops an idealist functionalism without deep-structure commitments.

Just as a thinker whose ideas are more consistently devoted to deep-structure themes is not likely to give these themes their most powerful expression, so a theorist who plays these themes down is not necessarily the best inspiration for the development of an alternative. Max Weber's work is a case in point. Weber may at first seem to differ from his companions in the canon by a less compromised devotion to antinaturalistic analysis. But this impression is mistaken. The parts of Weber's work that do not fit deep-structure social analysis fall mainly into one of two groups. On the one hand, there is the causally agnostic though immensely suggestive typology that occupies much of *Economy and Society*, ed. Guenther Ross and Claus Wittich, Bedminster, New York, 1968. On the other hand, there is the close study of obliquely expressed intentions exemplified by the famous essay *The Protestant Ethic and the Spirit of Capitalism*, which, when examined at close range, turns out to be similarly noncommittal in its explanatory posture. Many of the most interesting parts of Weber's work, and certainly the parts most aggressive in causal explanations, are precisely the writings closest to the blend of deep-structure assumptions and functionalist methods described in the text. One example is the previously mentioned discussion of the rationalization theme in *Economy and Society*. Another example is the argument of the early monograph *The Agrarian Sociology of Ancient Civilizations*, trans. R. I. Frank, New Left Books, London, 1976.

For a discussion of the functionalist element in the synthesis of deep-structure and functionalist ideas discussed here, see, for exposition, G. A. Cohen, *Karl Marx's Theory of History: A Defence*, Princeton, Princeton, 1978, pp. 249–296; Jon Elster, "Marxism, Functionalism and Game Theory: The Case for Methodological Individualism," *Theory and Society*, vol. 2 (1982), pp. 453–482; G. A. Cohen, "Reply to Elster on 'Marxism, Functionalism, and Game Theory,' " *Theory and Society*, vol. 2 (1982), pp. 483–496; Marshall Salins, *Culture and Practical Reason*, Chicago, Chicago, 1976; Anthony Giddens, *A Contemporary Critique of Historical Materialism*, Univ. of California, Berkeley, 1981.

MARXISM AS DEEP-STRUCTURE THEORY

96–100 Two major aspects of Marx's work exemplify the particular combination of deep-structure and functionalist ideas explored in the preceding section of the text. One of these aspects is the core analysis of the system-preserving and system-transforming laws that govern the capitalist mode of production. These laws form the chief subject matter of *Capital*. The other aspect is the placing of the analysis of capitalism within an inclusive but equally lawlike account of the evolution of modes of production in world history. See *Introduction to the Critique of Political Economy*, *The German Ideology*, and the

Communist Manifesto. This more comprehensive view has sometimes been discounted by people more sympathetic to the focused
analysis of capitalism. But it is hard to see how the smaller story
could be true unless something like the bigger story also held good.
The Marx that combines deep-structure assumptions with functional methods is the Marx expounded in G. A. Cohen, *Karl Marx's
Theory of History*.

There are many parts of Marx's writings that just as clearly do
not conform to the synthesis of deep-structure analysis and functional explanation. They include the following.

1. The criticism of English political economy. See especially,
The Poverty of Philosophy, chap. 2, section 1 ("The Method"), International Publishers, New York, pp. 103–126; *Grundrisse*, trans.
Martin Nicolaus, Vintage, New York, 1973, Introduction (Notebook M), section 3, "The Method of Political Economy," pp. 100–
108; *Capital*, trans. Samuel Moore and Edward Aveling, International Publishers, New York, 1967, chap. 1, section 4, "The Fetishism of Commodities and the Secret Thereof," pp. 71–93;
Capital, vol. 1, chap. 19, The Transformation of the Value... of
Labor-Power into Wages, pp. 537–552. The construction somewhat
betrays the critique.

2. The idea of the universality of human labor power, gradually
revealed through the long ordeal of class conflict. See, for example,
Grundrisse; *Theories of Surplus Value*, pp. 705–706; and *The Communist Manifesto*. This theme in Marx's work is in part an expression
of the idea that as the forms of human connection shake loose the
grip of rigid roles and ranks, people become the conscious authors
and beneficiaries rather than the unconscious objects of the "laws"
of history.

3. The thesis of the legal specificity of capitalism. See, for example, *Grundrisse* (Introduction), p. 109. See also Engels's letter to
C. Schmidt of October 27, 1890, in Karl Marx and Friedrich Engels,
Werke, Dietz, Berlin, 1967, vol. 37, pp. 488–495. The more mired
in historical particularity the definition of capitalism turns out to
be, the less plausible it becomes to identify capitalism as a universal
type of social organization, capable of being introduced at different
moments in the history of different societies.

4. The occasional historical writings such as *The Eighteenth Bru-
maire of Louis Bonaparte* and *The Class Struggles in France, 1848–
1850*. These writings emphasize the historical particularity of a
society's class structure and forms of class consciousness. The same
distinctive institutional and cultural facts that cannot be inferred
from a general category like capitalism are also crucial to the course
of conflict over governmental power and class relations. Thus arise
the problems mentioned later when I discuss the effort to rescue
Marxism from within by playing up the autonomy of "politics"
and group ideas. Particular states of affairs and trajectories of social
change begin to undercut the larger story about the succession of
modes of production. The more detailed the account of class struc-

ture, class conflict, and institutional change, the harder it becomes
to reduce this account to deep-structure and functional explanations. The less detailed the description, or the smaller the importance accorded to this particular set of details, the sharper the tension
between what the story says and what historical learning or contemporary experience seems to show.

MARXISM AS DEEP-STRUCTURE THEORY: THE TROUBLES OF THE CONCEPT OF CAPITALISM

101–113   For more detailed bibliographical references about this part of the
discussion, see the commentary on Chapter 4 of *False Necessity*, the
constructive work that follows this critical introduction. For the
definition of capitalism in Marx, see section 1, of *The Communist
Manifesto*; *Capital*, vol. 3, chap. 51, "Distribution Relations and
Production Relations," pp. 879–884; G. A. Cohen, *Karl Marx's
Theory of History*, Princeton, Princeton, 1978, pp. 180–193. Here
are a few examples of the discussion, beyond the narrow confines
of Marxist theory, about capitalist realities outside the periods or
the sequences that are generally labeled capitalist. For the contrast
between the Graeco-Roman and the modern Western worlds, as
illustrated by the status of the city, see M. I. Finley, "The Ancient
City from Fustel de Coulanges to Max Weber and Beyond," *Comparative Studies in Society and History*, vol. 19 (1977), pp. 305–327.
For China during the T'ang and Sung dynasties, see Stefan Balázs,
"Beiträge zur Wirtschaftsgeschichte der T'ang-Zeit (618–906)" in
*Mitteilungen des Seminars für Orientalischen Sprachen zu Berlin, Osi-
asiastische Studien*, vol. 34 (1931), pp. 1–92; vol. 35 (1932), pp. 1–
73; vol. 36 (1933), pp. 1–62; Dennis Twitchett, "Merchant, Trade
and Government in Late T'ang," *Asia Major*, New Series, vol. 14,
part 1 (1968): pp. 63–95; Yoshinobu Shiba, *Commerce and Society in
Sung China*, trans. Mark Elvin, Michigan Abstracts, Ann Arbor,
1970. For Islam and the Islamic imperial states, see Maxime Rodi-
son, *Capitalism and Islam*, trans. Brian Pearce, Pantheon, New
York, 1973; Peter Gran, *Islamic Roots of Capitalism: Egypt 1760–
1840*, Univ. of Texas, Austin, 1979. For the Mughal Empire, see
Irfan Habib, "Potentialities of Capitalistic Development in the
Economy of Mughal India," *Journal of Economic History*, vol. 29
(1969), pp. 32–78.

     The relevant issue for my immediate purposes is not under what
circumstances these situations would have issued in either the
institutional arrangements or the practical capabilities of the modern
Western societies that Marx labeled capitalist. Nor is the question
whether these societies might have attained modern European capabilities without accepting modern European arrangements.
(These matters, however, certainly are relevant to the theory of
context making presented in *False Necessity*.) The point in question

is simply the embarrassing theoretical implication of including or excluding these circumstances from the list of capitalist forms.

For the related matters presented by the debate within Marxism about the "Asiatic mode of production," see Karl Marx, articles on India and China in *Surveys from Exile*, Vintage, New York, 1974, pp. 301-333. See also Barry Hindess and Paul Hirst, *Pre-Capitalist Modes of Production*, Routledge, London, 1975; Lawrence Krader, *The Asiatic Mode of Production*, Assen, 1975; Anne M. Bailey and Josep R. Llobera, eds., *The Asiatic Mode of Production: Science and Politics*, Routledge, London, 1981; Stephen P. Dunn, *The Fall and Rise of the Asiatic Mode of Production*, Routledge, London, 1982. For the complementary body of literature about deviations within modern Europe from the stereotypical English route to capitalism, see once again the references to Chapter 4 of *False Necessity*.

<h2 style="text-align:center">MARXISM AS DEEP-STRUCTURE THEORY: PLAYING UP POLITICS</h2>

For discussion of the anomalous role of the "political" in Marxism, 113–117 see Ernesto Laclau, *Politics and Ideology in Marxist Theory*, Verso, London, 1979, pp. 51–80; Victor M. Perez-Diaz, *State, Bureaucracy and Civil Society: A Critical Discussion of the Political Theory of Karl Marx*, Humanities, Atlantic Highlands, N.J.,1978. For an attempt to revise Marxist theory from within by playing up *the relative autonomy of class situations and class consciousness* from the defining features of a mode of production like capitalism, see the writings of Gramsci cited under "General Background" earlier in these Notes. For a detailed historiographic example that inspires the remarks in the text about the different careers of *smallholders in early modern Europe*, see Robert Brenner, "Agrarian Class Structure and Economic Development in Pre-Industrial Europe," *Past and Present*, no. 70 (1976), pp. 30–75, the criticisms of Brenner published in later issues of that journal, and Brenner's response and restatement, "The Agrarian Roots of European Capitalism," *Past and Present*, no. 97 (1982), pp. 16–113.

<h2 style="text-align:center">ECONOMICS AS A NONEVOLUTIONARY DEEP-STRUCTURE SOCIAL THEORY</h2>

For a statement of the early *evolutionary element in classical political* 120–130 *economy*, see the discussion of stages of social and economic organization in Adam Smith, *Lectures on Jurisprudence*, Oxford, Oxford, 1978, pp. 14–17. For a view that moves economics toward a nonevolutionary version of deep-structure social theory, see the passage cited earlier in John Stuart Mill, *A System of Logic*, and *Principles of Political Economy*, Toronto, Toronto, 1968, "Preliminary Remarks," pp. 20–21. My discussion of the marginalist revolution as a several-step retreat to supposedly more defensible lines is indebted to Joseph A. Schumpeter's treatment in *History of Economic Analysis*, Oxford, New York, 1954, pp. 909–920.

On the problem of *systematic or recurrent disequilibrium*, see Keynes's *General Theory of Employment, Interest and Money*, Harcourt, Brace, New York 1964; and Axel Leijoninfvud, *On Keynesian Economics and the Economics of Keynes*, Oxford, London, 1968.

Classical political economy both recognized step-by-step *the institutional indeterminacy of the market conception* and circumscribed the consequences of the recognition. Thus, Mill acknowledged the principle in the sphere of distribution. See *Principles of Political Economy*, "Preliminary remarks," p. 21 (". . . unlike the laws of Production, those of Distribution are partly of human invention . . ."), book 2, chap. 1, pp. 199–200. Marx went much further by redefining the supposed laws of economics as relative to the particular institutional arrangements of the capitalist economy.

The most extensive appreciation of both the institutional indeterminacy of the market concept and the dependence of supposed economic laws on contingent institutional arrangements can be found in two sets of interwar writings. One group of writings grew out of the response of Western European economists to the economic crisis of the l930s. See, for example, some of the occasional writings of Keynes (where these insights appear more clearly than in his theoretical work), such as "Can Lloyd George Do It?" (1928), in *The Collected Writings of John Maynard Keynes*, ed., Donald Muggridge, Macmillan, London, 1981, vol. 19, part 2, pp. 761–834; Mihail Kalecki, *Selected Essays on the Dynamics of the Capitalist Economy*, 1933–1970, Cambridge, Cambridge, 1971; Mihail Kalecki, *Selected Essays on the Economic Growth of the Socialist and Mixed Economy*, Cambridge, Cambridge, 1970; Friedrich A. Hayek, *Profits, Interest, and Investment*, Routledge, London, 1939; Nicholas Kaldor, "Capitalist Evolution in the Light of Keynesian Economics," in *Essays on Economic Stability and Growth*, Free Press, New York, 1960, pp. 243–258. A second group of writings set the terms of the debate between right- and left-wing factions about the institutional context of Soviet industrialization. See E. A. Preobrazhensky, *The Crisis of Soviet Industrialization*, Sharpe, Armonk, N.Y., 1979; Nikolai Bukharin, *Economics of the Transition Period*, Humanities, Atlantic Highlands, N.J., 1971.

The idea of the institutional indeterminacy of the market concept has been emphasized in writings of the American Critical Legal Studies Movement. See, for example, Duncan Kennedy and Frank Michelman, "Are Property and Contract Efficient?" in *Hofstra Law Review*, vol. 8 (1980), pp. 711–770. On the other hand, the relation of particular institutional arrangements to economic regularities has been studied by the neoKeynesians. See, for example, Alfred S. Eichner, *The Megacorp and Oligopoly: Micro Foundations of Macro Dynamics*, Sharpe, Armonk, N.Y., 1976. Such work has lent new theoretical strength and practical urgency to the long forgotten concerns of German, British, and American institutional and historical economics.

The criticism of mainstream economics in the text should not be read as an argument that the sole tenable alternative to the economic analysis that resulted from the marginalist revolution is an economics that submerges its distinctive identity and concerns within the type of antinaturalistic social theory for which this book argues. Traditions of writing like those just cited demonstrate that a less superstitious theoretical practice need not await comprehensive theories. Such a practice begins and flourishes in particular disciplinary settings, and it can assume countless transitional forms.

POSITIVIST SOCIAL SCIENCE

The text treats positivist social science, like deep-structure social 130–135 theory, as a tendency defined by particular intellectual moves. Once again, the most developed and persuasive use of these moves is likely to occur in works that also use ideas and methods at odds with positivist assumptions.

For a characteristic formulation of the view of society as an agglomeration of problems to be solved and interests to be reconciled – a view that nourishes and is nourished by the positivist moves – see David Easton, *The Political System: An Inquiry into the State of Political Science*, Knopf, New York, 1953.

Positivist social science goes on in particular disciplines. In each of these disciplines its practice clusters around certain stock themes. One way to study this style of social analysis is therefore to examine these narrowly defined genres and to identify the methods and ideas they share: especially their assumptions about the framework–routine distinction and the stratagems by which they represent social reality as if this distinction were unimportant or uncontroversial. Political science, for example, has the study of voting behavior. In industrial sociology, social psychology, and management science there is a genre of work that studies the sources and dynamics of contention among members of an organization or a work team, the better to ensure cooperative attitudes and effective coordination. Sociologists are familiar with the study of networks and small groups, a study whose practitioners ask such questions as: Why do married couples in a particular society stay together or get divorced?

Notice that each of these standardized forms of social science can be quantitatively formalized or conducted in measurement-averse, discursive terms. Quantitative formalization is not the essence of the mode. But an ideal of quantitative verification is sometimes used as a basis with which to urge a particularly straitened version of positivist analytic practice. See, for example, Hans L. Zetterberg, *On Theory and Verification in Sociology*, Bedminster, New York, 1965.

Another way to study positivist social science and to distinguish its chief variants is to look for examples of each of the *techniques of avoidance*. As suggested in the text, the clearest distinctions in the use of these techniques can be found in the literature of economics. Thus, for *the technique of disclaimer*, see the more austere writings on general equilibrium analysis, e.g., Gerard Debreu, *Mathematical Economics: Twenty Papers of Gerard Debreu*, Cambridge, Cambridge, 1983. For *the technique of idealization*, see publicists such as Milton Friedman, *Capitalism and Freedom*, Chicago, Chicago, 1981, the writings of the Chicago School, and the sequel in "rational-expectations" theory. Or see historiographic counterparts to this brand of positivist social science, such as D. C. North and R. P. Thomas, *The Rise of the Western World: A New Economic History*, Cambridge, Cambridge, 1978. For *the technique of hollow concession*, consult the works of mainstream macroeconomists and especially the American Keynesians (as distinguished from the so-called neo-Keynesians): for example, Robert Solow, "Alternative Approaches to Macro-Economic Theory: A Partial View," *Canadian Journal of Economics*, vol. 12 (1979), pp. 339–354. For a typical example of policy analysis that both recognizes in principle and disregards in fact the particular institutional determinants of the tensions it explores, see Arthur Okun, *Equality and Efficiency: The Big Tradeoff*, Brookings, Washington, 1975.

Note that most criticisms of "positivism" in social science are in fact critiques of one or another version of what the text later describes as the scientistic prejudice. The point of the argument against positivist methods here is not to vindicate the legitimate role of general or not directly falsifiable elements in social thought. The point instead is to explore the consequences of the failure to come to terms with the formative yet trumped-up character of the institutional and imaginative frameworks of social life. The scientistic prejudice encourages and justifies this failure. But it is not the same thing.

For examples of the familiar controversy about positivism in Anglo-American, French, and German settings, see *Positivism and Sociology*, ed. Anthony Giddens, Heinemann, London, 1974; Theodor W. Adorno et al., *The Positivist Dispute in German Sociology*, trans. Glyn Adey and David Frisby, Heinemann, London, 1976.

HISTORY WITHOUT A SCRIPT

139–141 The *modest eclectic response* recurs in every field of contemporary social and historical thought. One of its most coherent and illuminating variants: (a) emphasizes the influence that the social structure of a society exercises on its politics (in the narrow sense of the term), an emphasis that provides a basis for general explanations, and (b) studies this influence comparatively, through a version of Mill's "method of concomitant variations." Some examples of this style of thought come from a Marxist background. See Barrington Moore, *Social Origins of Dictatorship and Democracy*, Beacon, Boston,

1966; Theda Skocpol, *States and Social Revolutions*, Cambridge, Cambridge, 1979; Theda Skocpol, "A Critical Review of Barrington Moore's 'Social Origins of Dictatorship and Democracy,' " in *Politics and Society*, vol. 2 (1973), pp. 1–34. Other instances develop out of mainstream positivist social science. See, for example, Harold L. Wilensky, *The Welfare State and Equality*, Univ. of California, Berkeley, 1975, a book that also represents positivist social science at its most illuminating.

It is important not to confuse the sense of politics in the slogan 144–151 "It's all politics" with the sense that Carl Schmitt gives to the primacy of politics in *The Concept of the Political*, trans. George Schwab, Rutgers, New Brunswick, N.J., 1970. Schmitt emphasizes the opposition between friend and foe as a force that harnesses and overrides all particular disputes. Not animosity but the defiance of structures, and of the tendencies and constraints that shape them, represents the key problem to which the cry "It's all politics" refers.

The thematic outline of an *antinaturalistic social theory* in the text 151–165 is restated as a "proto-theory" in chapter 1 of *False Necessity* and developed in the remainder of that book.

The conception of ultra-theory is more the announcement of an 165–169 intellectual hope than the description of a well-established practice of thought. But the spirit of what I call here ultra-theory has been prominent in the writings of many twentieth-century thinkers: Foucault, for example (despite the frequent sacrifice of critical or reconstructive aims to sheer delight in historical mis-en-scènes), or Gramsci (despite the fidelity to Marxism). Moreover, it would be wrong to associate ultra-theory solely with leftist or modernist intellectuals. Why not, for example, John Dewey (despite the gap between the commitment to institutional experimentalism and the slide into institutional conservatism)? See, for example, *Philosophy, Psychology, and Social Practice: Essays*, ed. Joseph Ratner, Capricorn, New York, 1965.

THE PHILOSOPHICAL AND SCIENTIFIC SETTING OF AN ANTINATURALISTIC SOCIAL THEORY

For a study of the history of *social laws* in early modern thought, 170–172 see Robert Brown, *The Idea of Social Laws: Machiavelli to Mill*, Cambridge, Cambridge, 1984. For a classic statement of the program of a "naturalistic" science of society, see the passage cited earlier in John Stuart Mill, *A System of Logic*.

For a crude formulation of the scientistic program in social thought, see William Catton, *From Animistic to Naturalistic Sociology*, McGraw-Hill, New York, 1966. For more refined statements, see, for example, George C. Homans, *The Nature of Social Science*, Harcourt Brace, New York, 1967; Neil Smelser, *Comparative Methods in the Social Sciences*, Prentice-Hall, Englewood Cliffs, N.J., 1976;

Arthur Stinchcombe, *Constructing Social Theories*, Harcourt Brace, New York, 1968.

For examples of the type of criticism of the scientistic prejudice that seeks to replace causal explanations with an explication of intentions and meanings, see R. C. Collingwood, *The Idea of History*, Oxford, Oxford, 1946, pp. 282–315; Peter Winch, *The Idea of a Social Science and Its Relation to Philosophy*, Humanities, Atlantic Highlands, N.J., 1969. For an early criticism of this point of view, see Max Weber, *Critique of Stammler*, trans. Guy Oakes, Free Press, New York, 1977.

NECESSITY AND CONTINGENCY

174–177 The thesis of *extreme necessitarianism* is best represented by the rationalist philosophers. Not even Kant's synthetic a priori will quite do.

177–180 For an account of the *cosmological theories* mentioned here, see D. W. Sciama, *Modern Cosmology*, Cambridge, Cambridge, 1971.

180–185 For discussion of the attack on privileged methods or representations and therefore also on *privileged representations of contingency and necessity*, see generally Richard Rorty, *Philosophy and the Mirror of Nature*. On *the empirical character of ideas about space and time* and *the occasional redefinition of things true by definition as only empirically true*, see Hilary Putnam, "Philosophy of Physics," in *Mathematics, Matter and Method: Philosophical Papers*, vol. 1, Cambridge, Cambridge, 1975, pp. 88–92; Putnam, "It Ain't Necessarily So," in *Mathematics Matter and Method*, pp. 239–243. See also Imre Lakatos, "A Renaissance of Empiricism in the Recent 'Philosophy of Mathematics,'" in *Mathematics, Science and Epistemology: Philosophical Papers*, vol. 1, Cambridge, Cambridge, 1978, pp. 24–42. The example of the kinetic theory of energy is drawn directly from Hilary Putnam, "The Analytic and the Synthetic," in *Mind Language and Reality: Philosophical Papers*, vol. 2, pp. 42–46. For the attack on *the distinction between the analytic and the synthetic* and between truth by convention and empirical truth, see Willard van Orman Quine, "Two Dogmas of Empiricism," in *From a Logical Point of View*, Harper, New York, 1961; Donald Davidson, "On the Very Idea of a Conceptual Scheme," *Proceedings of the American Philosophical Association*, vol. 17 (1973–1974), pp. 5–20; and Donald Davidson, "Truth and Meaning" in *Synthese*, vol. 17, 1967, pp. 304–323. On the elaboration by developmental psychology of the idea of *emergent frameworks of reasoning and perception* supervening on one another, see L. S. Vygotsky, *Mind in Society: The Development of Higher Psychological Processes*, Harvard, Cambridge, 1978. Jean Piaget, *The Language and Thought of the Child*, 3rd ed., trans. Marjorie and Ruth Gabain, Routledge, London, 1959; Piaget, *Genetic Epistemology*, trans. Eleanor Duckworth, Norton, New York, 1971. See Piaget's "Comments on Vygotsky's Critical Remarks," published as an attachment to L.S. Vygotsky, *Thought and Language*, trans. Eugenia Hanfmann and Gertrude Vahar, M.I.T., Cambridge, 1962.

HISTORICAL PARTICULARITY AND GENERAL EXPLANATIONS

For a classic statement of the problem, see Max Weber, "Roscher's 185–187 'Historical Method,' " in *Roscher and Knies: The Logical Problems of Historical Economics*, trans. Guy Oakes, Free Press, New York, 1975, pp. 55–91. See also Alexander von Schelting, *Max Weber's Wissenschaftslehre*, Mohr, Tübingen, 1934, pp. 335–343.

I owe the *geological example* to attendance at the geological lectures 187–188 of Professor Stephen Jay Gould of Harvard University. On the history of the example of the *South American marsupials*, see George 189–190 G. Simpson, *Splendid Isolation: The Curious History of the South American Mammals*, Yale, New Haven, 1980. For a discussion of 190–191 part of what the text calls *the property of divergent sequence*, see Richard Lewontin, "Is Nature Probable or Capricious?" *Bio Science* (Jan. 1966), pp. 25–27. Compare the distinction between *three types of* 192–194 *order* to Popper's three worlds. See Karl Popper, *Objective Knowledge: An Evolutionary Approach*, Oxford, Oxford, 1972, pp. 153–190. Here, as in Popper, the particular characterization of the third level reveals the point of the entire classification. For a discussion of the *self-referring and self-replicating type or order*, see Ernst Mayr, "Teological and Teleonomic: A New Analysis," in *Evolution and the Diversity of Life: Selected Essays*, Harvard, Cambridge, 1976, pp. 383–404; François Jacob, *The Possible and the Actual*, Pantheon, New York, 1982.

Proper-Name Index

Thematic Index

Absolute frame of reference
    idea of, 80
    repudiation of, 80–82
    Peirce's and Hegel's attempts to reestab-
        lish the idea of, 83
    as provided by naturalistic beliefs about
        society, 84
Absolute insight, Hegel's idea of, 83
Abstraction, 57, 58
    dilemma of abstraction and concreteness,
        102–109
Accumulation
    commitment to, as characteristic of capi-
        talism, 103–104
Acquiescence without commitment, 41
Agnosticism versus facing the empirical and
    normative issues,   (as styles of eco-
    nomic analysis), 125–128
Agrarian–bureaucratic societies, 105
Analytic and synthetic judgment (Kant),
    collapse of any significant distinction,
    181–182
Analytic truth, 182
Anarchy, 155
Artifact, society as, 1–17, 71, 80, 84–87,
    150, 155, 166, 200–202, 207, 224–225
    and the central problem that the radicali-
        zation of this idea presents to social ex-
        planation, 202–204
    as developed by ultra-theory, 9
    see also Social theory; Society
Association, human
    the basic activity of context making and
        context breaking exemplified in, 18–23,
        202–204
    as the subject of distinctive models of co-
        existence enacted in particular areas of
        social practice, 151, 155, 198, 208
    the conflict over the imaginative scheme
        of, exemplified in a Brazilian setting,
        73, 75
    see also Contexts as formative institutional
        and imaginative contexts of particular
        societies; Contexts of human activity
Avoiding framework–routine distinction,
    strategems for the disclaimer (skepti-
    cism), 133
    hollow concession (confession and avoid-
    ance), 134–135

idealization, 133–134
see also Contexts as formative institutional
    and imaginative contexts of particular
    societies

Big-bang theory (in cosmology)
    methodological implications drawn from
        discussion of (standard model), 179–180
    see also Cosmology
Biology, 188–190, 193–197
    Darwinian selection theory and microbi-
        ology, 188
    mammalian evolution, 189–190
    noncompetitive extinctions, 189
Books, writing books and doing politics
    a mirage of power, 31
    a sense of inadequacy, 78–79
    practical implications of a better theoreti-
        cal view, 159–165
    practical significance of theoretical error
        (as in Marxism), 117–120
Brazil, 67–79, 117
    as an example of constraints on transfor-
        mative action, 67–79
    as a testing ground for a way of organiz-
        ing government and the economy, 76

Capabilities
    their relation to frameworks (the failure
        of the functionalist thesis that there is a
        one-to-one relation between institu-
        tional frameworks and practical capa-
        bilities), 63–64, 95, 109–110
    see also Contexts as formative institutional
        and imaginative contexts of particular
        societies; Functional explanation
Capitalism, 90, 100–120, 139, 140, 232–233
    in Marx's system, 101, 232–233
    two different roles of the idea of capital-
        ism in Marx's theory, 109–113
    overinclusion and underinclusion in the
        definition of, 101–109
    changed from general type to unique
        constellation of arrangements, 101, 102,
        140
    defined in terms of independent wage-
        labor, 103
    defined through combination of wage-

243